CAUTION
TO THE WIND

FAITH LESSONS FROM THE LIFE OF
DON MCCLANEN

BY
JOE MURCHISON

CONTENTS

Acknowledgements

One author's name may appear on this book, but more than 100 have contributed to its completion–through their interviews, suggestions, support and prayers. My first thanks go to Don McClanen, along with his wife, Gloria, for having lived a story that begged to be told, and for all their grace to me as they modeled bold Christian discipleship. Special thanks also are due to Ann Parr for her numerous and invaluable editorial suggestions, above all impressing upon me time and again the power of active verbs and simple declarative sentences. I am equally grateful to Rose Berger for her advice and editorial review of the chapters, and to publisher Gordon Thiessen, who was so pleasurable to work with.

Kayla McClurg and Susan Bell supported this project in crucial ways throughout, offering encouragement, serving as sounding boards and proofreading chapters. I am greatly indebted to them. Larry Braak graciously contributed photographs he took of Don in Calcutta and Kenya and assisted in preparing other photos. Thanks also are due to many who offered valuable suggestions and encouragement, including Gordon Cosby, Bryan Sirchio, Les Steckel, Tom Rogeberg, Wayne Atcheson, Jeff Cruikshank, Michael Gorman, Katie Murchison, Sharon Pavelda and Randall Mullins, Don Remmey, Mur Carrington, Dorothy Devers, Jean Mathews, Dick Busch, Dixcy Bosley, Fred Taylor, Tom and Carolyn Hubers, Jim Knight, Dot Cresswell, Bill Price, Joe Collier, Terry Flood, Sydney Johnson, Margie Roberson, Yolande Ford, Catherine Gibson and Jim Hall. Numerous others from the Church of the Saviour community offered encouragement and information.

I am indebted to Andrea Wells Miller and her husband, Keith Miller, who graciously made available a large body of material they had collected about Don and Gloria McClanen, including transcripts of numerous interviews with Don and Gloria, as well as with friends and associates. Andrea Wells Miller also made available a draft she had written describing many episodes of the McClanens' lives, for which I am grateful.

Don and I thank several generous donors, who will remain

anonymous, whose contributions paid expenses associated with this project.

Finally, I thank my wife, Marilyn, for being a gracious, understanding and supportive "book widow" during the crafting of this book.

Note Concerning Names

During three decades of money ministry, Don McClanen helped thousands of people to become more open and forthright in dealing with their financial lives in the context of their faith. These people were emboldened to shatter a taboo and find new freedom and creativity by sharing their money details with others in a loving and safe community. In that spirit, a number of people in this book have graciously agreed to reveal aspects of their finances to show the impact of Don's ministry. In most cases they have agreed to do so under their real identities. In four cases that are indicated, this book employs pseudonyms to protect people from possibly harmful public exposure.

Note on Book Proceeds

All royalties from the sale of this book will be donated to ministries aiding the poor around the world with which Don McClanen has previously worked.

Dedication

To Gloria McClanen and Gordon and Mary Cosby

"Give your entire attention to what God is doing right now,
and don't get worked up about what may or may not
happen tomorrow. God will help you deal with whatever
hard things come up when the time comes."
(Matthew 6:33 *The Message*)

Foreword

The first time I met Don McClanen was at the second annual Fellowship of Christian Athletes conference at Estes Park, Colorado, in 1957. I was a college student and had been raised in the church, yet was not convinced that Christianity had much relevance to me. I loved athletics, particularly football, and sometimes had difficulty in relating to the image of Jesus as being a meek and mild person who called us to "turn the other cheek." I was much more interested in knocking people down in highly competitive sports. I also had difficulty relating to many of the people I saw in the church that I attended. Their lives did not reflect the excitement and passion that I found in athletics.

During that week at the Fellowship of Christian Athletes camp, I heard Christianity articulated in a way that I could relate to. I saw a vitality and a challenge in Christianity that I had not seen before. Being around many well-known athletes whom I respected made a huge impact. There were football players from the University of Oklahoma, Louisiana State University and many other major universities. I was from a small Nebraska school, Hastings College, and felt somewhat insignificant comparing what I had accomplished athletically to what many of these athletes had accomplished. I still occasionally see people such as Clendon Thomas and Bill Krisher, both All-American players at Oklahoma, who attended the conference. I also remember football players Doak Walker and Donn Moomaw, pitcher Carl Erskine, pole vaulter Bob Richards and many other prominent athletes.

Don McClanen spoke at the conference and I remember him as a very humble, mild-mannered, unassuming person. Don appeared to be one who was more comfortable staying behind the scenes. I later learned that Don had been a successful basketball coach at Eastern Oklahoma State University. While there, he envisioned the influence that athletes could provide in promoting Christianity among young people. He and his wife, Gloria, sacrificed their finances, time and energy in engaging prominent members of the athletic community in their fledgling ministry. Don persisted and eventually enlisted the help of such athletic figures as Branch Rickey, Otto Graham and many others. His vision, determination and effort in getting the Fellowship of Christian Athletes off the ground became a harbinger of his efforts in establishing other Christian ministries such as Ministry of Money and Harvest Time.

I have been one of several million young people who can trace their Christian conversions to a Fellowship of Christian Athletes event, so I can attest personally to the power and the scope of this movement. It transformed the landscape of athletics in the United States, serving as the launching pad for team chaplains, team Bible studies and chapel services which are now common for so many high school, college and professional teams. Those of us from the athletic community will always be grateful to Don for his vision and his leadership in establishing the Fellowship of Christian Athletes.

As time went on, I became better acquainted with Don. His son, Michael, served as a graduate assistant football coach for me at the University of Nebraska for a period of time. As I visited with Don, I began to understand better the nature of his faith. Don is one of the most spiritual people I have ever met. He spends much time in prayer, meditation, fasting and the Scriptures, and is keenly aware of the leading of the Holy Spirit. What sets Don apart from so many Christians is that he is willing to move in whatever direction he sees the Spirit leading him, whereas most of us find it very difficult to leave our "comfort zones."

Don, through his acquaintance with Mother Teresa, began to realize that the obsession with material possessions that so many of us have in the United States is a major obstacle to spiritual maturity. Mother Teresa, at one time, indicated that she felt that the greatest mission field in the world was the United States because of our preoccupation with material wealth. In an attempt to address spiritual poverty, Don launched Ministry of Money, which connected people of wealth in the United States with the poverty and suffering of people in various Third World countries. Don's vision was that these types of "reverse missions" benefited the wealthy in terms of creating a greater awareness of the disproportionate distribution of wealth throughout the world and also benefited those impoverished people whom the wealthy were able to assist through philanthropy.

Don usually contacted me around the time of the football bowl games each year. Since his brother lived in Ft. Lauderdale, he would usually attend the Orange Bowl game in early January if Nebraska was playing in Miami. When Nebraska played the University of Miami in the 1995 Orange Bowl, Don was there. It turned out that we had been undefeated that year and would win the national championship if we were able to beat Miami, which was a "tall order" since Miami had lost only once on their home field (the Orange Bowl) in more than 70 games. That evening we managed to come from behind to win the game and the national championship. The game did not end until nearly midnight and, by the time we had gotten back to our Miami Beach hotel and had talked to family, players and friends, it was very late. I had gotten into my pajamas and was just ready to go to bed at 2:30 a.m. when there was a knock on my hotel door. It was Don. After a brief congratulatory conversation, he began to talk to me about taking a trip to Haiti as part of the Ministry of Money. At that point, in the middle of the night, I was probably not listening real closely and agreed that this sounded like a good idea and that maybe sometime we should take the trip. Don left and I thought little more about it. A few weeks later, I received a phone call from him informing me that the trip was all set, that he had bought the airline tickets and that I would really enjoy the trip. At that point I was fairly well committed and agreed to go, even though I was not enthusiastic about leaving my family after a long, hard season and was not at all sure what I was getting into.

In terms of its spiritual impact, the trip to Haiti was similar to my Fellowship of Christian Athletes experience at Estes Park many years before. Don and I visited Cité Soleil, a cardboard and tin-shack community built on a dump in the bay of Port-au-Prince, Haiti. I had never seen living conditions so bad. There was no running water or sewage disposal. Children were running around in what had to be highly contaminated surroundings, living in abject poverty. Don distributed money to some of the people with whom he maintained contact at Cité Soleil and did what he could to make their lives better. However, we both realized that the need was much greater than available resources.

We then visited two of Mother Teresa's hospitals in Port-au-Prince. One was for adults who were mostly terminal patients. These people were picked up at night as they lay on the streets around

Port-au-Prince and their situation was quite desperate. Next we visited a hospital for infants and small children, nearly all of whom were dying of AIDS and other fatal diseases. I remember talking to one of the Missionaries of Charity sisters at the hospital and asking her how she could endure working in such conditions day after day, year after year. She indicated that the sisters spent several hours a day in prayer, meditation and worship, and that this time was what renewed them and made their life not only bearable but a work of true meaning and joy. That lesson concerning the importance of spiritual discipline stuck with me and certainly has been important in my own spiritual walk.

Don had made the acquaintance of then-President Aristide, who had presided over Haiti for a number of years after a major uprising. Don decided that we should go to Aristide's headquarters and see him. After we spent a couple of hours waiting on the Mardi Gras parade viewing stand at the president's palace with other dignitaries, Aristide had not appeared. We started back to our living quarters and got caught in a huge crowd of people celebrating the festivities. I remember Don and I trying to cross a human river moving down the street, and we were in some danger of being knocked down and trampled. Don was 70 at that time and I was almost 60. I am sure that the revelers were amazed at these two old white guys attempting to go against the flow.

The Mardi Gras event in Port-au-Prince is somewhat symbolic of the way Don has lived his life. Through trips to Bosnia and the Middle East, living in the midst of Washington, D.C., inner-city violence, adventures on a submarine in World War II and even combat with a Marine platoon during that war, Don has never been one to avoid danger. His faith in God's providence has enabled him to transcend the mundane and routine lives that so many of us live.

Tom Osborne
Lincoln, Nebraska
University of Nebraska athletic
director, former head football coach
and former member of Congress

Introduction

"If you love me, you will keep my commandments."–John 14:15 (NRSV)

Don McClanen has founded five major Christian ministries, including the two-million-person Fellowship of Christian Athletes (FCA) and influential Ministry of Money. But at the age of 83, he is not yet done. Don has moved on to his next calling, named Second Journey, in which he is exploring the implications of a quote by Meister Eckardt, a 14th-century mystic, who said, "There are plenty to follow our Lord halfway, but not the other half."[1] Despite reaching the autumn of an extraordinary life, Don still seeks to follow Christ all the way home.

His life has been one of throwing caution to the wind or, better said, to the Spirit, since wind and spirit are the same word in the Old Testament. It's been a circuitous path, from coaching basketball at a junior college in eastern Oklahoma to founding FCA, followed by sod farming; initiating a ministry to inner-city youth in Washington, D.C.; starting a church-renewal ministry; creating Ministry of Money to help people follow Christ in their financial lives; becoming a spiritual tour guide for numerous groups of pilgrims to sites of Third-World poverty; embarking on humanitarian adventures to war-torn Bosnia and Iraq; ministering to the wealthy; and raising millions of dollars for projects to aid the poor around the world.

Along the way he has worked with, and often influenced, such notable people as Mother Teresa, college coaches Tom Osborne and Dean Smith, Christian writers Richard Foster and the late Henri Nouwen, and social reformers Jim Wallis of Sojourners and Millard Fuller, founder of Habitat for Humanity.

Don never hesitated to knock on doors, whether of sports celebrities, religious leaders, the poor or the rich. As Mur Carrington, a friend and spiritual director of Don's, noted, "He doesn't have a shy bone in his body." Carrington then added, "But he's humble." That combination of boldness and genuineness, placed in the service of callings that he has perceived from God, has resulted in Don's remarkable ministries. When Don heard those calls, which most others might have considered implausible or even impossible, he responded with an adventurous, emphatic "yes." One of Don's favorite sayings is from British philosopher Alfred North Whitehead: "Without the high hope of adventure, religion degenerates into a mere appendage of a comfortable life." Time and again he has followed the call, despite financial risk, opposition, suffering and, in some cases, physical danger. And as he plowed ahead, he repeatedly saw the Spirit preparing the soil ahead of him.

Don's ministries have changed lives and, for that matter, the national culture. When Don founded FCA in 1954, he noted that religion was generally a private and individual matter in the nation's locker rooms. Today, pro and college teams have chaplains and Bible study groups, the players often pray before games and star athletes frequently testify to their Christian faith. Ministry of Money, founded in 1975, and its successor ministry, Harvest Time, have influenced contemporary thought on the relationship of money and faith—a crucial if underappreciated issue amid America's affluence. Don pushed past the tithing and money-management approaches that so often passed as Christian wisdom to explore deeper issues: the tithe as a starting point rather than the standard, the role of money in Christian conversion and freedom, and the need for rich and poor to be in relationship with one another.

All strong personalities have their shadow side, and with Don it has been no different. He has excelled in vision and action, but at times his single-minded intensity and occasional fits of anger have alienated others and ruptured relationships. He has suffered periods of anguish, doubt and depression. Don's self-understanding is that his life has been that of a deeply flawed individual who nevertheless became an instrument that God could use in numerous powerful ways.

Through periods of both triumph and despair, Don has lived deeply, passionately, abundantly. To some, Don's spiritual life and achievements can seem far beyond reach. Many may feel as if they are hardly out of the gate in the Christian life, much less passing the halfway point. Not all can be Don McClanen, whom God endowed with unique gifts of personal warmth, energy, fearlessness and devotion. But if his life is worth the telling, it is to underline that all people, according to their gifts, can accomplish great things. Or more properly said, those grafted into a small community of serious disciples can be opened to God's indwelling Spirit and be used to accomplish great things.

This book tells the story of Don's life, distilling principles and lessons that can advance the path of anyone seeking to follow Christ. As God has put Don to good use, so the Lord wants to use all people. May the reading of this book help in that high adventure.

1

Blessed Encounters

"Knock and the door will be opened to you."
–Matthew 7:7 (NIV)

August 1954

"Mr. Rickey will see you for five minutes." With these words, an assistant ushered Don McClanen into the office of Branch Rickey, the general manager of the Pittsburgh Pirates and one of the most important figures in American sports.

Don, 29 years old, had been trying for months to see Rickey. An obscure basketball coach and athletic director at Eastern Oklahoma A&M College, Don had dreamed up the idea of creating a movement of Christian athletes who would lead youth to Jesus, capitalizing on the nation's worship of sports heroes. A dozen well-known sports figures had said yes to an initial letter, but Rickey had not bothered to respond.

Rickey seemed to be the main cog he needed to get his organization into motion. First, Rickey had great influence in the sports world. His brilliance as a baseball executive had powered his previous teams, the St. Louis Cardinals and Brooklyn Dodgers, to eight pennants and four World Series championships, plus numerous additional titles in the years following Rickey's departures. Essentially Rickey had invented modern baseball: he formed the first minor-league farm system, dismantled pro baseball's color barrier by hiring Jackie Robinson to play for the Dodgers, initiated the use of batting helmets and marketed the game to women as well as men. Equally important, Rickey was a devoted Christian with strong Methodist roots–his mother had named him Wesley Branch Rickey. Don had also noted the clause Rickey negotiated in his management contracts absolving him from attendance at Sunday games.

But Don had faced clear obstacles in getting to Rickey. The Pirates' executive might assume Don was little more than "something out of a box of Cracker Jacks." Also, Rickey, 72, suffered from an inner-ear disorder called Meniere's Disease, and he was preoccupied trying to resuscitate a team that was mired in the National League cellar. Don had made numerous prior calls to the Pirates' executive offices trying to speak with Rickey, but the manager's assistant, Ken Blackburn, and Rickey's son, Branch Rickey Jr., had told him repeatedly Rickey just had too much on his plate.

Undeterred, Don, the folksy young coach, called Blackburn again from his parents' home in Morrisville, Pennsylvania, where he, his wife Gloria and their two children were visiting. Don told Blackburn he would be passing through Pittsburgh the next day while driving home—not exactly a straight line to Oklahoma, but a detour that might pay off. "Is Mr. Rickey going to be in town tomorrow?" Don asked.

"As far as I know, he's scheduled to be here," Blackburn responded.

"What time do your offices open?"

"Eight o'clock."

"I'll be there at ten of eight."

Early the next morning Don drove from a motel to Forbes Field, the home of the Pirates, leaving Gloria and the kids "to cover me in prayer." Sitting in the Pirates' outer office at eight o'clock, Don watched a slightly stooped elderly gentleman hobble in and, without looking Don's way, enter a corridor of executive offices. Don recognized him immediately—the bushy eyebrows, grey suit, white shirt, bow tie and, clamped in his hand, an unlit cigar. About ten minutes later, Blackburn announced to Don that Rickey would see him for five minutes.

The meeting lasted five hours.

As Don entered the office, Rickey sat behind his desk. Behind him, a row of glass-block windows filtered light onto an oversized bulletin board on another wall that contained columns of names: one column for the Pirates' roster and the other dozen or so containing every player on the organization's minor-league teams. Rickey welcomed Don and asked him to take a seat. Don leaned forward, laid out his dream of bringing ball players together to influence youth for Christ and mentioned the Rev. Louis Evans Sr., former pastor of a Presbyterian church in Pittsburgh who supported Don's idea. "Yes, I know of that man Evans," Rickey said.

Don ran down a list of athletes he had contacted, and others who he knew were Christian. "Do you mean Robin Roberts is a Christian?" Rickey exclaimed when Don mentioned the Philadelphia Phillies pitcher who had faced the Pirates' Vernon Law, a devout Christian, the previous evening. "You mean these were two Christian men pitching against each other?"

"Yes," Don answered, "and there are lots of others like them."

Now Rickey also leaned forward. He began to grill Don about his faith. "Do you really believe in Jesus Christ?" Satisfied with Don's answers, Rickey asked if Don had any money. Don explained that, no, he had taken out a $1,000 loan using his white Pontiac as collateral to pay for trips to visit athletes that summer. This prompted Rickey to reminisce about taking over the impoverished St. Louis Cardinals during World War I. When visitors came to the Cardinals' office, Rickey said, he would bring a rug from home to dress up the place. Soon Don thought to himself, *This guy wants me to hang around. I'm not burdening him.*

"You're going to need some money," Rickey said. He pledged to help Don raise $10,000. Between phone calls about player trades, Rickey continued to brainstorm with Don. "This thing has the potential for changing the youth scene in America in a decade," he exclaimed.

"Would you put that on your stationery?" Don asked.

Later, following lunch with Rickey and Vernon Law, Don left with a four-sentence Rickey endorsement. Little did he know that the organization growing out of that meeting, the Fellowship of Christian Athletes, would become the world's largest Christian sports organization.

January 1963

"Good evening, sir. What brings you here?"

Don had just slipped into the door of a small Washington, D.C., storefront church about the size of a small living room and had taken a seat in the back row. The large woman who addressed him stood in front of a dozen or so worshippers. She wore a dark dress and black, no-nonsense shoes and exuded a commanding presence. The worshippers turned around to face Don. He explained that he was taking a course on Christian ethics at a nearby church, and that the pastor that evening had told the class to "take their ethics to the street"—to go out and see what they might find. Don had wandered eight blocks into the inner-city and wound up here on Seaton Place, a dilapidated, trash-strewn block one resident described as a place of "rats, roaches, winos and fights."

If any drinking or disturbance was going on that evening, Don didn't see it. Instead, he had heard the sounds of tambourines, clapping and singing coming from a building in the middle of the block. The sign said "Sacred Heart Church," and there was a cross over the door, but it was the music that drew him to step inside, he told the small group.

"Wonderful," responded the woman, whom Don sized up to be 300 pounds. "Do you mind giving us your testimony?"

"I would be glad to," Don said. He described his conversion experience at college in Oklahoma and how God had eventually led him to Washington, D.C., to join a congregation called the Church of the Saviour. He told how he worked as a farmer at a retreat farm the church owned in Germantown, Maryland, 25 miles away. Don did not mention his founding of the Fellowship of Christian Athletes, which he had left one-and-a-half years earlier.

The pastor thanked Don for his words, then continued the service. *This is the first time in my life I've been in the midst of a group of black people,* Don reflected. There were none in his schools growing up in Pennsylvania. Two had been on his submarine during World War II, but they were steward mates largely segregated to the officers' quarters. The colleges that he attended and where he coached basketball had not admitted blacks, and even his work with athletes through FCA had put him into contact with a limited number. Only a few middle-class blacks were members of his own church.

Don, a minority all by himself, sat in a room of inner-city residents. He looked around. The pastor stood at a small podium topped by a Bible. Behind her, various pictures of Jesus hung on the wall, along with a cardboard heart painted red. In front of her, worshippers sat in four rows of folding wooden chairs. Some in the front row had tambourines. Fifteen minutes later the service ended, and Don stepped forward. "We're glad you came," the pastor said. As they chatted, he learned that her name was Bishop Marie Reed and that her special concern was for the 124 children who lived on that block. "Is there any chance the retreat farm could host a summer camp for some of the children?" she asked. Don said that he would like that, and would check with leaders at his church.

"Can I come back and worship with you next week?" Don asked.

"Of course," Reed responded. Don had been hungering for a new mission since leaving FCA. A similar electric sense of possibility–a chance to create a ministry that would immerse him, not in the world of celebrity athletes, but in a community of people hemmed in by bigotry–thrilled him. Soon Don would be eating a weekly dinner with Reed's family, sleeping occasionally in a house across the street and mentoring some of the children of the neighborhood. Eventually he founded a ministry to train and empower inner-city youth leaders.

January 14, 1979

"Is it possible to set up an appointment with Mother Teresa for seven people from America?" Don asked the woman who answered the phone.

"Well, this is Mother Teresa," stated the voice on the other end of the line.

Don and Gloria had arrived in Calcutta (now named Kolkata), India, the previous night with a group from the Church of the Saviour. They were almost three weeks into a month-long tour of India, on which the McClanens hoped to gain a greater understanding of Third World poverty. The group hoped to talk with the Catholic nun who had gained worldwide renown for her work with the poorest of the poor. They also were hot, tired and disoriented from their travels. They did not realize that all the deprivation they had seen already in India–the filth, people dressed in rags living on the street, beggars, amputees–would be even more brutally displayed in Calcutta.

Mother Teresa told Don she could see them that day if they came to her Missionaries of Charity Mother House. The excited group set out by taxi from their hotel, where a half-dozen waiters had hovered about them at breakfast. The streets were jammed with traffic: packed buses with riders on the outside as well as clinging to window sills; taxis with horns blaring; rickshaws ferrying the rare well-to-do; an occasional cow wandering down the middle of the street; and snake-charmers galore.

People in ragged, dirty clothes who had nowhere else to live covered the sidewalks. Some lay asleep on sheets of cardboard, others on worn pieces of fabric. Some bathed, splashing themselves from buckets or with water that gurgled out of open pipes. Some cooked over stove pots on cow-dung fires, the smoke curling into the dust-filled air. And out of large pits workers clambered with baskets of dirt on their heads–Calcutta's stunningly primitive way of excavating for a subway system. The group encountered the omnipresent beggars, the cripples and the mournful children who approached them saying, "*bhukha, bhukha*"–"hungry, hungry." After two weeks in India they resisted these entreaties, having been told that giving to the beggars only supported the "pimps" who often controlled them.

When they arrived at the Mother House, they walked down a short alley and knocked at a simple wooden door. Don noticed a tile by the door that said, "Mother Teresa," with a slat underneath that slid to cover either the word "in" or the word "out." At that moment the word "in" was visible. *This is like going to the White House and seeing a sign that the president is in*, Don thought. A sister dressed in a white-and-blue sari and headscarf opened the door and told them that Mother Teresa was visiting with some businessmen and would be with them shortly. The sister seated them on benches along the wall of the small, bare antechamber. In an alcove off the antechamber, dozens of blankets were piled. After 20 minutes, the group saw a half dozen Hindu men in business suits walk through the antechamber and out the door. Shortly after, the group's rising expectancy peaked as Mother Teresa appeared.

"She's so tiny," Gloria McClanen commented to the group later. Don had a different thought: *She looks so strong.*

Mother, as Don came to call her later, was dressed in her usual white sari and headdress, both trimmed with three blue stripes. Just over five feet tall, she was slightly hunched, feet bare, face furrowed with wrinkles. She greeted them with a warm smile and reported her enthusiasm about her visit with the departed businessmen, "These good men have given us all these blankets!" She then invited the group into another room with a map on the wall displaying the dozens of Missionaries of Charity locations around the world.

Mother spent almost an hour with the group, asking about their mission, speaking of loving God and loving the poorest of the poor, commenting on America's material wealth but also on its poverty of love toward so many of its citizens, and telling of her order's work in Calcutta with infant orphans, lepers and the destitute and dying. She was not an erudite speaker, Don noticed. In truth, she was very simple, very plain and "very present." He was in awe.

Mother described Kalighat, or the House for the Destitute and Dying, where the sisters cared for terminally ill men and women they had picked up off the streets. Don was captivated and was determined to see it before the group departed for New Delhi. The following day he and several others arrived at the entrance to the house, a former hostel for pilgrims who had traveled to see the adjacent temple devoted to the Hindu goddess Kali. The door of Kalighat stood open, without a guard or greeter. Don walked up three steps into a long room with 50 men lying in three rows of cots. A separate room for 50 women, with their own rows of cots, lay to the right of the entrance. The scene reminded Don of a battlefield hospital he had seen during World War II. "I saw bodies and starving people and dying people, and sisters and volunteers feeding and bathing and medicating," he said. "There was misery, poverty, hunger, death." There was also, Don felt, an unmistakable "aura of love and joy."

After the trip, Gloria, a nurse, wrote about her impression of the house, where the sisters put the McClanens to work feeding and bathing residents. "I set the bowl of rice on the floor beside her cot and gathered the old dying woman in my arms," Gloria wrote. "It was obvious she was not physically hungry, but starving for love and warmth from another human being as she finished her dying. My thoughts went to the little woman in the blue-bordered sari I had met the night before at the Mother House. ... I wondered how that simple, uncomplicated and totally dedicated nun felt when she picked up her first patient covered by ants and half-eaten by rats.

Surely she had to be convinced that it was Christ she served in that broken body. ... I looked down into the face of the woman in my arms and tried to believe it was Christ in her that I was serving at that moment." When she returned to America, Gloria would try to adopt that attitude of serving Jesus with all her nursing patients.

Don, similarly moved while tending to the broken poor, knew deep in his soul that he had come "home" and would return to this place. He didn't have an inkling, though, that during the next quarter century he would bring almost a thousand people with him, not only to Calcutta, but also to other sites of destitution in Haiti, Thailand, the Philippines, Kenya, Sudan, Ethiopia, Mexico, Nicaragua, Egypt, Bosnia, Kosovo, Jordan, Palestine and Iraq.

Summer 1983

"What's your reaction?" Don asked the woman on the other end of the phone line.

"Mary" [not her real name] answered, "I'm sitting here crying."

Don had met Mary three years before at a conference where Don spoke about the Church of the Saviour and its ministries. Don had mentioned that he was involved in an outreach called Ministry of Money. At the next break, a middle-aged woman with high, Katherine Hepburn cheekbones and an unmistakable vivaciousness approached him and asked, "What in the world is a Ministry of Money?" Don explained that its mission was to help affluent people deal with their wealth from a biblical perspective, and that its work was done primarily through workshops and "pilgrimages" to the Third World.

"Oh, that's just what I need," Mary exclaimed.

She attended a Ministry of Money workshop in 1982. As their friendship grew, Don learned that Mary was a multi-millionaire. She had grown up in a wealthy family and had attended an elite boarding school. Her marriage ended in divorce, and she had raised two children with the help of a nanny. With a home in an exclusive California community, she was searching for meaning in her life. Don also learned about Mary's empathy for the poor. Having grown up in the Depression, she recalled peeking out the window of her home at beggars who came to the back door to ask for food and being driven by chauffeurs past bonfires that poor people had built on a lakeshore to keep warm and cook meals.

Mary consequently made substantial gifts to Church of the Saviour ministries, amounting to tens of thousands of dollars, in addition to other charities she supported. But Don believed she was ready to make a more high-impact gift to help the poor. In a phone conversation, Don described a dream of some members of the Church of the Saviour: to buy an abandoned apartment building in an inner-city area of Washington, D.C., and turn it into a shelter for the homeless. Don told Mary that the building was now used as a crack house, but that two staff members of a church-operated medical clinic in the neighborhood envisioned it redeemed into a place that gave the sick and homeless a new opportunity and freedom from the streets. There was just one major hurdle: to buy and refurbish it required at least $1 million.

Moved to tears by the idea, Mary said, "Fine, get to work."

As plans proceeded, cost estimates rose. Within a few months, at a meeting with church leaders that included one of its best-known supporters, urban developer James Rouse, Don learned that the new price tag was going to be more like $2 million. Don called Mary and asked if he could fly out to California and discuss it with her.

The morning after his arrival, Don and Mary sat in the living room of her elegant, hillside home, praying and reading Scripture. The picture windows afforded a beautiful view of wooded slopes. In back of the house were a pool and nanny cottage. They agreed that, before Mary decided on what she might give, they would each take a separate walk on paths that traversed the surrounding slopes, asking God to direct Mary. As Don strolled through a forest area, occasionally resting on a tree stump or rock, he felt calm. There was nothing for him to do, no pressure to apply, no expectation to hold. *Two dollars or two million dollars,* he found himself thinking, *it will be okay. This is clearly the work of the Holy Spirit.*

An hour later, they shared a cup of tea in the kitchen. Mary sat on a stool, Don stood at the counter. "I know what it ought to be," Mary said.

"What should it be?" Don asked.

"Two and a half million," Mary said.

The announcement seemed almost anticlimactic. The two continued their conversation without particular emotion or celebration—almost as if they had been discussing the price of a carton of eggs.

Two years later, when the homeless shelter opened with the name Christ House, the cost for purchase, renovation and furnishing came to $2.4 million. The extra $100,000 paid for hiring an initial staff. "It was one of the most amazing miracles," Don said later.

Boldness

Many Christians may make the mistake of believing that they cannot accomplish much of significance beyond the small influence they might have on people with whom they interact day to day. When it comes to larger challenges where boldness is required—convincing a large group to witness for Christ, bringing change to inner-city neighborhoods, seeking the support of an influential person for a ministry, raising a large sum of money—they often shrink back.

Many of us lack Don's natural adventurousness and embrace of risk-taking. But these three principles can increase our confidence to take risks for God's kingdom:

1) We can know that God is waiting to jump in and help us when we get in over our heads. The Rev. Ray Hammond of Boston's Bethel A.M.E. Church notes that if we only attempt to do what we know we can achieve, we are essentially telling God, "I don't need you; I can do it myself." But if we have a God-inspired vision to do what we know is beyond our normal capacities, then we give God room to work and fill our inadequacies. Don and others who have attempted great things for God have found that their risk-taking has multiplied their faith as they felt God lift them over hurdles they couldn't leap by themselves.

2) We work best in community. Don initiated powerful ministries, but he could not have advanced without support from others. We rarely achieve anything of significance alone. As Ecclesiastes 4:12 says, "And though one might prevail against another, two will withstand one. A threefold cord is not quickly broken" (NRSV). Working as a team is crucial to provide mutual encouragement, gen-

erate ideas, hold each other accountable and carry out the work. God often answers our needs and fills our inadequacies through other people who come alongside. The team doesn't have to be large; in fact, small is often better. Anthropologist Margaret Mead said, "Never doubt that a small group of thoughtful, committed citizens can change the world. Indeed, it's the only thing that ever has." Gordon Cosby, Don's pastor at the Church of the Saviour in Washington, D.C., notes that a small group of highly committed people can accomplish a lot more than a large group of half-committed people.

3) We can be unapologetic about our cause. To recruit a highly committed team, raise money and convince influential people to alter what they are doing all require that something important be at stake. We may shrink back from proclaiming that our cause is important because we believe that we as individuals aren't that important, or believe that our cause isn't seen as important by the larger culture. But we can seek to refine our message to express the essence of the kingdom work that we are undertaking: "Babies are dying...," "Children's souls and futures are at stake...," "The sick and mentally ill are being left untended...," "We wouldn't allow our families to live in that kind of environment...." We won't be surprised that some close their ears to what we say, but we can be confident that some will hear and respond. For every one who turns away, we are that much closer to the one who will say, "Yes."

2
Founding the Fellowship

"Your young men shall see visions."
–Joel 2:28 (NRSV)

Born on February 3, 1925, Don grew up in Morrisville, Pennsylvania, a town across the Delaware River from Trenton, New Jersey. Don's father, a carpenter and home builder, and his mother were members of a Presbyterian church, but limited their personal piety to Sunday-morning worship and church meetings. Once, when Don expressed enthusiasm about a sermon and suggested that he might want to become a pastor, his father chided him as being impractical. Don's parents certainly would not have guessed his future impact in the Christian world.

Don was an average student and an above-average athlete who played end on his high school football team. At a slender five feet ten inches, he was not destined for a major college program. Clean-cut good looks, a warm smile and a fun-loving personality made Don popular with his fellow students, who elected him president of his junior and senior classes and president of his church youth group. However, his antics and practical jokes frequently landed him in the principal's office. A local justice of the peace described him as "the orneriest kid to ever graduate from Morrisville High School," and occasional displays of impetuous risk-taking, such as walking with his dog across the ice-covered Delaware River one winter–near where George Washington made his famous Christmas eve crossing–worried his parents.

If Don was always up for a good time, he also had a strong sense of right and wrong. When he heard pro baseball manager Leo Durocher's quip, "Nice guys finish last," Don knew the aphorism was not only unfair, it was simply a lie. He harbored in his young soul a determination to prove that winning athletes could also be winning people, which became the first stirrings leading to the creation of the Fellowship of Christian Athletes. Don also was outraged by the Japanese attack on Pearl Harbor, which occurred three months into his high school senior year. He burned with a desire to join the military and exact revenge. But his parents refused to grant permission, required for under-age recruits. Don spent a year at Admiral Farragut Naval Academy, a prep school on the New Jersey coast. Afterward he entered navy flight school but was scrubbed because of an oversupply of fliers. He ended up training as a gunner's mate for the submarine service. In 1945, the final year of the war, his ship, the U.S.S. Chub, patrolled the Java and South China seas, sinking several enemy vessels, diving frequently to escape Japanese bombs and rescuing three downed pilots.

Two experiences during Don's Navy years showed his impetuosity. As he completed submarine school in New London, Connecticut, in the fall of 1944, Don panicked that a crew position on a submarine might not be available and his chance to fight in the war might slip away. He learned that the U.S.S. Chub, a new submarine, was to leave for the Pacific just after his graduation. Violating military protocol, Don located the New London home of the skipper, Captain Cassius Douglas Rhymes Jr., and knocked on the door. A 33-year-old man with a Mississippi drawl came to the door in street clothes. "May I come in and talk to you for a few minutes, sir?" Don asked.

The startled captain stared at Don for a moment before answering, "Yeah, come in." Don began, "Captain, I realize this is highly unusual, but I want to go to sea so bad I can taste it. I will sleep in the bilges, I will mess-cook, I will do anything to go with you on the Chub." After several seconds of silence, Rhymes squinted at Don and asked, "What did you say your name was, sailor?" For a sickening moment, Don thought the captain was going to call the shore patrol and have Don arrested for insubordination. He answered, "McClanen, sir." Rhymes's surprising response was, "You're the kind of boy I want on my sub. But there's not a chance in the world for you, because we're all commissioned. The crew is at full complement, has already been on the shakedown cruise and we're leaving in three days." Don replied, "Captain, I'm aware of that. That's why

I'm here. Because I want to go with you." Two days later Don received orders to report to the Chub to replace a sailor who had fallen ill.

The second experience was far more foolhardy. In June 1945, Don's submarine sailed into the Philippines' Subic Bay for a two-week rest and refitting stop. Don, now 19 years old, had heard scuttlebutt from shipmates about how some sub sailors hunted for the enemy on the islands where their subs landed for rest stops, some at the cost of their lives. This idea seized his imagination. On his first night in Subic, Don quietly left his rest camp, hitchhiked 55 miles to Clark Air Force Base outside Manila and managed to find out which planes were going where. When he found one that was to take off for Okinawa, he thought, *That's got my name on it.* U.S. forces had invaded the Japanese island, 900 miles north of the Philippines, in March 1945, and some of the fiercest fighting of the Pacific campaign was taking place there. When no one was paying attention, Don climbed aboard the plane and hid behind some large boxes. When the plane landed at Naha Air Force Base in Okinawa, Don walked off trying to look nonchalantly like part of the crew, despite his sailor uniform.

The U.S. military had largely occupied the island, but Japanese soldiers continued to fight. The air base crawled with tanks, trucks, jeeps and troops, all headed in different directions. The surrounding terrain was a moonscape of rock, volcanic ash and artillery-shattered trees. A soldier pointed Don in the direction of the front, and Don began walking backward on the road with his thumb out. When shore patrol officers stopped to question him, Don responded, "I'm on one of those ships in the harbor and I'm going to see my brother." An officer replied, "This is no picnic. Get back on your ship." After the jeep drove off, Don continued hitchhiking. Eventually an Army truck stopped for him, and he slipped on a dirty Army jacket he found on the vehicle's floor.

When they reached a Marine camp, Don got off and left the jacket in the truck. The Marines looked suspiciously at Don's navy uniform, so he told them a lie. "My brother, a Marine, was killed. I came here just to be with you guys and to get revenge for his death." A lieutenant said his platoon would take Don on patrol the next day, and gave him a flak jacket, helmet, grenades and a rifle. In the tropical heat of the following morning, Don was quickly exhausted by the weight of his equipment and fell out from the patrol and stumbled back to camp. At dawn the next morning, the lieutenant placed Don with a machine gun on a perimeter line of Marines guarding the camp. Don took his place among some scrub trees. Within 15 minutes, he saw a Japanese soldier rise from the brush 80 feet away and cock his arm to throw a grenade. Don lifted his machine gun and fired, and the soldier fell dead. As Don walked up to the soldier's body, two Marines came up beside him. One unsheathed his knife and cut off the soldier's ears, and the other pulled out pliers and extracted the soldier's teeth. When they offered these to Don, he backed away and declined. His years of frustration in seeking revenge for Pearl Harbor had ended. Killing the enemy on a submarine with torpedoes was one thing; hand-to-hand combat was another. When Don would later recount the adventure, he would appreciate its adventurousness, but also acknowledge that it was his introduction to the deep depravity of war. After Don hitched a flight back to Subic Bay, word filtered up to his executive officer. "McClanen, there's only one thing I should do with you—court-martial you," the officer said "I'm not going to do that. You just keep your mouth shut and don't mention this to anybody else."

In February 1946, the day Don was discharged from the Navy, a Navy lieutenant standing on a train platform asked him offhandedly, "What are you going to do now, sailor?"

Don replied, "Well, I'm probably going to go to college."

"Where?"

"Probably University of Pennsylvania. That's closest to where I live."

"Why don't you come to a *good* school?"

"Where's that?"

"Oklahoma A & M."

The suggestion grabbed Don's attention. He knew the Oklahoma A & M football team ranked third in the country, behind Army and Navy, led by All-American halfback Bob Fenimore. And its basketball team, coached by the legendary Henry Iba, had just won its second straight national title—the first college to achieve that feat—behind the game's first seven-footer, All-American Bob

Kurland. So Don wrote to Iba, saying he wanted to go to college and become the best coach he could be. Don admitted that his high school grades were unimpressive, but added that he had served on a submarine during the war. Iba wrote back an encouraging letter. "You're a veteran, you've matured and you're ready to go to school. We don't concentrate on the past; we look to the future."

Don arrived for school in Stillwater, Oklahoma, with his new wife, Gloria Clark, who had been valedictorian of their high school class. They lived in a trailer they had hauled out from New Jersey because of a Stillwater housing shortage and began attending a local Presbyterian church. One day, the youth pastor visited them in their trailer and asked Don to give a three-minute talk on making his vocation Christian. He agreed, but was puzzled. As a physical education major, how was he supposed to marry his faith with his aspiration of coaching sports teams? The question lodged in Don's soul, awaiting an answer along with the Durocher quote about nice guys finishing last.

In April 1947, during the spring of Don's freshman year, Don's and Gloria's first child, Douglas, was born on Easter Sunday. But two days later, their joy turned to grief when their son died, apparently from injuries during a difficult labor. "Your baby just died," the obstetrician announced brusquely as he stuck his head in the door of Gloria's hospital room before hurrying on to his next patient. Days later, with Gloria recovering from the Caesarian section, Don made a lonely trip to Morrisville, flying in a plane with Douglas's body stowed in the cargo hold in a small coffin. Douglas was buried in a McClanen family cemetery plot with three grandparents present. For some, this tragedy might have shaken their faith. But for Don— with Gloria, his pastor and his church community gathered around him—it deepened his search for Christian meaning.

Later that spring, Don attended a physical education conference in Oklahoma City, 60 miles from Oklahoma A & M. One of the speakers was H. Clay Fisk, a school principal from Tulsa who had played football for the University of Kansas, coached state championship squads at two high schools and been a decades-long lay leader at First Presbyterian Church in Tulsa. There was nothing overtly religious about Fisk's talk. But Don was moved and inspired by Fisk's challenge that coaches, in the way they live their lives, can "lead a young person up a mountain or down a drain." An anguished sense of sin awakened in Don–that he was failing to be the Christian model he wanted to be. The words of St. Paul rang in his ears: "For I do not do the good I want, but the evil I do not want is what I do" (Romans 7:19 NRSV). After the talk, while others went to lunch, Don slipped out of the hotel to ponder what he had heard. After walking four blocks, he saw an open door to a church, knelt in a back pew and prayed simply, "Lord, I surrender my will to you." That was it–no deep emotion or grand spiritual insight. Yet Don came to call that moment his real "conversion," the beginning of a shift from belief to obedience. He was struck by the wondrous way God worked: converting a Presbyterian in a Catholic church through a school principal's non-religious presentation during a secular conference.

With his deepening commitment to follow God's will and his musings about how to do that as a future coach, Don started to take note of prominent athletes who were Christians. He collected articles about them from newspaper sports pages, magazines such as *Life* and the *Saturday Evening Post*, and from *Guideposts*, a national magazine that printed inspirational stories about people of faith. Don stuffed each new article in his top dresser drawer. He continued this collection through his graduation from Oklahoma A & M in 1950; during a year of coaching basketball at a high school in Norfolk, Oklahoma (a rural crossroads near Stillwater); and after he was hired as basketball coach and athletic director at Eastern Oklahoma Agricultural and Mechanical (now Eastern Oklahoma State). As Don's clippings mounted, an idea took shape: that Christian stars could harness the worship of sports heroes into a positive influence on youth. The need was great, Don felt. After all, FBI Director J. Edgar Hoover had said, "Juvenile delinquency is largely the result of a lack of spiritual emphasis in the home." And in *A Man Called Peter*, a best-selling book by Catherine Marshall about her husband and chaplain of the U.S. Senate, the Rev. Dr. Peter Marshall, Don read that 30 million American youth were going without religious training of any kind.[1]

Don experimented with this idea at Eastern A & M. He posted clippings in the locker room, and he implemented a team prayer before games. He often called on six-foot four-inch Jim Howell, one of the team's forwards, to say the prayer. Howell, who later became a lawyer, judge and state senator, once worded a prayer, "Help us to help those who can't help themselves." When he finished, Don had tears in his eyes. In spring 1954 on a team trip, Don had another chance to make an impression on Howell. Eastern A & M had won the Oklahoma junior-college title and was invited to the national tournament in Hutchison, Kansas. En route, the team spent the night in a motel, and Don shared a room with Howell. As they watched TV, Don said, "Wouldn't it be great, Jim, if an athlete would get on TV and advertise his faith similar to the way they advertise tires and cars and other things? An influential athlete talking about his faith would have quite an impact."

Don's personality and character were doing their own kind of advertising with other players, most of whom were not church-goers. Curg Laughlin, a five-foot ten-inch farm boy who had played guard for Don at Norfolk High before following him to Eastern A & M, was one of those. Don, as Laughlin's young coach, provided an older-brother figure. Laughlin's father had died when he was seven and he lived alone with his mother on a farm. Don did not favor or coddle him; on the contrary, Don was an intense, demanding coach who pushed Laughlin and the rest of the team hard with condition-ing and defensive drills taken from Henry Iba, for whom Don had been team manager for three years. But Don did not demean his players or utter a profanity. He believed in their perfectibility. "You've got the talent and you need to work at it," he told Laughlin and others, leaving the players encouraged by the idea that they were valued.

At Norfolk High, which was five miles down a gravel road from the nearest highway, the McClanens lived in a "teacherage," a school-furnished house with only one bedroom. The kitchen had no electrical outlets, so extension cords hung down from the overhead light fixture to run appliances. Gloria broke into tears at the sight when she first arrived with Don and their children, Michael, two, and Judy, an infant. They lived on a $2,600 annual salary. Gloria and the kids went to all the games, and Don took a mediocre program to a first-year 29-2 record in 1951. After his first loss, a one-pointer late in the season, Don was so distraught that he drove to a drugstore in a nearby town and bought a bottle of Hadacol, a patent cure-all medicine, to get himself to sleep. He showed this same competitiveness in the second, season-ending loss in the regional finals, when Laughlin sprained his ankle in the last quarter. "You're not hurt; get back in there," Don told him.

Don stopped by when Laughlin was plowing a field the next summer and asked him to come to Eastern A & M, where Don had taken a new coaching job. Laughlin had never heard of the school, but he jumped at the chance to follow Don. Iba had arranged the job for Don at the college, which was 70 miles from the Arkansas line in Wilburton. The job was a step up from the one at Norfolk, but not exactly a leap. Wilburton was a town of about 2,000 people in Oklahoma's southeastern hill country, the poorest part of the state. Don's salary increased to $3,600, and the family moved into a college-supplied teacherage—an apartment with two bedrooms, rather than one, and actual electrical outlets in the kitchen. It was located in a former military Quonset hut that had been relocated just off campus. The children played in a front yard largely devoid of grass.

Don worked hard, Laughlin recalled. "He was a trainer. He wrapped our feet. He did everything. ... It wouldn't surprise me if he even mopped the floor." During games Don was so animated, stomping his feet at mistakes or leaping into the air, that fans came partly to watch his gyrations.[2] Gloria fixed breakfast for the players before they left for away games and then climbed aboard the bus, with the two children in tow, to cheer the team on. Don became a profoundly shaping force in Laughlin's life. When Laughlin made the mistake of shoplifting "a shirt that didn't fit and a belt that was too small," Don found out and sent him a letter withdrawing his athletic scholarship. Don stated that if he ever saw Laughlin again, he would turn away from him. Laughlin, devastated, carried the letter in his pocket for two years as a token of shame and a spur to redemption. Twenty years later, by this time a physician, he reconnected with Don, who had contacted him about a reunion of their team. Don had forgotten about the shoplifting incident, and was distressed to learn how severely he had treated Laughlin. "Thank you for having a tremendous influence on my life," Laughlin later wrote.

In March 1954, Don's third year at Eastern A & M, he picked up the *Daily Oklahoman* newspaper as Gloria prepared breakfast for the family. Don read something that jolted him to attention. A small announcement said Dr. Louis H. Evans Sr., national minister-at-large of the Presbyterian Church, would be speaking on the following Thursday evening at First Presbyterian Church in Oklahoma City. Don immediately thought of a *Life* magazine clipping in his top dresser drawer about Evans, a former all-conference basketball player at Occidental College in Los Angeles, whom *Life* had listed as one of the country's ten leading clergymen. *He is the perfect person to help me realize my vision,* Don thought. Don knew he had to go hear and meet Evans. But a moment later, when he realized his basketball team had a game scheduled on that night, his spirit sank. He slammed the clipping back into the drawer and swore, *God, I thought this was something you wanted.*

The day after Evans appeared in Oklahoma City, Don, Gloria, five-year-old Michael and four-year-old Judy climbed into their four-door white Pontiac and drove 190 miles to Oklahoma A & M in Stillwater. They planned to stay with their old campus minister, the Rev. Bob Geller, and his family. Don continued to brood over his lost opportunity of the previous evening. When the McClanens pulled up at the Gellers' home a couple of blocks north of campus, Bob's vivacious wife, June, hurried out to the driveway. "I'm so glad you are here early," she said. "Come in and put your things away; we're having a guest for supper."

"Who is the guest?" Don asked.

"Dr. Louis H. Evans," June replied.

Don's heart almost stopped. "What is he doing here?" he blurted out. June explained that Evans had come to speak during the campus's Religious Life Week.[3] About an hour later, Evans arrived. A handsome man with a square jaw and outgoing personality, he spoke with an easy authority befitting one of the Presbyterian Church's most prominent clergymen. He also looked the part of a former basketball player, his business suit enclosing a six-foot four-inch frame. While the McClanens' children ate in the kitchen with the Gellers' seven-year-old daughter, the adults sat down to a dinner in the dining room. At one point Bob Geller said to Don, "Tell Dr. Evans what you've been sharing with me."

Don launched into his vision. "It's an attempt to witness for

Christ through Christian athletes, capitalizing on the hero worship phenomenon in society," he explained. "I've been hanging on to these clippings about Carl Erskine and you and Otto Graham, Doak Walker and Branch Rickey." (Carl Erskine was an all-star pitcher with the Brooklyn Dodgers, Otto Graham an all-pro quarterback with the Cleveland Browns, and Doak Walker an all-pro halfback with the Detroit Lions.)

"Don, that's a great idea," Evans said. "It must already be going on, it's so great."

Don replied that he had no interest in duplicating what might already be happening, but noted that he had been on the lookout for such activity for several years and had not found it. (One precursor that Don might have mentioned was Billy Graham's crusades. At the evangelist's first crusade in 1947 in Charlotte, North Carolina, Graham arranged for the reigning American mile champion, Gil Dodds, to run a simulated race around a makeshift track and then give his testimony. Dodds was so well-received that Graham frequently included athletes in his crusades thereafter. But of course the athletes were a side event to Graham's preaching.)[4]

"So why don't you write these guys and see what they say?" Evans told Don.

That's all the encouragement Don needed. Back in Wilburton, he began drafting a letter. But what could he say to get their attention? That he had been on a county runner-up high school football team? That he had gone out for the Oklahoma A & M football team and ended up a "seventh-string meatball"? That he had tried to develop his placekicking to make himself useful to the team, practicing long hours with Gloria holding the ball for him and Dusty, their cocker spaniel, chasing the kicks, but that A & M coach Jim Lookabaugh had been unimpressed in an era prior to kicking specialists? That he had finally dropped off the football team his sophomore year? That he had been manager of the basketball team for three years, soaking up the coaching strategies of Henry Iba?

At least Don could point to his success at Eastern Oklahoma, guiding the team to one Oklahoma junior-college championship, two second-place finishes and an 11th-place finish in the National Junior College Tournament. With Iba's continuing encouragement and influence, Don was well-positioned to move up to a major-college coaching job. But what did these trophies mean to professional ballplayers who were at the top of the athletic world? Otto Graham, for instance, had led the Browns to four straight All-America Football Conference championships from 1946 to 1949 and then guided them to the NFL championship in 1950 when the Browns joined that league. Graham went on to make the NFL title game his last five seasons, winning two more championships. With a career regular-season record of 105-17-4, he was such a phenomenon that Peter King of *Sports Illustrated* would later name him the best quarterback of all time, higher than No. 2 Joe Montana and No. 3 Johnny Unitas.[5] (King was writing in the era before Tom Brady of the New England Patriots staked a claim to belong in that pantheon.)

Carl Erskine had led the National League with 20 wins and 6 losses in 1953, and had set a World Series single-game strike-out record of 14 against the New York Yankees that year. Doak Walker had been the Heisman Trophy winner as a Southern Methodist University halfback and had helped lead the Detroit Lions to National Football League championships in 1952 and 1953. Stars in Cleveland, Detroit and New York City would hardly be impressed by a small-time coach from the hill country of eastern Oklahoma.

In the end, Don didn't mention Iba or his coaching record. He wrote a two-page letter that would seem to have little chance of success. It was heartfelt, but awkward and rambling. "I have a problem on which your observation and thought can give tremendous insight," Don began. "I am enclosing a list for your information of names of others to whom this same letter is being written to gain their opinion. Let me start by saying that as a coach I am of course interested in many of the same things you and other athletes and coaches are interested in, but, recently I have become so overwhelmingly interested in one particular thing we as coaches and athletes can further that I am considering devoting my full time efforts to organization and development of the opportunity." After dropping Dr. Louis Evans's name, Don finally revealed the purpose of the letter: the founding of "some type of organization which would provide an opportunity for those of us (athletes and coaches) who are so inclined to speak and witness for Christ and the wholesome principles of good character and clean living to the youth of our nation." Such an organization "might actually be one of the greatest contributions ever made to the youth of our country," he said in a flourish of hyperbole (that nevertheless held a touch of prophecy as to the movement's eventual size).

Acknowledging that he didn't know how such an enterprise would be arranged or financed, Don did suggest some possible activities. "Along with publications which would be sent to organizations of campuses and in public schools we might hope to send a name athlete or coach to talk to the school. ... The opportunities to speak and witness at scout camps, churches, banquets, military camps, etc., would also be great no doubt." Don then asked the prominent athletes to let him know if they would cooperate and if they knew any other athletes or coaches who might be interested. He requested that the athletes "answer immediately ... as I will have an opportunity in the next week or so to do considerable study on the matter and your prompt reply will be of the utmost importance. As a closing statement I want to say that I make no apologies for having written such a lengthy letter and consumed so much of your time in consideration of it. Many of you no doubt have a much keener appreciation than I of the need for help that our young folks have today."

Gloria typed copies of the letter on Eastern A & M letterhead, and Don signed them as athletic director. The letters went out in April 1954 to 19 people, most of them professional or All-American football, basketball and baseball players, Olympic stars and national-title-winning coaches.

They were, in addition to Otto Graham, Carl Erskine, Doak Walker and Branch Rickey:

- Amos Alonzo Stagg, legendary football coach who had directed teams for 54 years at the University of Chicago and College of the Pacific.
- Bob Mathias, who had won back-to-back Olympic decathlon gold medals in 1948 and 1952.
- Bob Richards, a gold medalist in pole vaulting in the 1952 Olympics.
- Glenn Cunningham, University of Kansas graduate and former Olympic competitor who held the mile world record for three years in the 1930s.
- Dean Cromwell, legendary track coach who had won 12

NCAA titles at the University of Southern California before retiring in 1948.

- Dan Towler, running back for the Los Angeles Rams who had been chosen all-pro from 1951 to 1953.
- Bud Wilkinson, head football coach at the University of Oklahoma, which had claimed the national title in 1950 and had won eight straight Big Six league titles.
- "Biggie" Munn, Michigan State athletic director who had coached the Spartans' football team to national titles in 1951 and 1952.
- Alvin Dark, shortstop for the New York Giants who was named an all-star in 1951 and 1952 and whose hitting helped the Giants win the National League pennant in 1951.
- Tom Harmon, a sports broadcaster who had won the Heisman trophy as a halfback at the University of Michigan in 1940 and, after serving in World War II, played for the Los Angeles Rams in 1946 and 1947.
- Red Barber, well-known sportscaster for the Brooklyn Dodgers.
- Roe Johnston, a Presbyterian pastor and All-American end on the Naval Academy football team in the 1940s.
- Donn Moomaw, a two-time All-American linebacker at UCLA in 1950 and 1952 who was studying to become a minister.
- R.J. "Jack" Robinson, an All-American basketball player from Baylor who led his team to the NCAA finals in 1948 and then played on the gold-medal U.S. Olympic team that year.
- Louis Zamperini, an Olympic track star.[7]

With this list, Don certainly wasn't slouching. He was out to skim from the cream of the sports world, even though those men "didn't know me from a bar of soap."[6] He did not have to wait long for responses to begin arriving in Wilburton. The letters were short but positive. Within weeks, 14 of the 19 had replied that they supported the idea. Don was elated. One letter particularly intrigued him: Otto Graham's brief expression of enthusiasm, climaxed by his unforgettable signature: a big O, two t's, and another O, like a tic-tac-toe drawing in cursive.

Now that Don had famous athletes willing to help, he had to ask the next question: Help with what? He talked to school administrators in Oklahoma City and Tulsa, who were enthusiastic about the idea of sports stars coming to speak at their high schools. Officials at the University of Oklahoma, Oklahoma A & M and the University of Tulsa also quickly climbed on board. "You mean you can really provide people like this for us at no expense?" was their general reaction. Athletes espousing a Christian message in public schools and universities was not an issue in the mid-1950s in the nation's Bible Belt.

However, elation quickly turned into terror. Don began to awake in the middle of the night in a panic, wondering, *Oh, my God, what have I done?* He hadn't met any of these athletes he was promising to deliver. Would they really decide to come? How would he pay their airfare and hotel costs? Don knew he had to talk face-to-face with those who answered his letter to gauge their level of commitment. Lacking travel money, Don took out a $1,000 loan, using his car as collateral.

On a weekend in early summer, he and his family headed north to meet the Rev. Roe Johnston, the former football player at the Naval Academy who was now pastor of First Presbyterian Church in Indianapolis, Indiana. Johnston, who was a brother-in-law of the McClanens' former senior pastor when Don was at Oklahoma A & M, put them up overnight, enthusiastically encouraged them and invited them to attend a service at his church the next morning.

The next stop was Cleveland. After staying in a motel overnight, Don walked into the downtown insurance agency where Otto Graham worked in the off-season. When Graham came out to meet him, Don recognized him immediately from having watched Browns games on TV: the dark hair and eyebrows and compact build slightly taller than Don's. Even though Graham was dressed in a shirt and tie, Don felt immediately at ease with his welcoming, down-to-earth manner. In their 30-minute conversation, Graham said, sure, he would be glad to come to Oklahoma to speak with school kids. At one point he asked Don how he had gotten to Cleveland, and Don answered that it was by taking out a loan on his car. Graham later told Don that this risk-taking had convinced him of Don's genuine faith. Gloria, who had quietly fretted about the $1,000 loan, began to think that maybe her husband's crazy idea had some potential after all.

Don then traveled to New York City to visit Len LeSourd, managing editor of *Guideposts* magazine. Don walked into LeSourd's office on East 46th Street in downtown Manhattan without an appointment. "I apologize for not contacting you in advance, but do you have any time for us to meet now?" Don said when the managing editor presented himself. Not only did they meet, but LeSourd invited Don to lunch. Don told how *Guideposts* articles had helped him identify recruits for his cause, and asked LeSourd for permission to reproduce clippings and photographs. LeSourd expressed his desire to be supportive. He also furnished background information on the man Don was most eager to contact: Branch Rickey. It turned out that Rickey had been the baseball coach at Ohio Wesleyan University when LeSourd's father played on the team, and had become a close friend of the LeSourd family. LeSourd had spent weekends at Rickey's home in Saint Louis during World War II when LeSourd was stationed in the area and Rickey was general manager of the Cardinals. Later, on visits to New York, Rickey had accompanied LeSourd to Marble Collegiate Church, where *Guideposts* founder Norman Vincent Peale was pastor. LeSourd's information about Rickey reaffirmed Don's sense that Rickey was a crucial element to the whole enterprise.

Don's next destination was Philadelphia, to grab a visit with Brooklyn pitcher Carl Erskine on a day when the Dodgers were playing the Phillies. When Don learned where the Dodgers were staying, he headed downtown to the Warwick Hotel, a first-class English Renaissance building just off Rittenhouse Square, one of Philadelphia's most fashionable addresses. Entering the ornate lobby, he recognized Erskine, dressed in his street clothes, chatting amid a group of people. Don walked over to the group and stood in its outer ring, waiting patiently for his opportunity. As the group began to disperse, Don touched Erskine on the arm and said, "Carl, can I have a word with you?" In his book *Tales from the Dodger Dugout*, Erskine recounts his reaction. "I had just come off my best big-league season and the 'red-hot' deals were coming my way. I had learned to be wary of most of them. McClanen, however, was so soft-spoken and laid back that he impressed me. When he told me about his idea to organize pro athletes to speak at high schools, colleges and other youth settings—endorsing their faith and church relationship–I listened with a different kind of interest."[8] Don told Erskine about his contact with Otto Graham and with Len LeSourd, who had interviewed Erskine for a *Guideposts* article two years earlier. By the end of their 15-minute conversation, Erskine was on board. And Don was becoming convinced that the Holy Spirit was visiting these people ahead of him.

Back in Oklahoma, he called others of the 19 who had received his letter, as well as more Christian athletes he was just learning about.[9] When Don reached Doak Walker, the top running back in the NFL at the time, Walker told him that speaking about his faith in public was difficult for him. "It doesn't come naturally to me," he said. But Walker added that he would cooperate anyway; "I know I need to do it."

A further encouragement for Don, amid his financial uncertainties, was a donation of $1,000 from Westminster Presbyterian Church in Oklahoma City, allowing him to pay off his bank loan. Don had shared his vision with the church's pastor, the Rev. G. Raymond Campbell, when they met at an eastern Oklahoma church where Campbell was a guest preacher. Once again with money in their pockets, Don, Gloria and the two children headed to Pennsylvania for a family visit in August 1954. On the way back, Don had his fateful meeting with Branch Rickey. Rickey's letter of endorsement then helped bring University of Oklahoma football coach Bud Wilkinson on board. The idea was gaining momentum.

In September, Campbell again came through with a $600 donation from the Oklahoma City Christian Laymen's League, a group in Campbell's church. The money paid travel expenses for the new organization's first advisory board meeting in Oklahoma City. Attending were, among others, Louis Evans, Roe Johnston and Bob Geller. Choosing the organization's name dominated the agenda. "Athletes for Christ" had been proposed, but the group decided it was too similar to that of another organization, Youth for Christ. One member suggested "Religious Athletes," but Evans responded vehemently, "If you take the C out of this thing, you take me out of it." He wasn't about to let the name of Christ be pushed aside. The group settled on the name "Fellowship of Christian Athletes."[10]

Word about this new organization began to spread in the athletic world and beyond. Ed Sullivan, the famous TV show host who was also a columnist for the *New York Daily News*, derided the idea of the fellowship, saying he was surprised Branch Rickey would back a movement that threatened animosity between Christian and Jewish ballplayers. Don forwarded the clipping to Rickey, who wrote back, "Don, I would treat that like a fly speck on your nose and flick it off."[11]

In October 1954, the fellowship launched its own publicity offensive, announcing itself to the nation via an eight-page pamphlet produced by Len LeSourd of *Guideposts*. Fifteen thousand copies displayed pictures of six sports figures on the cover: Bud Wilkinson, Olympic pole vaulter Bob Richards, Carl Erskine, Doak Walker, Otto Graham and Branch Rickey. Inside, Erskine was quoted, "I know only too well, of course, that my no-hit victory against Chicago and my 14 strike outs against the Yankees in a World Series game belong to yesterday. They mean little today since each day calls for a new effort. I have much to be grateful for, a lot to learn still, but I do know the most important asset a person can have–faith in God."

Donn Moomaw, a two-time All-American linebacker at UCLA, also was pictured and quoted. "For two years of my college career I had no contact with the church," he said. "I was living from pleasure to pleasure. ... In the middle of my junior year at UCLA I first set out to find the answers to this game of life. ... I counseled with Christian friends. Then I attended some meetings of a campus Christian group. I could see in these Christians a certain peace, a profound assurance that showed on their faces and in their lives. It was something I had never experienced on the gridiron or in any phase of my life. Any honors I have been fortunate to receive on the gridiron have brought me no thrill that could hope to compare with the thrill I have in knowing Christ. He is my Coach in this greater game–this game of life. I can honestly say with the blind man of old, 'Where once I was blind, now I can see.' "

Don turned to Roe Johnston, a member of the organization's new board, for help in raising money. Johnston gave the following account of naively stumbling into success: "I was new in Indianapolis. I had heard that there was a wealthy man in Columbus, Indiana, named J. Irwin Miller. I called him up one morning and got right to him. I couldn't believe it. I didn't know any different than you arranged a meeting for this sort of thing. I just told him I had a story to tell him that I thought he would be interested in if he had a minute. I was only 35 miles away, I said, and I told him I would be there after lunch if he wanted to see me. He said come on down."[12] In fact, Miller wasn't just "a wealthy man." He was the head of the Cummins Engine Co., a maker of diesel engines and power equipment that Miller had led to Fortune 500 prominence. Miller also was one of the founders of the National Council of Churches and a leader in recruiting the world's top architects to design a series of buildings for his hometown, bringing Columbus the nickname "Athens of the Prairie."

Johnston continued his story: "I went into his office and I knew that when you make a financial pitch, you make it right now. You try and wrap it up within two minutes and if you haven't sold him by then, you aren't going to. I hit him right between the eyes. I said we've got this great idea of athletes who are Christians who can tell their story and link together across the country in the field of athletics. It'll be a tremendous influence. We need some money. I want $20,000. He looked at me and pushed the button on his desk. The door opened and a guy walked in and Mr. Miller said, 'Richard, listen to this. Say that again.' So I told the story again. He said to Richard, 'Doesn't that sound pretty good?' Richard said, 'Yea, that sounds great.' So Mr. Miller said to me, 'Okay, you'll get your money, but with it you get this guy,' whose name was Richard Stoner, his financial adviser. Then Mr. Miller said to me, 'He's going to teach you how never again to do what you just did.' "[13]

In all, Miller gave FCA three annual gifts of $20,000 each. But the first payment didn't come until 1957. Meanwhile, Don continued to coach, teach physical education and serve as athletic director at Eastern A & M, as well as juggle FCA's shoe-string finances. FCA's puzzle-pieces kept falling into place, but Don remained impatient and anxious that the pieces also might fall apart at any moment. Meanwhile, Gloria prayed silently that FCA wouldn't result in her family's bankruptcy.

Don accepted Louis Evans' invitation to come out to the West Coast to meet more sports figures who might help FCA. With Don's coaching responsibilities, he could only swing a trip during the

Christmas holidays. All he had was $100 that Charles Dowell, a pastor and former all-American football player for the University of Oklahoma, had given him. So Don borrowed another $100 from a bank. He dressed in his Naval Reserve uniform and traveled by bus through a snowstorm to Tinker Air Force Base outside Oklahoma City. Don spent the night in a barracks, went out to the airfield early in the morning to hitch a flight and discovered to his delight that an incoming plane would be flying nonstop to Los Angeles. He learned that a general was aboard and wanted him to join in a hand of bridge. Don apologized that he didn't know the game, but left a winner when the general shared that he was heading to the Rose Bowl football game in Los Angeles and could bring Don back to Tinker on a return flight.[14]

During Don's three-day stay in Los Angeles, Evans took him to the Rose Bowl, where they sat with Dean Cromwell, a legendary former University of Southern California track coach. Evans also introduced him to Donn Moomaw, the former UCLA linebacker who had just entered seminary, and gave Don $100 to repay the bank loan.[15]

Soon, however, Don applied for another loan, this time $1,000 to bring athletes to Oklahoma for the first FCA speaking tour in late January and early February 1955. FCA's real kickoff had finally arrived. Otto Graham flew in from Cleveland, Carl Erskine from Indiana, Doak Walker from Dallas, Bob Richards from Los Angeles and Glenn Olds, the chaplain of Cornell University and a former boxer, from New York. In addition, Don recruited Robin Roberts, all-star pitcher for the Philadelphia Phillies, and Oklahomans Bob Fenimore, an Oklahoma A & M football All-American, and Pepper Martin, a member of the colorful "Gashouse Gang" that had brought the St. Louis Cardinals four World Series titles in the 1930s and '40s. Martin, whose wild antics had been tempered by a later Christian conversion, lived on a ranch not far from Eastern Oklahoma A & M, and Don had previously asked him to speak to his basketball team.

The speakers split up into groups that appeared at high school assemblies in Oklahoma City and Tulsa, as well as for evening appearances at four colleges: the University of Oklahoma, Oklahoma A & M, Tulsa and Eastern Oklahoma A & M. The theme for the assembly programs was "Stand for Something." Don paired

Erskine with Roberts, a frequent foe in Dodgers-Phillies games, to speak at an Oklahoma City high school. "There was no script, no prompting and no format," Erskine recalled. "I'm telling you, I agreed to do it, but I told Don I'd never done much of that before. Speaking in those days was difficult for me anyway, but speaking about your faith to young people in a strange place—that was a big assignment.

"So I always remember a significant thing happening. Robin was ahead of me. He said, 'When I was a kid I could throw the ball real hard. My buddies, they tried, but they couldn't throw it as hard as I could. After I had played a couple of seasons, I began to realize I had something special; that I'd been gifted. I thought, "If God gave me the ability to throw hard, then maybe God should have something to say about how I use it."'

"That just gave me the most courage to go ahead and do my piece," Erskine said, "because that was such a down-to-earth, practical application of faith. It was just right down where I lived."

The Tulsa Tribune reported, "Three outstanding athletes visited Tulsa today speaking to all male groups at Tulsa's Central, Rogers, Webster and Booker T. Washington high schools. All represented the newly organized Fellowship of Christian Athletes movement, which numbers among its members some of the greatest athletes of all time." It quoted Glenn Olds as saying, "We're not trying to get youngsters to join anything. We just want them to stand for something."[16]

After a day of high school assemblies in Oklahoma City, Otto Graham, Doak Walker and Pepper Martin spoke to 75 athletes at the University of Oklahoma in Norman. Chuck Bowman, a member of the football team, recalled the meeting vividly. The whole Oklahoma football team was gathered in a meeting room in the university's football dormitory, and their coach, Bud Wilkinson, introduced the three visitors. Walker, a Texan, looked liked Roy Rogers in his blue jeans, jean jacket, cowboy boots and cowboy hat. Graham, dressed in a three-piece suit, looked like a New York businessman. Martin, dressed in a sports shirt and slacks, looked like he might have come off a golf course. Bowman noticed how small the visitors seemed. The Oklahoma players were a confident bunch, having just come off a national championship season, and a number of them were going on to play in the NFL. But they definitely were wowed by the presence of the league's best quarterback and best running back.

Walker, Graham and Martin each spoke for 20 minutes, spending five minutes on athletics and the other 15 on their faith. Bowman remembered how each mentioned his mother as being a key spiritual influence, something Bowman could relate to. The visitors noted that they represented a new organization called the Fellowship of Christian Athletes and they wanted the Oklahoma players to consider being a part of it too. Bowman, like many of his teammates, came from a strong church background, but the meeting showed him something new: prominent athletes being bold and speaking out about their faith. When he walked out of the meeting, he thought, *I want to be part of that.* He later became an FCA staff member for 31 years. Two other players in the room also would have long associations with FCA: Bill Krisher, a future All-American and pro player who later worked for FCA for more than 25 years, and future All-American Clendon Thomas, who became a longtime FCA volunteer.

Doak Walker also appeared at Eastern A & M and public schools in Wilburton, along with Bob Fenimore and Bob Richards. At the college, the athletes spoke as part of a larger event that Don had put together to coincide with the FCA assemblies: an Eastern A & M Sports Jamboree. They gave their testimony, and Bob Richards put on an impressive pole-vaulting exhibition in the field house. The jamboree also featured an Eastern Oklahoma A & M basketball game and appearances by Yankees slugger Mickey Mantle and Milwaukee Braves all-star pitcher Warren Spahn, both off-season residents of Oklahoma.

By the end of the appearances, the FCA speakers had appeared before 18,000 students in Oklahoma City and Tulsa. Two weeks later, Richards received a letter from Latimer County schools Superintendent Delbert Garner. "Never in 20 years has there been anything which had the impact on youth for good as your visit to us in Wilburton," Garner said. "I wish it were possible to pass on to you all the comments I have heard from these boys and girls about your talk and the fine performance of your athletic ability in the field house. Only eternity will reveal how many lives were changed by your visit."[17]

Don, elated by the success, remained rattled by debt and his struggles to organize FCA in addition to all his Eastern A & M duties. As for money, in addition to paying off his latest $1,000 loan, he needed another $1,000 to fly athletes to Pittsburgh for a fund-raising event Branch Rickey had pledged to host. On a Saturday morning in April 1955, Don packed Gloria and the two kids into their Pontiac and headed 165 miles north to Bartlesville, where he had arranged to visit Bill Doenges, owner of a Ford dealership. He did not know Doenges personally, but had heard he was a leading layman in Oklahoma Methodist circles, had been a standout football player for Oklahoma City University and was a big sports fan. Arriving at the dealership, Don left Gloria and the children in the car to cover him with prayer as usual. In a brief meeting, Don described his FCA vision and the organization's financial needs. Doenges pulled out a checkbook on the spot and wrote a check for $2,200. The family rode happily back to Wilburton.

With the necessary finances, Don scheduled the Pittsburgh fund-raiser for the evening of June 7, 1955. Earlier in the day the advisory board met and chose Don as FCA's official administrative director. Don had pictured a nationally prominent sports figure as director, but the fact that no one came forward and that others urged him to take the position convinced him to accept.[18]

Rickey hosted a dinner for several dozen people in a small, chandeliered dining room at the exclusive Duquesne Club. Rickey had expressed to Don his hope for a sizable donation from Mike Benedum, an 85-year-old oil and gas magnate whose success in finding and acquiring new oil fields had made him one of the nation's richest men of the time.[19] But Benedum, an active Methodist layman, asked Rickey to invite instead his nephew, Paul Benedum, who worked in Uncle Mike's oil operations. Paul, a dapper dresser with silver hair, waxed mustache and a silk handkerchief in his coat pocket, was sports-minded but less of a church-goer than his uncle.[20] In addition to members of the business elite, Don and Rickey had arranged for Pittsburgh Pirates pitcher Vernon Law to be present, as well as Brooklyn's Carl Erskine, since the Dodgers were in town for a game. They also invited the Rev. Sam Shoemaker, pastor of Calvary Episcopal Church in Pittsburgh. During the 1920s and 1930s as rector of a church in New York City, Shoemaker had been the American leader of The Oxford Group, an international Christian renewal movement, and was instrumental in the formulation of the twelve-step program adopted by Alcoholics Anonymous.

Emceeing the gathering was Gary Demarest, a former baseball pitcher and student body president at the University of California, Berkeley, who was now a Presbyterian pastor. Louis Evans introduced Don to Demarest, who had developed a standup-comedy routine during his years of youth ministry in Seattle. Demarest was to soften up the crowd with one-liners and then turn the podium over to Rickey and Evans for the financial solicitation. But at the end of Demarest's routine, one of the potential donors said Demarest should stay at the mike: "I want to hear the pitch from 'Bob Hope.'" Demarest nevertheless nimbly passed the baton to Erskine and Law, who spoke about the promise of Don's idea to tap into the hero worship of sports stars, with athletes endorsing their faith instead of merchandise. Evans spoke about the promise of the new organization to improve the lives of athletes, coaches and youth. At one point he pointed to Erskine and Law and said, "These men have the muscle to make this work; you have the money. We need to get the two together."[21]

Paul Benedum grew enthused about what he heard and wrote a $10,000 check–an amount equal to $80,000 in today's inflated dollars. He told Don, "I think it's the most remarkable thing I've heard of." Benedum became a leading angel for FCA during the next two decades, funneling $467,000 to the organization through a family foundation.[22] Finally, FCA's finances rested on something more secure than the state of Don's bank credit. Two months later, Don resigned his job at Eastern A & M to become full-time FCA administrator.

Call

That God has a special calling for each of us that utilizes our best gifts and showers us with our greatest fulfillment seems too good to be true. It is unbelievably good news that we think happens only to special people like Don. Yet truly it is God's desire for each one of us. Our call may be temporary, rather than life-long, giving way to another call, or a series of calls. Our call may involve a job or it may take place outside the nine to five of our working lives. But God has work for us to do that will electrify us with aliveness. After all, Jesus came to give us life, and life more abundantly.

Discerning call is not easy. We may sense a call that is "important" and will win us the attention and praise of others. This may not be God's call; it could be our ego's call and, if so, it is false. Myra Thompson Flood of Wellspring, a mission of the Church of the Saviour in Washington, D.C., once noted in a newsletter that the ability to discern call comes after one has progressed in the inner life: "You must have some experience of being in [God's] presence in the lonely places and hearing his word in scripture speaking to your life. You need experiences of being filled with love for God and overwhelmed by his love for you. You must come to know Jesus as companion on the journey, as friend, lover, brother, saviour. You must experience the Spirit's power as he moves across the face of your deepest places, leads you to the desert and sometimes leaves you there to wrestle with the choices you must make about your own life."

Yes, answering call may lead us to suffering as well as joy. Call often comes at the point where pain in our lives intersects with the world's needs around us, and it often entails financial risk.

The Church of the Saviour has identified the following "Marks of Call":
• "It's Good News. It feels life-giving and energizing. It is exciting and filled with possibilities. We want to do it. And joy is dominant.
• "There is a sense of mystery and awe. ... It is not my idea and is not an ego trip. God in me connects with God in the world.
• "It can be very simply stated. It will be seen in global terms, yet will be clear and focused. For example: Feed the hungry! .... Open a hospital!
• "It seems impossible. In human terms, that is. We feel resistant and inadequate. We ask, as did Moses, 'Who am I to do this?' This throws us back on God's grace.
• "But it feels right. There will be an inner knowing; a sense of being made for this task.
• "It's risky. We will question whether we have heard it right. We may fail. We may succeed. We are called to be faithful–not suc-

cessful!
- "It's persistent! It just will not go away.
- "It will always need a community of God's people to do it. (At the Church of the Saviour we will not allow a new call to happen until there is at least one other willing to commit to the project.)
- "It is countercultural. As is Jesus! It will be an alternative way—a third way—to the way secular society would conceive it. This might (will) cause conflicts and misunderstandings. It could seem irrational to 'the world.'
- "But although it is costly—it may cost you everything!—it is growing and will enhance our inner being. It will stretch us, heal us and be our salvation."

Each of these marks applies to Don's founding of the Fellowship of Christian Athletes. It was audacious, it was risky, it defied norms, it persisted and it was impossible without a group. As with Don's call, so it may be with ours. Few of us are called to start a national organization and recruit famous people for a cause. Our call may be more local. But it will matter, it is likely to scare us, it will call forth our best gifts and it ought to lead us to others who share our dream. And we will find God going on before us, preparing the way.

3

Success and Failure

"A time to seek, and a time to lose."
–Ecclesiastes 3:6 (NRSV)

Leaving his coaching career behind, Don moved with Gloria and the children, six-year-old Mike and five-year-old Judy, to Norman, Oklahoma. Besides being home to the University of Oklahoma and its national championship football team, Norman also was close to the Oklahoma City airport, from which Don could travel to see athletes in other parts of the country. The McClanens rented a three-bedroom Cape Cod just north of campus for $85 a month. Gloria reveled in their first real house as Don opened FCA's first national headquarters, a one-room office in the First National Bank Building provided by a bank officer and FCA supporter.

On a large, wall-hung blackboard by Don's desk, he listed athletes scheduled to make FCA appearances. Written at the top was "Expect Great Things from God–Attempt Great Things for God." A large U.S. map above the blackboard pinpointed cities that FCA would visit.[1] Plans for a national rollout of city campaigns modeled on the successful Oklahoma rallies filled much of the board, beginning with Denver in January 1956.

The start of the Denver campaign was shaky. A kickoff community rally on Sunday afternoon drew only a few dozen people. Emcee Gary Demarest joked to the audience, "There are more of us on the platform than there are of you in the audience." But the next day, the athletes played to big crowds with school appearances, averting a public-relations disaster. *Sports Illustrated* had sent a reporter who wrote that an "all-star lineup ... were exhibiting what they considered to be the least of their talents: public speaking before audiences of high school and college students."[2] Top professional athletes told their stories: Carl Erskine of the Dodgers; Robin Roberts of the Phillies; Vernon Law of the Pirates, who would go on to be a Cy Young Award winner and lead the Pirates to their 1960 World Series title; George Kell, an all-star third baseman and slugger for the Chicago White Sox; "Deacon" Dan Towler, a pastor and former Pro Bowl running back for the Los Angeles Rams; and Adrian Burk, quarterback of the Philadelphia Eagles and one of the few NFL players to throw seven touchdown passes in one game.

Don pushed them hard, setting up speaking engagements at four high schools, Denver University, the University of Colorado at Boulder, the Air Force Academy, a boosters' club luncheon and a Sunday school class. "Sometimes the athletes got tangled up in their own words, but their sincerity won them their listeners as few polished speakers could have done," the *Sports Illustrated* article said.[3] Demarest added polish with his comedic gifts and poise behind a microphone. He introduced Robin Roberts at East High School by joking that Roberts "had thrown more homerun balls in one season than any big leaguer since Abner Doubleday invented baseball," a *Denver Post* article noted.

"Roberts went right along with the kidding," the article continued. "Perfectly deadpan, he told about what a satisfaction it had been to bring joy to the hearts of so many of his opponents by serving up pitches they could clout out of the park. Then for ten minutes he spun baseball yarns while the audience listened in fascination. The audience listened with the same rapt attention when Roberts slipped smoothly into the serious windup of his talk. 'In professional sports as well as in life,' he said, 'there are times when the burden we are called on to bear seems to be a lot bigger than one man can carry. Many times I've asked Christ to help me. Not necessarily to win, but to guide me and give me strength. And he always has. Those of us on the platform are Christians and we are not ashamed of it. You have heard of athletes endorsing merchandise for pay. Tonight my friends and I are endorsing something else, Christianity, the biggest thing in our lives, and we are not getting a cent for it. We are proud to be here telling you what Christ has meant in our lives.'"[4]

Following the rallies, the Rev. David Colwell, president of the Denver Council of Churches and former All-American fullback at

Yale, wrote Don, "When I first learned of the organization, I had certain very real reservations about how effective it would be, but my experience with you during the weekend that you were in Denver has caused me to be an enthusiastic supporter. It seems to me you have an extremely promising idea for affecting for good the youth of our country."[5] Don left Denver with more than good wishes. Palmer Hoyt, publisher of *The Denver Post*, hosted a luncheon, announced a donation of $1,000 and invited the athletes to speak to his editorial staff. He later wrote, "Anyone who reads the daily papers knows how necessary it is for our youth to hear such a [Christian] story today. I consider this a frontal attack on juvenile delinquency." Another Denver businessman also donated $1,000.[6] Don followed up the Denver success with city campaigns in Houston, Indianapolis and Lincoln, Nebraska.

Later that spring, Louis Evans invited Don to Estes Park, Colorado, where Evans was attending a conference at a camp called the YMCA of the Rockies. Located on a hill, the camp was surrounded on three sides by Rocky Mountain National Park. A large meadow stretched out from the administration building, providing a great place for ball games and other athletic events. Three peaks covered with Ponderosa pine rose beyond the meadow. Farther in the distance was the Mummy Range, crowned by 13,514-foot Mt. Ypsilon. Don and his supporters had talked of holding a national conference. Don quickly decided this would be the location. He booked cabins for 500 people for August 19 to 23.[7]

Fortunately, the camp did not require a deposit. After the expenses of the city campaigns, FCA's and the McClanen family's finances had returned to a meager level. As Gloria prepared breakfast one morning after Don had returned from Estes Park, Don stood in the living room jangling the change in his pocket. The coins added up to 22 cents—all the money he had at that moment. Bills totaling $300 lay on a filing cabinet at work with no money in the bank to cover them. Don came into the kitchen, showed Gloria the coins and said jokingly, "This may be our last meal." They sat down to breakfast, where their daughter, Judy, having overheard her father, said with concern, "Mommy, is this going to be our last meal?" Gloria responded, "Yes, eat your oatmeal." Gloria was immediately stung by remorse at burdening their child with the family's financial insecurities, but also realized the toll such worries were taking on herself.

Gloria had tried hard to be encouraging and supportive to Don in his idealistic undertaking. But the struggle dredged up the nightmares of her childhood. Gloria's father, Ernest Clark, an Australian rubber manufacturer, married an American, Myrtle Johnson, in Chicago. The couple moved to Brazil, where Ernest had a rubber factory. Gloria and a sister were born in Brazil, where they lived in a three-story home with maids and a chauffeur. Ernest sold the business while Gloria was still young, and the family returned to the United States, occupying a beautiful hilltop house in West Orange, New Jersey. Gloria and her sister were cared for by a Brazilian maid. But two years later, in 1929, Ernest lost everything in the stock market crash, and the family moved to an apartment.

During the winter, Gloria's father sometimes fell behind on utility payments, and the electricity and gas would be cut off. At one point the family succumbed to burning their living-room furniture, piece by piece, in a coal stove in the kitchen to keep warm. When Gloria graduated from high school and landed a good job with the telephone company, she left behind her life of poverty. FCA's financial uncertainties dragged her back into the specter of a hand-to-mouth existence.

As usual, Don found a way to keep things going. He called Bill Payne, an oilman and active Presbyterian in Oklahoma City, whom he had heard about but never met. "Mr. Payne, I know you don't know me, but I know of you from our Presbyterian circles," Don said. "I'm trying to start an organization of Christian athletes, and we're in a real financial bind."

"What does that amount to?" Payne asked. Don told him $300. "I'll send you a check today," Payne replied. Payne continued to support FCA thereafter with annual gifts.

The turning point in Gloria's struggle with anxiety came from a spiritual turn of events rather than a financial one. In June 1956, evangelist Billy Graham held a month-long crusade in an Oklahoma City stadium. Don went most nights with a missionary friend who was visiting from Africa, but Gloria showed little interest. She had been a church-goer all her life, and she didn't think Graham's invitation for people to walk forward and commit their lives to Christ had anything to do with her. Still, she relented and went with Don and their friend the last night. The event was so crowded that they couldn't find seats together, and Gloria ended up sitting on the grass in front of the podium where Graham was speaking. When Graham finished his sermon and gave his invitation, Gloria didn't give it a second thought. She got up and went forward. Gloria had prayed and read the Bible all her life, but somehow this was different. This was her version of Don's prayer in the Catholic Church in Oklahoma City. She turned over her concerns to God and experienced a mysterious deliverance from fear about the future. Looking back years later, she said, "I'd not only given my life to Jesus, I'd given myself to FCA."

If Gloria's anxiety dissipated, Don's mounted. He had notified every FCA contact he knew about the Estes Park conference. The fee was only $25 a person. Yet a month before the conference date, only 38 people had registered. Lining up speakers also was difficult. Fortunately, Len LeSourd of *Guideposts* was running a cover story on Robin Roberts, the Phillies pitcher, in his August 1956 issue based on Roberts' experience at the Denver rallies. At the end of the article LeSourd printed a short sidebar about the Estes Park conference under the title "Inspiration and Perspiration." The article named Otto Graham, Doak Walker and Branch Rickey as some of the prominent sports figures who would be there.

Before the opening of the conference, Gary Demarest, who had been appointed the conference "dean," picked up Branch Rickey and "Biggie" Munn, the Michigan State athletic director, at the Denver airport. During the two-hour drive to Estes Park, Rickey asked Demarest how big a crowd was expected, and Demarest gave an evasive answer. Rickey brushed this aside and asked again. Forced to come clean, Demarest revealed that fewer than 100 people had pre-registered. Rickey responded, "Don't forget, Jesus started with 12!"[8]

Donn Moomaw, now a student at Princeton Theological Seminary and one of the conference staff, was apprehensive about how things might go. Moomaw knew about youth conferences and evangelical outreaches, having accompanied Billy Graham on a three-month England crusade the previous year. But FCA was different. Moomaw didn't know what to expect from a group of coaches and athletes, many of whom probably came from minimal church backgrounds and weren't used to open expressions of faith.

On registration day, a long line of cars streamed into the camp from all over the country, many driven by high school and college coaches bringing their players without having pre-registered. *This is an absolute miracle,* Don thought to himself. As the conference opened that night, Don counted 256 people, all male. Few girls played sports in that era. Don had approached Patty Berg, a nationally prominent golfer who would later help found the Ladies Professional Golf Association, about being involved in FCA. But she was his sole female contact. It was, after all, 16 years before the passage of Title IX, the federal law that required women be given equal opportunity to participate in school sports.

At an opening assembly in the camp chapel that evening, Demarest and Moomaw, good friends through West Coast church connections, put the audience in stitches ragging on each other. "When I hear the name Moomaw, I don't know whether to milk him or what," Demarest said. "Hey, Gary, the bus is leaving at 3 p.m. tomorrow; be sure to be under it," Moomaw answered back. Later in the conference, Moomaw misspoke just as he reached his message's climax: "It's tough to be a Christian and to be an athlete. You have to have an anchor. You have to have your ... Bibie." Demarest howled in the front row, and soon the whole crowd was guffawing. Demarest did not miss an opportunity for the rest of the conference to tell the youth not to forget their Bibies.

Bill Mann, music director of First Methodist Church in Dallas, led the singing. Moomaw had low expectations for the music; he anticipated mumbled words and off-key pitches from a bunch of semi-churched athletes. But when the youth opened their mouths, a rich, full, enthusiastic sound filled the chapel.

Rickey gave the keynote address. Wearing his trademark outfit of a suit and polka-dot bow tie, he delivered a rambling, hour-long meditation on the role of athletics in society (overemphasized) and the role of Christianity in society (underemphasized).[9] At one point he talked about reading Giovanni Papini's *Life of Christ* to Jackie Robinson before bringing him to the Brooklyn Dodgers in 1947. Robinson "was not an ideal man [to break the major-league color barrier]," Rickey said. "He was resentful of criticism, quickly retaliating to insults by nature. Had a sense of injustice that any should discriminate against him because of different pigmentation of skin. ... I read [from the book] to Robbie six months before anybody knew he was signed. We were talking about what would be said to him on the field of play, of the nasty things that would be imputed to him, and they were. ... Papini says that one way to react to force is to fight back and he treats it as a fruitless way to do. And he says that the second way to resist force is to run away. And he points out the unfortunate vulnerability of that. And then, you know, he comes to the biblical injunction about turning the other cheek."[10]

Rickey also declared his absolute allegiance to Jesus. "Jesus is not a myth," he told the audience. "He's not a fraud. He's not the plausible but illogical philosopher. He's the light of the world. ... He died at 33, a young man, the very age that ballplayers, with their knowledge and agility, are at their best–this man died. It's been a revealing thing to me all my life." As he closed, Rickey assessed FCA's potential. "I don't think I've ever been faced with a situation that seemed to me to be so pregnant with the immediate possibilities of a great crowd of young men coming to feel the presence of God and the duty of service to the King of Kings."

Don, Demarest and Moomaw had mapped out full days of activities for the rest of the conference. The mornings were dedicated to "inspiration," with chapel at 6:45 a.m., a half-hour of private devotional time after breakfast, assembly speakers and a small-group "huddle" discussion. The afternoons were dedicated to "perspiration," with coaches' clinics, games and competitions in what came to be called the "Dogpatch Olympics." An evening assembly led by Louis Evans closed out each day.

A group of coaches and athletes, corralled by Don, gave clinics. Rickey taught about baseball. Otto Graham was in charge of football, assisted by Doak Walker. Phog Allen, who had just retired from 39 seasons as a legendary basketball coach at the University of Kansas, winning the national championship in 1952, took basketball. Dean Cromwell, whose Southern California track teams had dominated the nation for a decade in the 1930s and '40s, led track and field. "Biggie" Munn and Tad Wieman, athletic director from the University of Denver, presided over all the clinics as "deans of athletics."

The huddle discussion leaders were not athletic pikers either. Seven of the ten were All-Americans or Olympians: Donn

Moomaw, Bill Krisher and Clendon Thomas; Olympic skier Keith Wegeman; Bill Glass, a football player at Baylor; Eddie Southern, a 400-meter Olympic hurdler; and Rafer Johnson, an Olympic decathlete. Amazingly, Southern and Johnson participated despite having only two months of training left before the Olympic Games in Melbourne, Australia, where both won silver medals.

Louis Evans, Roe Johnston and Branch Rickey also led huddle sessions for coaches and pros. Gloria McClanen led the wives' huddle. Don mostly directed the logistics, although he did co-lead huddle sessions for visiting clergy and other adults.[11] Don sat in the back of assemblies and was content with his low-profile role.

Paul Benedum had obtained a $10,000 contribution from Gulf Oil to make an FCA movie.[12] The 22-minute film featured footage of Doak Walker, Carl Erskine, Bob Richards, Otto Graham, Robin Roberts, Dan Towler and Rafer Johnson in competitive action, after which they gave faith testimonies. Benedum was present for the first showing at the conference. The film then went into national distribution with Billy Graham's World Wide Pictures.

Pole vaulter Bob Richards had just returned from a two-month tour of exhibitions in Asia sponsored by the U.S. State Department, and was delayed in reaching Estes Park, where he was scheduled to vault. Well into the evening, Richards performed with the glare of automobile headlights directed at the uprights and crossbar as his only illumination.[13]

The camp had a powerful impact on many gathered there. Athletes and coaches, coming from all types of Christian backgrounds—and some from no church background—let down their guards and bonded, listening to each other, praying for each other and sharing their faith with each other. "I knew we were in the right place, it was of God and we weren't going to stop it," Moomaw recalled. Krisher, as one of the huddle leaders, said, "There were all the different denominations, and nobody was questioning anybody else's faith but just keeping the focus on Jesus and just moving ahead. As the week went by, we watched the Holy Spirit open up people's lives and enable them to share together. It was a new deal for everybody."

Otto Graham and Doak Walker made themselves available at meals and in huddle-group discussions, where "they took their facemasks off," Chuck Bowman recalled. "We got to see them where they were human beings just like we were." After graduating as a football All-American from the University of Oklahoma, Bowman spent 14 years coaching high school and college teams before joining FCA's full-time staff. Each summer during his coaching years he took a van load of players to Estes Park. "We'd bring back a different bunch of kids when we'd come back home," he said.

For Gloria McClanen, it was the final confirmation that her husband's risk-taking had been God-inspired. Decades later, thoughts of the opening night still brought tears to her eyes–the memory of hundreds of youth laughing uproariously at the jokes and listening raptly to the messages.

Others, such as Bev Graham, wife of Otto Graham, came to the event with skepticism. She had not met Don McClanen, and still wondered about the cause into which Don had roped her husband. But she came along with their four children. Despite being a lifelong church leader and choir director, she was deeply moved at hearing high school and college youth speak "from their hearts" about their faith. In the glow of that atmosphere, she opened up in the wives' discussions in a way she rarely had before.

The previous April, Don brought Dan Towler to Kansas State University to talk to athletes about FCA. Impressed by Towler's message and Don's "quiet faithfulness," Jack Parr, a six-foot nine-inch center for the basketball team, decided to attend the Estes Park conference. Parr wanted to hear more about Don's take on the Christian life and to bask in the personal interest Don showed him. Parr was also inspired by speakers such as Evans, Rickey, Moomaw and Demarest.

Parr had grown up in a church-going family, but he had not heard the gospel expressed in such a dynamic way. At the end of this "mountaintop experience," he left with new friendships that would last his lifetime and a fresh commitment to live his faith more deeply. He became more active in his church and began to mention his Christian faith at athletic banquets and youth events where he was invited to speak. After college he launched an annual FCA conference in Kansas that attracted hundreds. He named one of his children after Donn Moomaw. And his association with Don McClanen became "one of the most important relationships of my life."

During Parr's senior year, in 1958, despite being named an All-American, he struggled with depression. Kansas State was ranked No. 1 in the nation during the season, and the team made it to the Final Four. But Kansas State lost in the semifinals, with Parr playing poorly. Shortly after, the depression became so severe that Parr was hospitalized. "Don was the first individual I heard from expressing concern and a willingness to be helpful," Parr recalled. "It was very significant to me that at that point somebody really cared about me."

Fast-forward to May 2006. Parr, in his 37th year of a successful career as a management consultant, was flown to Houston to be treated for a sudden heart ailment. As the plane descended, "my aorta ruptured. That's 96 percent fatal. I ended up on the operating table with three liters of fresh blood in my chest cavity." Miraculously, with a top aortic surgeon performing the emergency procedure, Parr survived. "And the morning I awaken from my surgery, I look at the foot of my bed and there stands Don."

The Estes Park conference grabbed national attention at a whole new level. President Dwight D. Eisenhower and Secretary of State John Foster Dulles had learned of the event from Louis Evans, who had preached that summer at a church they attended, National Presbyterian in Washington, D.C. "Please give delegates gathered at Estes Park my warm greetings," Eisenhower telegrammed. "You will be invigorated for the months ahead by your work together, by mountains around you, and the devotion within you. I wish you a successful meeting." Dulles said in his telegram, "I feel confident that those of you who have won a reputation and influence in the field of athletics can equally exert Christian leadership, and I am delighted that you are undertaking this. It will, I am sure, serve the interests of our nation, which has from the beginning been strengthened by the Christian principles of its people."

Life magazine, *Newsweek* and *Sports Illustrated* covered the conference.[14] *Life* noted, "In the mornings [the participants] took part in thoughtful discussion and prayer. In the afternoons they jarred each other's brains out." It concluded, "When a quarterback from Tulsa U. became discouraged with his fumbling handoffs, Otto Graham told him, "Look, Christianity and football are just alike–they both take hard work." The Estes Park summer conference, off to a great start, would continue annually until 2004. Summer camps and conferences would become so central to FCA's mission that, in 2007, the organization held 240 camps around the country attended by 42,000 youth.

Don, exhilarated but also exhausted, stayed with his family in Estes Park for another week to vacation. But then they had serious work to do: the family was moving from Norman 400 miles north to Kansas City. The sports editor of the *Kansas City Star*, Ernie Mehl, an FCA supporter, sold Don on the advantages of relocating. Kansas City was right in the center of the country, had a major airport, boasted a new major-league baseball team and served as the head-quarters of the National Collegiate Athletic Association and National Association of Intercollegiate Athletics, which together oversaw most of the country's college athletics.[15]

The McClanens became homeowners for the first time. In 1956, they purchased a modest rambler for $13,500 in Roeland Park, Kansas, a suburb just west of the Missouri state line. Little did they know that it would be the only home they would ever own. With three bedrooms, the house was in a convenient neighborhood where the children and parents could walk to school, to a neighbor-hood shopping center and to their Presbyterian church. Gloria found Roeland Park to be a friendly and comfortable place to live.

Don drove seven miles to a two-room FCA office located on the fifth floor of the downtown Traders National Bank Building. Planning for city campaigns continued. That fall, a series of appear-ances began in Columbus, Indiana, the home of FCA benefactor J. Irwin Miller, whose concern was juvenile delinquency. An article in the *Philadelphia Inquirer Magazine* noted that Robin Roberts of the Phillies came to this town of about 20,000 people in the fall of 1956. "In 24 hours he talked to every junior and senior high school student in the community in informal meetings," the article said. Carl Erskine, Dan Towler and Bill Glass made follow-up visits in subse-quent months. Glass was an All-America defensive end at Baylor who would become an all-pro player for the Cleveland Browns. "It would be naïve to suggest that hoodlumism has been stamped out by the appearances of these sports greats," the article said. "But reports indicate that the situation has improved. Many Columbus kids apparently have been impressed by men whose athletic achievements prove that they know the score."

In the article Roberts related how, when Don had approached him the previous summer about participating with FCA, Roberts's reaction was, "'I'd like to, but I'm not sure of my speaking ability.' 'Don't worry,' McClanen replied. 'Kids are interested in what you say, not how you say it.' 'But there's so much I don't know about the details of religion.' 'We don't want you to preach sermons,' McClanen said. 'These kids want you to talk about baseball. And you'll be surprised how interested they'll be in hearing about your Christian beliefs, too.'" The article ended with Roberts declaring, "'I feel that this is the most rewarding experience of my life.'"[16]

Throughout 1957 and 1958, Don continued to organize citywide campaigns and annual Estes Park conferences. In 1959, he recognized an opportunity to reach hundreds of college coaches who attended the American Football Coaches Association annual convention in January at a Cincinnati hotel. Don organized an FCA breakfast, a modest event drawing only 13 people. One of those at the breakfast was Don's old friend Otto Graham, who at that time had retired from playing and was coaching at the U.S. Coast Guard Academy in New London, Connecticut. "Who's that fellow over there?" he asked Don, pointing to a coach he did not know. The fellow was Paul Dietzel, football coach at Louisiana State University, who had just won a national championship. The convention was honoring Dietzel as national Coach of the Year. Don asked Dietzel to speak at the annual Estes Park conference that coming August and later recruited him to address a fund-raiser in Philadelphia in early 1960.

Don picked up Dietzel at the airport for the Philadelphia event and drove him to his hotel, where they chatted in Dietzel's room about donor prospects. Dietzel told Don he had prepared a written speech, which even included some passages of Scripture. Before heading off to the event, Don invited Dietzel to kneel on the floor and pray with him. Dietzel, who had not experienced one-on-one prayer since high school, was moved by Don's spiritual intensity. As they were leaving, Don told Dietzel, "Just leave your speech here."

"What?" exclaimed Dietzel.

"Just leave your speech here," Don reiterated. Dietzel spoke extemporaneously at the dinner. Afterward Don told him, "That was the best I've ever heard you speak. You weren't giving a speech; you were sharing from your heart." Don's example prompted some self-examination, and Deitzel concluded that he wanted to grow beyond his Sunday-only Christianity. He became active with FCA, where he was inspired by friendships with other Christian football coaches such as Frank Broyles at Arkansas and Bobby Bowden at Florida State. He continued to be a frequent FCA speaker and served two terms as FCA board president.

Despite its modest beginning, the FCA breakfast at the football coaches' convention would come to draw as many as 1,300 coaches annually. In fact, by 2007 FCA, whose staff now numbered 860, would host events at 11 national coaches' conventions drawing 5,300 coaches. Such numbers were hardly imaginable in 1959, when Don felt fortunate to expand his staff by one. That summer the FCA board hired Gary Demarest from his youth pastor position at a Jacksonville, Florida, church to become Don's first program director. Demarest took over the organization of the citywide campaigns, which during the next 12 months included appearances in Jacksonville; Dallas; Tulsa, Oklahoma; Springfield, Massachusetts; and Odessa, Georgia. Demarest also launched FCA's first regular publication, *The Christian Athlete*. And in an FCA-inspired wedding, Demarest married Marily Evans, daughter of Louis Evans Sr., in August. Marily's father helped preside at the ceremony.

While Demarest traveled the country organizing events, Don spent much of his time on fund-raising. The budget for the fiscal year of July 1, 1958 to June 30, 1959 was $109,480—an ambitious amount, given that Don had raised only a little more than that during the previous three years combined. The fiscal 1959 budget included salaries for six full-time and part-time staff people: Don, Demarest, an office manager and three support personnel. The budget also included $7,500 to pay back loans needed to bridge gaps in income.

The need for money was constant and stressful. Don approached individuals, churches, businesses and foundations. He managed to land a series of grants from the Kellogg Foundation in Battle Creek, Michigan, with Michigan State athletic director "Biggie" Munn's help. The Lilly Endowment in Indianapolis, where Roe Johnston was a pastor, also gave a series of annual grants, as did the Pew Charitable Trusts in Philadelphia. Paul Benedum, the

Pittsburgh oilman, continued to support Don. "Feel free to call me if you have a real need," he said. "I may not be able to give it to you on the spot, but I'll get it." Don resorted to this ace in the hole on several occasions.

As stressful as fund-raising could be, Don and Gloria faced a much tougher situation: the health of their daughter, Judy. From infancy she had suffered a persistent digestive problem that caused frequent vomiting. Her body remained small and frail; she looked like a delicate china doll. But what she lacked in physical strength, she more than made up for in sweet disposition and spirit. Judy loved Jesus, and she often would inspire her parents at family devotionals with her earnest and eloquent prayers. Don and Gloria considered her their "angel." She especially delighted in the Estes Park conferences, enjoying the attention of the young athletes and standing on a bench in the chapel assemblies singing heartily "How Great Thou Art" and other hymns.

The McClanens' pediatrician in Norman, Oklahoma, had diagnosed a heart murmur, but said Judy would outgrow it. In the fall of 1959, when Judy was nine, their Kansas City pediatrician X-rayed her when she contracted strep throat. Afterward he stunned Gloria by saying, "Are you aware that Judy has a congenital heart condition?" The doctor arranged to do further tests, which revealed that an atrium of Judy's heart—one of the chambers that receives blood returned from other parts of the body—had a hole in the outer wall, and one of her heart valves wasn't closing properly. Open heart surgery would be required. With their doctors' concurrence, the McClanens put off the operation until after Judy's tenth birthday on February 10, when Judy invited all her best friends to a square dance party in the McClanens' recreation room. Several days later, Don and Gloria checked Judy into the University of Kansas Hospital, five miles from their home.

Judy had five days of pre-operation tests and procedures. On Sunday, the next-to-final day before the operation, the McClanens went to see her after church. Judy was in tears. "Mommy, I want to go home," she told Gloria. Her mother recalled Philippians 4:13, a verse that had comforted her when she was coping with the uncertainty of the early FCA days. "Honey, when you get feeling like this, just remember that you can do all things through Christ who strengthens you."

On Tuesday, Don and Gloria waited anxiously through the three-and-a-half-hour surgery. One of the doctors on the operating team was an intern who belonged to their church, and in the late morning he brought good news. The surgery had gone well, and while Judy was coming out of her anesthesia she sang, "Onward Christian Soldiers." But when Don and Gloria were finally permitted into the critical care unit at midnight, the sight was excruciating. Judy was unconscious, lying naked with ice packed around her from head to foot to combat her high temperature. A raw L-shaped scar ran the length of her breast bone and across the bottom of her left rib cage.

The next day, doctors told the McClanens that Judy should be out of the hospital within two weeks, restricted to home for less than a month and then be back in school. Her parents began a daily watch at Judy's bedside, with Don going in early and staying till 4 p.m., and Gloria replacing him from 4 p.m. to midnight. By the end of the week Judy was able to sit in a wheelchair. But on Saturday, Judy cried and fussed, totally out of keeping with her normally sweet spirit. Doctors began to give her blood transfusions. The following day, Don and Gloria arrived at the hospital to find a sign on Judy's door reading "Staphylococcus Infection."

Doctors tried every antibiotic available, but the staph infection didn't respond. The following Thursday evening, Gloria was in the hospital room and Judy seemed to be sleeping. All of a sudden, she raised her head off the pillow and exclaimed, "Oh Jesus, oh Jesus." She laid her head back down, then raised up again and, staring off into a distance, said, "Oh Jesus, I'm coming, Oh Jesus, I'm coming."

On Friday, when Gloria arrived at the hospital, doctors told the McClanens that Judy had developed staph pneumonia, they were putting her in an oxygen tent and her survival would be a miracle. When Don and Gloria entered the room, Judy was in the tent shivering, with hot water bottles stacked around her body. Gloria went to a wash basin and splashed water on her face, trying to disguise her tears. Judy said, "Daddy, come hug Mommy. She doesn't feel good." Turning to Gloria, she said, "Mommy, remember, you can do all things through Christ who strengthens you."

She's dying and she's worried about me, Gloria thought.

Don and Gloria had cots put in the room, and throughout the night they could hear Judy murmuring. The next morning, March 5, 1960, a nurse came and asked that they leave the room so that she could tidy up. Gloria took her Bible and went into an unoccupied room to read and pray. Meanwhile, Don talked with Gary Demarest and his wife, Marily, who had come to support them. Shortly after, Don ran into Gloria's room, grabbed her and exclaimed, "Judy's dying." Then he ran back up the hall. By the time Gloria reached Judy's room, her daughter was gone. Don told Gloria that, as he watched Judy shivering and suffering at the end, he had heard her repeating her last words: "God is love, God is love."[17]

Devastated, the McClanens took Judy's body back to Pennsylvania and, as with Douglas 13 years before, buried her in the McClanen family grave plot. Dick Armstrong, a Presbyterian pastor on the FCA board and a good friend, spoke at the funeral. He and his wife had lost a child to leukemia just before they had come to know the McClanens. As Armstrong spoke and looked at Don's and Gloria's drawn faces, the grief of his own loss flooded in and he was halted by emotion for several moments. Gloria later told him, "Your tears meant more to us than your words."

In the devastation of losing a second child, the McClanens found solace in the embrace of their church and friends. Condolences poured in from their FCA network. "You can be sure you and your family are in the prayers of every one of your friends in FCA," wrote Carl Erskine. "You will never know how great a Christian influence you've been to thousands of people through FCA."

"There is just no use of my trying to tell you how much my heart goes out to you, and all of you, who are so grievously afflicted," Branch Rickey wrote. "I have this sort of consolation–that you, more than anyone, know where to go for the only comfort that can possibly assuage your sorrow at a time like this."

"Words just fail me here and now, but be sure, dear fellow, that you are in our love and prayers mightily," Louis Evans wrote. "I know that that faith that you have shared with so many others will be displayed in courageous measure now to those who call you friend."

Especially solicitous was Sam Shoemaker, the Pittsburgh pastor who had become Don's informal spiritual director. Shoemaker telegrammed immediately, "Tears came when I heard how ill Judy was, but when I heard she had been released I could only think of her joy in the land of light and fellowship of the saints. I know you are feeling this even with the heartbreak." Within the month he wrote more letters. "You have been much in my mind, and I am so eager for a word from you. ... I don't think I've ever known a time when more people were going through really terrible trouble than right now, and yet there is a wonderful breaking through on all sides of the Spirit of God, giving people victory in the midst of difficulty" (March 18). "I'm so glad for [the letter of] yours of March 24th. What God does to help people face the real anguishes that come into life and turn them into triumphs is to me the most mysterious and in some ways the most glorious thing that happens. There is nothing else on earth that does this. No science can do it. No mere will power can do it. Only the Grace of God can do it" (March 28). Shoemaker's encouragement might have seemed callow had it not come from a man of such spiritual depth. Don took great comfort in his eternity-colored view of their loss.

Indeed, the McClanens sent out a circular letter on March 25 that was filled with grace and hope. "As we reflect first on ten years of wonderful life with Judy we can only try to thank God enough for His goodness to us. We can only now really understand what the great prophet Isaiah meant when he said, 'And a little child shall lead them.' ... The reality of the Cross and our Master's words of compassion, 'Father, forgive them ... not my will, but thine be done,' have added at this time a new dimension to our understanding of God's grace and giving of His ONLY Son for each of us." The letter ended, "We will merely conclude by saying, thank you again, and asking any who have been so moved from within through this event to join with us in the rededication of our lives to the only one who can give us 'new life' and 'eternal life' ... Our Lord and Saviour, Jesus Christ. We know nothing could bring a warmer smile to His face or Judy's at this time."

Despite those words, Don, Gloria and their son, Michael, felt deep pain. Gloria wept frequently and struggled to get through each day. Don and Michael kept their emotions more hidden, but Don could not totally repress his grief. One day in early summer he was home alone when a surge of emotion washed away his defenses. He began screaming at God, using every curse word he could think of. When his rage was spent, he sank onto the couch, surprised by the outburst. *Where did that come from?* he thought. But he also felt exhilaration—a sense that he had been real with God and that God, despite being reviled, loved him for his honesty. It was as if, Don thought, his own son Michael had come to him to express anger over some grievance, trusting in his father's ability to work through their differences rather than hiding his hurt.

Work at FCA did not allow Don much time to grieve. The city-wide appearances continued, and Gary Demarest gave notice that he would be leaving at the end of the year to become pastor of a church in Hamburg, New York. Don and the board had decided, in addition to Estes Park, to hold a second summer conference that August in Wisconsin. Fortunately, Don was able to hire Bob Stoddard, a high school coach from Carmel, New York, as associate executive director to succeed Demarest. Stoddard, one of the most successful high school football coaches on the East Coast, had become a staunch FCA supporter after attending the Estes Park conference in 1958.[18]

The new conference at a YMCA camp on scenic Lake Geneva, Wisconsin, drew 345. At the Estes Park conference the following week, 589 were enrolled, with 75 turned away. Bill Bradley, a high school basketball player from Crystal City, Missouri, attended the Lake Geneva conference. He also attended an Estes Park conference the following summer before becoming an All-American at Princeton followed by a career with the New York Knicks and a seat in the U.S. Senate.

Bradley reflected on FCA's impact on his life after he joined the Knicks. "I first met Christ at a Fellowship of Christian Athletes' summer conference after my junior year in high school," he wrote. "I met Him through the talks of Jim Jeffrey, Don McClanen and others, and through the huddle group leader, Fran Tarkenton." (Tarkenton was quarterback for the University of Georgia football team at the time, and would go on to become an NFL star with the Minnesota Vikings.) "I was moved that these men would share such personal experiences," Bradley said. At Princeton, "I had broken my foot that year and I didn't think I was going to play basketball very well. Also I was worried about my studies, and it was the first time that I was away from home for any length of time. After Christmas vacation at the University, I took an examination in French. It was an oral exam and I did miserably. I walked back to my room and flopped on the bed. I didn't know where to turn. I thought I'd call home, but that was 1,200 miles away. I considered talking to my friends, but would they really be concerned? I thought of turning to the Bible, but where would I look? I finally thought of a record I had from the summer conference of the year before and, as I listened to it, I heard a man speak whom I've always kind of idolized–Bob Pettit [Hall of Fame basketball player for the St. Louis Hawks]. I heard him say: 'We are not trying for the state championship, nor are we playing for the national championship. We are playing but for one thing–the victory of Christ in the hearts of men.' Here I was worried about my academics, my basketball, and everything else, while neglecting the one thing that counts most. I never did receive that bolt of lightning but, at that moment when I heard those words roll off that record, I knew I had been giving my life to the wrong goals. I knew then that I wanted to give my life to Jesus Christ and His service."[19]

Despite FCA's growth and impact on young lives, Don and the board diverged in their views of the future. Some board members urged that FCA become a membership organization, with chapters in communities, colleges and high schools across the country. They thought this would promote growth and spur more donations. Don adamantly opposed the idea. He believed this would place FCA in competition with church youth programs, rather than act as a supporter of churches, and also would encourage a type of nominal Christianity in which an FCA card–rather than a changed life– served as evidence of devotion. By 1960 the board had swung on the issue and passed a membership plan over Don's objections.

At the same time, the FCA office had tensions among some of the staff members. Disagreement surfaced on how to operate the office and also on some religious issues. Despite FCA's success at blending people from various theological and denominational backgrounds, Don found himself caught up in such trivial matters as which version of the Bible to use. Don used the Revised Standard

Version, but another thought he should use the King James Version. Don suspected he was being criticized to board members.

On the home front, Don and Gloria went through the roller-coaster process of adopting a child in early 1961. Following the medical thinking of the time, Gloria had undergone sterilization after her third Caesarian section, so she could not have another baby. The idea of adoption came from Michael, who broke his silence about Judy's death one day by asking his parents, "Why can't we have more kids?" The McClanens approached one adoption agency, but the agency suggested it was too soon after Judy's death and that Don and Gloria might be unwittingly trying to replace their daughter in a psychologically unhealthy way.

Unexpectedly, they soon got a call from the county adoption service, which had heard of their search. Don and Gloria agreed to take a child who was due to be born to an unwed mother in March. But March came and went and there was no baby. An adoption official told them the mother must have miscalculated her pregnancy. Indeed, on April 26, 1961, while Don was giving an FCA talk to a civic group in Nashville, Tennessee, Gloria got the call: their baby, whom they named Laurie, had arrived. Gloria contacted Don's Nashville host, who waved him the happy news from the back of the room while Don was speaking. The audience broke out in cheers. Laurie joined the McClanens a week later.

Caring for a newborn added to the family pressure, and the incessant strain of fund-raising and overseeing a continually expanding roster of events took a toll on Don. Always intense about his work, Don wound himself even tighter, causing greater fatigue. In May 1961, the board took steps to relieve the pressures in the office by creating a new administrative director position that would supervise the FCA staff and day-to-day operations. This would free Don to concentrate on fund-raising, special projects and keeping the organization true to its vision, the board told him. A search to fill the new position continued in August 1961 when the sixth Estes Park conference took place. Don arrived with his family and his parents, who had flown from Pennsylvania to help Gloria take care of Laurie.

FCA's board scheduled a meeting for the opening night after the evening convocation. As board members waited in a meeting room for the stragglers to arrive, Don heard some talking with each other about the FCA office situation. Something in him snapped. Don hit his hand on the table and heatedly told the board members to stop whispering among themselves. "What are you saying about me?" he exclaimed. "Say it to me right now. Let's be real!" An awkward silence fell over the room, and board members reassured him that they considered FCA to be doing well. The meeting proceeded as if nothing had happened.

Don slept poorly that night and arose early. He realized he had left his Bible in the meeting room. When he entered the room to retrieve it, four board members were there having a discussion. Don excused himself and began to leave when the board's chairman, University of Denver Athletic Director Tad Wieman, said, "By the way, I'd like to talk with you later this morning." When they met, Wieman acknowledged that the four board members were discussing staff discord. "You're exhausted," Wieman said. "We want you to take a rest and go abroad for at least three months. We'll pay for all expenses." Then Wieman added that Don should schedule a psychiatric consultation, at FCA's expense. Board members, friends of Don, wanted him to get help. But Don was shocked by this proposal. He felt that, given this era and the culture of athletics, being referred to a psychiatrist was tantamount to being labeled insane. He said he would think and pray about it overnight. He told Gloria he felt inclined to resign, but she counseled him to wait, pray and talk to others before burning his bridges.

The next morning, Don told Wieman that he would agree to the two conditions, but that he didn't think he was the only person who should see a psychiatrist. "I have come to believe that there are other problems that are not all of my own making," he said, referring to a staff person with whom he had the most friction. He would see a psychiatrist if that person went, he said. For the rest of the conference, Don pretended, as best he could, that nothing was wrong.

Several weeks later, Don and Gloria drove 280 miles to a psychiatrist in Ponca City, Oklahoma. The psychiatrist mailed a diagnosis of "compulsive personality," stating that his perfectionist tendencies and ability to take on huge amounts of work made it difficult for others to work with him. The psychiatrist added that Don needed psychotherapy and that an appointment would be held open for him two weeks from that date. Don wrote back, "I will use your findings as a guide to corrective procedure in the days ahead. I will not need the appointment you are holding for me." The FCA board did not require the other employee to seek counseling and, in fact, gave the person a raise.

Don confided in Sam Shoemaker, who wrote back in an indignant letter. "Whoever got anything done that didn't have a compulsive personality? Is anybody so naïve as to think that St. Paul didn't have one, or that John Wesley didn't? ... I would wager that some people who don't want your evangelical emphasis continued in FCA find you difficult to work with. They certainly would find me difficult, or anybody else who upheld the things that you and I believe in."

Shoemaker volunteered to intercede on Don's behalf with board members. But Don was already exploring other options. The final straw came on October 2, 1961. As the McClanens prepared to travel to Europe, which Gloria had always wanted to visit, Don received a call. A bill had arrived at the FCA office for books by Catherine Marshall and another Christian writer that Don had ordered to send to sports figures to encourage them in their spiritual growth. Don was told that such an expenditure needed board approval. "I need to think about this," Don responded, "because this is invalidating a big chunk of my ministry in educating these people."

When Don told Gloria about the incident, she exploded. "That's it. I'm through. I don't want to go on the trip. I don't want anything to do with FCA anymore." Don hugged her and said she had spoken the words he was waiting to hear. "I would have resigned, but I couldn't bear to do that to you," he said. The next day Don wrote to the board that he had returned the books, canceled the reservations for Europe and would inform the board of his future plans after adoption court proceedings for Laurie concluded October 19. On that day, with the adoption completed and the McClanens having no further need to show adoption officials a steady source of income, Don sent his resignation letter to FCA.

"As a result of the Lord's guidance, we are planning on moving to Richmond, Indiana ... to start graduate work in the Earlham College of Religion," he announced. "In faith we know He will provide for our every need." This clean break and new direction gave Don and Gloria some relief. Mostly, however, they felt like another death had occurred in the family: a severing from the great cause to which they had devoted their lives.

Still, as with Judy's death, they sent encouragement to their FCA friends. In a general letter sent out in November, Don wrote, "Gloria and I are indeed grateful to God for the part He has allowed us to share with you in the development of the FCA movement. His grace has been more than sufficient to do all that He has indicated He wanted to do through such a movement from the outset. ... For the evidences of renewal in the life of the Church we can only stand in awe of the power of the Holy Spirit to use even a grain of mustard seed.

"From the outset we have felt and tried to be true to the fact that God had entrusted this great FCA ministry to not one, or a few, but to many Christians in the athletic arena of life. It is with this continuing conviction that we feel the movement will now go on to its rightful and greater fulfillment. ... We know all who have made FCA what it is will continue to give their utmost support to the staff and board of directors."

Suffering

Don has experienced suffering in his life, including the deaths of two children and the loss of his first ministry. One of his favorite Bible verses is 1 Peter 4:13, "But rejoice that you participate in the sufferings of Christ" (NIV). Don believes suffering is not only an inevitable part of life, but a positive one.

We may not consider suffering redemptive. We may try to cope by not acknowledging our suffering or by trying to dampen its pain. First, some of us attempt to minimize it by telling ourselves, "I'm not really suffering. I haven't lost a child, and my house hasn't burned down. Many people are worse off than I am." But suffering is not a competition. Difficult undertakings involve suffering. For example, sacrificing sleep for a newborn or staying true to a difficult friend or working long hours on a project with an uncertain chance of success can involve suffering. To acknowledge that we have given of ourselves is to imbue our undertaking with an appropriate sense of worth–to recognize that we are doing something important enough to suffer for it. And if we acknowledge that kind of sacrificing by others, they and what they do are ennobled.

In 2007, Don visited with FCA President Les Steckel at his Kansas City headquarters. After hearing Steckel describe his rigorous travel schedule, Don acknowledged that this involved suffering for Steckel. Steckel's eyes lit up in gratitude that someone had recognized the sacrifice of his long absences from home, long waits in airports and long nights of fitful sleep in unfamiliar hotel beds. They both understood FCA's mission as a cause worthy of Steckel's suffering.

Imagine if we halted for a day from our relentless activities, turned off our TVs and musical devices, left our books and magazines unopened, and spent the time alone focusing on our interior life. Some would protest how *boring* this would be. But boredom might not be the real reason such a day would be unattractive; the real reason could be fear. For in all likelihood, we would come face to face with unwanted feelings of inadequacy, fear, anger, futility–the stuff of suffering. If we allowed these feelings to surface, we might discover what is unresolved in us, what drives us. In other words, we might give ourselves a chance to grow. As St. Paul says, "We also boast in our sufferings, knowing that suffering produces endurance, and endurance produces character, and character produces hope" (Romans 5:3-4 NRSV). Don also recalls a saying of Mother Teresa: "Suffering opens up space within that otherwise would not be there– so that God can come in and fill it."

Acknowledged suffering also can knit us together. Opening up to another person about the pain in our lives can form a bond that is deeper than amiable conversations and shared good times. Suffering is one of two profound aspects of our human experience. The other is love, and it is inextricably tied to suffering. That which we love we suffer for. And when we endure suffering for the sake of love, we paradoxically experience joy. As the writer of Hebrews points out, "For the joy set before him [Jesus] endured the cross" (Hebrews 12:2 NIV).

We often consider suffering to be an occasional and unwelcome visitor to our modern lives, endowed as we are with unprecedented affluence and ability to control our environment. Instead, we can accept suffering as a constant companion in ways large and small and, indeed, even a constant friend.

4

The Wilderness

"Leave your country ... and go to the land I will show you."
—Genesis 12:1 (NIV)

At the age of 35, Don had pursued—and ended—two careers, and had little idea what might be next. He and Gloria moved their furniture into the basement of a house of friends and, in October 1961, loaded their Ford station wagon with clothes, two children and a few other belongings. They headed 550 miles eastward to Richmond, Indiana, an industrial town on the Ohio border. Richmond was the home of Earlham College, a small Quaker school with a new School of Theology where Don would take classes and explore a call into the ordained ministry. The school's founder, Elton Trueblood, a professor of philosophy and author of national prominence, had invited Don to the school.

In addition to the college, Richmond, population 44,000, boasted the Whitewater River Gorge running through the middle of town and a cluster of factories that made auto parts, school buses and caskets. The McClanens moved into a two-bedroom apartment in a Victorian house separated from campus by Route 40, a national east-west highway. The college, a pleasant swath of green lawns spotted with academic buildings mostly of red brick and white wood trim, welcomed Don, one of the older students. He arrived a month after the opening of the semester, but nevertheless enrolled in three theology courses, including a philosophy of religion course taught by Trueblood, who was 61.

That class, with fewer than 10 students, met in the Teague Library, a small, one-room building on campus built for Trueblood by a businessman supporter. It was an intimate, home-like space, lined with floor-to-ceiling wooden bookshelves and with a fireplace, where the class gathered on sofas and easy chairs for discussions. Trueblood, in dark suits and wire-rimmed glasses, was both methodical and outgoing. He led animated discussions, which ended precisely at the sound of the campus bell that marked the change of classes. Don enjoyed his teaching. On occasion, Trueblood and his wife, Virginia, had Don and Gloria to dinner.

Don admired Trueblood from having read his books. Trueblood had earned a theology degree from Harvard and a Ph.D. in philosophy from Johns Hopkins. Before coming to Earlham in 1945, he had gained a national reputation as the chaplain at Stanford University, which led to a steady schedule of speaking engagements across the country. Trueblood's writing was prolific, resulting in 33 books. Among other themes, his lectures and writings critiqued the superficiality of "churchianity" and called for a "fellowship of the committed" who would work across denominational lines for spiritual renewal and societal reform.[1] This concern for deeper Christian commitment led Trueblood to found the Yokefellows movement in 1949.[2] The name referred to Jesus' commandment, "Take my yoke upon you and learn from me" (Matthew 11:29 NIV). The movement included conferences, a network of people seeking to deepen their commitment to Christ and a nationwide ministry to prison inmates.

Before Trueblood met Don, he had read about and admired Don's work with the Fellowship of Christian Athletes. Their acquaintance began in 1959 when Trueblood invited Don to speak at a Yokefellows conference, and they remained in touch thereafter. After Don arrived at Earlham, Trueblood broached the possibility of Don becoming executive director of Yokefellows. Don thought about the offer only for a moment. While it would have given him a secure job and a measure of solace from the sting of his unhappy departure from FCA, Don had no interest in returning to such an administrative position. He sensed that God had something new—something unique—for him to do, and he wasn't going to grab onto what seemed merely pragmatic.

It wasn't that he didn't need a job. His FCA salary continued through December, but the McClanens were making mortgage payments on their Kansas City house, which had not sold. Money was tight. Don and Gloria lived off savings, and also with a little help from a few benefactors. Among those were Carl and Julia Vrooman, an eccentric elderly couple who lived in Bloomington, Illinois. Carl had been assistant secretary of agriculture under President Woodrow Wilson, and Julia was an heiress, writer and jazz musician. They lived in a four-story, 36-room mansion that Julia had inherited, whose grounds included a "Lincoln Oak" where Abraham Lincoln reputedly had addressed the Bloomington citizenry during a presidential campaign. The Vroomans were major financial backers of Faith at Work, a renewal movement founded by Don's friend, the Rev. Sam Shoemaker, to encourage the application of Christian faith to daily life.

Bruce Larson, the movement's executive director, suggested to the Vroomans that they might want to help Don in his exploration of a new call, and arranged for the McClanens to pay the couple a visit in December. There was a major glitch, however. The week before the scheduled trip to Illinois, Don felt a terrible pain in his stomach. It turned out to be appendicitis, and he went into the hospital for an emergency operation. Twenty-four hours after surgery, Don felt much recovered and announced to his doctor that he planned to travel to Illinois. The doctor was aghast, but finally consented on the condition that Gloria drive their station wagon the 240 miles with Don lying on a makeshift bed in the back.

The Vroomans were gracious hosts, in their own strange way. The McClanens learned that Julia didn't believe in using soap when washing her dishes to avoid leaving a residue on them, and the Vroomans were quite frugal about using their heat. Don and Gloria were shown to separate bedrooms, where they spent a cold, unpleasant night. The house was old, musty and ill-maintained, and Gloria was apprehensive about what germs they all might catch. But the privations proved to be worthwhile. The Vroomans listened with interest to Don's description of a paper he was working on for one of his Earlham courses. He envisioned a conference ministry that introduced people to some of the Christian movements that had sprung up just after World War II. FCA, Faith at Work and Yokefellows were prominent among these. Don thought of these movements as fresh new streams through which the Holy Spirit was flowing, and he called his ministry concept "Wellspring," based on John 4:14: "The water I give him will become in him a spring of water welling up to eternal life" (NIV). The McClanens soon received a letter from Carl Vrooman with a $700 donation in it.

The McClanens joined First Presbyterian Church in Richmond and, as they had done in Kansas City, initiated a small Bible study group. They also participated in a small group on campus led by Keith Miller, a friend of Don's from Oklahoma who had left the oil business to study at the School of Theology. Miller would later write best-selling books such as *A Taste of New Wine*. Earlham also introduced the McClanens to Quaker meetings that took place at the campus Meeting House in a plain, unadorned room with white plaster walls, large clear-glass windows, exposed ceiling beams and five benches against each wall facing the middle. With 30 to 50 other worshippers, Don and Gloria sat in silence for 20 minutes at a stretch before someone "spoke out of the silence," sharing a thought or a message for the group. No one answered or questioned what the speaker said. The McClanens had been introduced to periods of communal silence at Faith at Work and Yokefellow meetings, but they were still neophytes at this form of Christian spirituality. The meetings were certainly different from the FCA chapel services where youth sang, laughed and applauded speakers with loud enthusiasm.

Always interested in experiencing new things, Don was intrigued by the Quaker meetings. He enjoyed their emphasis on quietness, receptiveness and humility. For Gloria, the meetings were even more of a revelation. Without a pastor telling her what to do and say, without written prayers and hymns, without a prescribed liturgy, she felt freed to experience God directly in silent prayer. It was as if she were worshipping for the first time. In the future, silence became a central Christian discipline for both McClanens.

In a different spiritual experiment, Don drove 435 miles to Green Lake, Wisconsin, to attend a four-day National Training Laboratory session. Therapists and facilitators helped clergy and lay leaders develop keener insights into their, and other people's, emotions. A clergyman in New York during Don's FCA days had once observed to him that he seemed out of touch with his feelings. Surprised, Don asked what he could do about that, and the pastor recommended the National Training Laboratory program.

The lab took place at the national conference center of the

American Baptist Church, located on the picturesque shoreline of Wisconsin's deepest lake. Don shared in group sessions with about eight others. The sessions were touchy-feely, but not exactly warm and fuzzy. When others in the group were asked to give a one-word metaphor for Don, some of their responses were a "glass of milk," a "drawn shade" and a "ghost"–suggesting he had a closed and unrevealing personality. In one session the facilitator, an ordained pastor, told Don that he had come with a lot of baggage. Don naively responded that he had only brought one small suitcase, which brought a gale of laughter from his fellow session members. At another point the facilitator prodded Don harshly by saying, "McClanen, you couldn't smell [feces] if it was smeared all over your face." Don's angry response to this provocation–telling the facilitator not to curse at him–drew a cheer from his fellow session members. The session confirmed for Don what the pastor had told him in New York: he was out of touch with his feelings, just as he had been after Judy's death. This was a surprise to him, because he had always thought of himself as an open person. And he didn't know what to do about it.

Don enrolled in more religion courses the second semester, but he increasingly realized his heart wasn't in it. He went through the motions. His studies at Earlham principally taught him that he was not cut out to be an ordained minister. Meanwhile, Gloria missed her friends and activities in Kansas City. A change in direction came in May 1962, when Don took a trip to New York and dropped in on Len LeSourd, editor of *Guideposts*. LeSourd had recently married Catherine Marshall, one of Don's favorite Christian writers. LeSourd invited Don to stay overnight at their home in Carmel, New York, an hour north of the city. During dinner, the conversation turned to the question of how to breathe new life into churches. Marshall, an attractive and direct woman with deep blue eyes and light, wavy hair, told Don, "You know, the kinds of things you're saying and questions you're asking make me think of Gordon Cosby and the Church of the Saviour. Have you ever met him?"

"No," Don replied, "but I've heard about him." In fact, Don had read an article about the pastor of this unusual Washington, D.C., church in a Faith at Work magazine, and kept hearing mentions of the church at conferences and in informal conversations. Elton

Trueblood also was impressed with this church, having become acquainted with it while he worked in Washington in the 1950s as chief of religious policy for the U.S. Information Agency under President Eisenhower. Catherine Marshall had occasionally attended services at the Church of the Saviour when she and her first husband, the Rev. Dr. Peter Marshall, lived in Washington, and she had found Cosby to be a helpful advisor on spiritual matters. In 1953 she had written an article about Cosby and his church for *Reader's Digest*, which brought a flood of attention to the church.[3]

"If I call Gordon Cosby and he is available, would you like to see him?" Marshall asked Don. The next morning, Marshall picked up a phone beside the breakfast table and dialed Cosby, who said yes, he could see Don that afternoon. Don quickly rearranged his plane tickets, had the LeSourds drop him off at the airport and flew to Washington. A taxi dropped him off at the Church of the Saviour's headquarters at 2025 Massachusetts Avenue, a three-story, 25-room brown-stone Victorian house in a neighborhood dominated by elegant foreign embassies. Cosby, age 45, nine years older than Don, wore a flat-top haircut and a dress shirt and slacks—no coat and tie. During their meeting, he focused in on Don so completely that, years later, Don would compare Cosby's ability to "be present" with that of Mother Teresa.

In response to Don's questions, Gordon described some of the characteristics of the Church of the Saviour. Its members were low in number—about 50—but high in commitment. To join, members agreed to live lives of both inner spiritual development and outward ministry, especially to the poor of the city. Before joining, prospective members completed two years of courses at the church's School of Christian Living. Cosby believed seminary-type training wasn't just for prospective clergy; it was for everyone. Upon joining, members pledged to read their Bibles, pray, write in a spiritual journal and spend time in reflective silence every day, and become active in one of the church's mission groups, with which they would meet, worship and study once a week. Church members also contributed at least a tithe—ten percent—of their income to the church and its missions, and pledged to confess and seek help from their groups should they fall short in any of these commitments.

At one point, with his FCA departure in mind, Don asked Cosby about the problem of conflict within churches. Cosby's answer surprised and intrigued him. "We have plenty of that here," Cosby said. "Chaos is the norm of the Christian life. Just look at the conflict that cropped up between Jesus and his disciples, and between Paul and Barnabas." By the end of their conversation, Don was energized in a way he hadn't been since leaving FCA. He wanted to find out more about this church. Upon returning to Indiana, he wrote Cosby thanking him for their time together and asked if he could return for a ten-day visit.

Several weeks later, Don flew back to Washington. The church had arranged for him to stay in a small apartment on the church's third floor, and had lined up members to talk with him and show him the church's School of Christian Living and some of its missions. The missions, each with their own mission group, included the Potter's House, a coffee house located on the edge of one of the city's mixed-income areas, and an adjoining art center called the Potter's House Workshop. There was also Dayspring, a 175-acre farm and retreat center 25 miles away in the Maryland countryside.

Among the individuals Don met were Frank and Dot Cresswell, who had been among the church's nine founding members in 1947. Despite Frank's workload in medical school at George Washington University and later during an intern year at Walter Reed Army Hospital, Frank and Dot dove into the activities of the church. In 1950 they left the Washington area for Georgia and then for their beloved Mississippi, where both had grown up. But the influence of the Church of the Saviour was so deeply implanted in their souls that in 1958 they moved back to Washington, now with six children, to rejoin the church. When Don came, Dot served on the church council and Frank was active with the Dayspring ministry.

Don also spent time with Elizabeth O'Connor, in title the church secretary but in function one of the pillars of the congregation. A vivid and lyrical writer, she was just completing a book about the church entitled *Call to Commitment*. The book was the first of eight that O'Connor eventually wrote evoking the life of that community. The foreword for the book was written by Elton Trueblood. When Don asked if he could read the galley proofs, O'Connor quickly agreed.

What Don learned about Gordon Cosby fascinated him. Cosby

had grown up in Lynchburg, Virginia, an ardent Southern Baptist. As an early teen he and his brother, P.G., agreed that they would pay each other a dollar each day one of them failed to talk to someone about Jesus. Frequently Gordon remembered his failure after going to bed, so he would rise and sneak out of the house to find someone to whom he could witness. One day Cosby, 15, and P.G., 19, were wandering a backwoods area in the foothills of the Blue Ridge Mountains just west of Lynchburg, trying to find a farmer to lend them a greased pig for a church youth-group event, when they came across what seemed to be an abandoned two-room church. An elderly black man appeared and explained that he was deacon of the church, which was without a minister. Cosby offered that he and P.G. could be its pastors. The deacon was skeptical, but arranged for Gordon to preach a trial sermon on a subsequent Sunday. A dozen people showed up. They urged Cosby on with "amens" as he talked about Revelation 3:15-16: "I know your works; you are neither cold nor hot. I wish that you were either cold or hot. So, because you are lukewarm, and neither cold nor hot, I am about to spit you out of my mouth" (NRSV). The congregation invited the Cosbys back, and they stayed on as the church's ministers for several years. The flock, growing to 40, embraced Gordon as their own, and he fell in love with them.

After high school, Cosby simultaneously worked on degrees at Hampden-Sydney College near Lynchburg and at Southern Baptist Theological Seminary in Louisville, Kentucky. In 1942, when he had completed both, he married Mary Campbell, the daughter of the pastor of Cosby's childhood Baptist church. The newlyweds moved to Arlington, Virginia, just outside Washington, D.C., where Cosby began pastoring a small church. But World War II intervened. Cosby enlisted in the Army as a chaplain, and was sent with the 101st Airborne Division to Europe to participate in the Normandy invasion. Ministering to soldiers facing imminent death and forging a Christian fellowship that cut across all denominational lines profoundly affected his view of what church should—and had to—be. There was no room for sectarian niceties, nor for a vague, half-hearted faith.

O'Connor told of a particular encounter Cosby had with a soldier the night before his unit was to assault an enemy-held hill. After

Cosby had crawled into a foxhole to check on him, the soldier said, "I have a premonition that I am going to die tonight–that I will meet God before the night is over, and I don't know Him. I want you to talk to me about Him." Then the soldier added, "Don't give me any stuff about philosophy or theology. I just want you to talk to me about God." Groping for an adequate reply, Cosby said, "I would like to talk to you about a verse of Scripture which means a lot to me: 'For God so loved the world ... '. The chaplain talked to the soldier for a few minutes about that verse from the gospel of John, and left. The next morning he checked the unit's casualty list, and the soldier was dead. Cosby returned from the war with a vision: to open a church in Washington, D.C., that would welcome people of all denominations, evangelize the quarter million citizens of the nation's capital who were unchurched and lead members in developing a faith deep enough to hold firm through the inevitable crises of existence.[4]

On the third day of his stay, Don visited Dayspring. The farm and retreat center immediately enraptured him with its rolling countryside, half fields and half woodland, farmhouse, barn, lake, retreat lodge and "inn" with 18 bedrooms for those on retreat. Don learned the origin of Dayspring. In 1952 Cosby began to speak about buying a farm within an hour's drive of the church to use as a place of silence and solitude in which to seek God's guidance. Growing crops or raising cattle would help pay the mortgage. The idea seemed fantastical, though, as the church had only 35 members and 100 worshippers, and had just taken on almost $100,000 in debt with the purchase and renovation of its headquarters building. But the dream grew in the imaginations of the members. A widow, Dorothy Ham, came into Cosby's office with a check for $1,300, saying it was for the Retreat Farm fund. "I don't know what you are talking about," Cosby told her. "We don't have such a fund."

Ham responded, "Well, Gordon, haven't we said that we need a place to pray?"

"Of course we do, but we owe $100,000, and anyway, you are a widow. You lost your husband in World War II. You are bringing up your little girl. You are bringing your mother here and buying her a house for her to help you bring up your child so that you can go to work. Where did you get this money, anyway?"

"If it is any of your business, it is my retirement up to this point."

Cosby said, "I don't feel good about this."

Ham said, "Well, Gordon, feel any way you like; this is for the Retreat Farm Fund."

Two days later, Cosby's secretary came into his office with her husband just before they were to leave for seminary. They had no car and no place to live. The wife was just out of high school with few marketable skills. They put a check for $750 on Cosby's desk. He said, "What on earth is this for?"

"It is our way of saying thank you to the Church of the Saviour. This is for the Retreat Farm Fund."

"Where did you hear of that?" Cosby asked.

The couple replied, "Don't we need a place to pray? This is for the Retreat Farm Fund."

"Where are you going to live when you get to seminary?"

"We don't know."

"How are you going to get to seminary?"

"We will go on the bus."

"Do you have bus fare?"

"We'll get it."

"Why are you giving this $750 when this would give you a week's motel expenses?"

"Gordon, whatever you want to think is fine, but this is for the Retreat Farm Fund."[5]

The church council appointed three young women to be a search committee. During the next six months they visited 50 farms without finding a suitable property. Still, by Easter 1953, the church was convinced the "treasure in the field" was near at hand and decided to designate the Easter offering as a down payment. Members already tithed, and few had substantial incomes. But some took second jobs and others took loans to make their contributions. The Easter offering came to $9,000.

A month later, in May 1953, the committee approached a new real estate agent, who called Gordon Cosby and said, "We have three girls here, who have indicated that your church is in the market for a farm. If you will send a responsible person, we will be glad to talk to him and show you what we have." Cosby responded that the church had no one more responsible than those three girls and if the agency wanted to do business with the church, it would have to do business with them. That very day, the committee was taken to view Dayspring, and a sale was later negotiated for $35,000–$5,000 under the ceiling price the church council had set.[6] The church took the farm's name from Luke 1:78-79: "The Dayspring from on high has visited us; to give light to those who sit in darkness and the shadow of death, to guide our feet into the way of peace" (NKJV).

Don learned that church members had built the wood-paneled retreat lodge on the edge of a field, half-nestled in a grove of oaks, maples, tulip poplars and hollies. These handymen and handy-women called it the Lodge of the Carpenter. Don also learned that the retreat Inn, whose single bedrooms featured quilts, comfortable reading chairs, desks and windows opening out to the forest, had been designed in consultation with retreat masters from around the world. And he noticed that Dayspring's farmhouse appeared unoccupied.

Don called Gloria later that day and told her, "Honey, I think I've found where we're supposed to be!" Don knew, however, that Gloria was not likely to be enthused. She had made clear to him throughout their marriage that she had no interest in farm life; she was a city girl. As Don described Dayspring to her, she did not protest. They had to go somewhere, she figured, and she didn't have any other plan. Besides, she assumed that any stay at Dayspring would be short and that they would quickly move to a nice suburban home.

Before returning to Indiana, Don hatched a plan. The McClanens would request to live in the farmhouse for the summer, and Don would find a job teaching or coaching. By fall, when the farmhouse was to be converted into a pastoral counseling center, they would find another place to live. Meanwhile, they would immerse themselves in the life of the Church of the Saviour and perhaps develop Don's Wellspring conference ministry idea. When he outlined this plan to Cosby, the pastor told him to write a letter of request to the church council when he returned home. Don's letter prompted a lively discussion at the next council meeting. Some of the members were skeptical about this person who seemed to be hopping about since leaving FCA, with no clear idea about what

God was calling him to do. However, Elizabeth O'Connor voiced the opinion that Don had spent considerable time exploring what the Church of the Saviour was about, and would not come in blindly. Dot Cresswell argued that perhaps Don was a modern-day Abraham, journeying in faith without knowing exactly where he was going. The council offered the Dayspring farmhouse to the McClanens for the summer at a rent of $25 a month.

In early June 1962, Don and Gloria left 12-year-old Michael with a friend's family in Indiana for the last few weeks of school, loaded one-year-old Laurie and their belongings into their station wagon and a small trailer, and headed 500 miles to Washington, D.C. To get final directions, they stopped in Germantown, Maryland, the town closest to the farm. The town consisted of a general store, a bank and a railroad crossing. They entered the general store and found all of the town's saleable goods: groceries in the middle and farm implements and clothing on the left, with a post office in the back and a small lunch counter on the right. The McClanens sat at the counter for their first Germantown meal. The folksiness of the people in the store reminded Gloria of the Oklahoma hospitality she had enjoyed early in their marriage.

Using the directions they got at the store, the McClanens pulled off the highway beside a white country church and made their way down a mile-long gravel road. Woods closed in on both sides of the road, with tall trees arching together overhead to form what almost appeared a leafy vaulted cathedral ceiling. At the bottom of a hill they came upon a house where Gloria was greeted by Carolyn Hubers and her two-year-old daughter, Martha, who would become a playmate for Laurie. Carolyn was one of the three women on the Dayspring search committee, and she and her husband, Tom, were the last people to live in the farmhouse. The Hubers had just finished building their own home six months before. Carolyn Hubers took a quick reading of Don, who was sunburned from having been at the Indianapolis 500 a few days before. His comments about the auto race showed him to be an intense, passionate person, she thought. She pointed the McClanens to the top of the next hill, the entrance to Dayspring.

Right at the crest, Dayspring opened up before them. Behind the Dayspring sign and a split-rail fence, a lawn sloped down to the farmhouse, large and white with a wide porch wrapped around two sides. Beyond the farmhouse stood a barn, with its stone foundation, weathered boards and steep tin roof. Next to the barn were a corn crib and a stable. Beyond these lay mown fields and, in the distance, forests. It was a lovely setting. Gloria left Laurie sleeping in her car seat, stepped out into the fierce heat of the day and entered the back door of the farmhouse. A musty smell and a layer of dust every-where greeted her. Wandering through the downstairs, the McClanens found a dead bird lying in a chair, old plastic furniture and two boxes for firewood that looked like coffins. In the kitchen, light flooded through the large windows, revealing old linoleum flooring and old-fashioned, worn countertops. Above the counter-tops were a row of cabinets. As her eyes were drawn upward, Gloria saw painted on the wall just below the molding these words:

> Lord Jesus, come be our guest,
> Our morning joy, our evening rest,
> And with this meal and bread impart
> Your loving peace to every heart.

It was a blessing that her daughter Judy had spoken frequently before family meals. As Gloria gazed through tears, she sensed Judy's presence, greeting them to their new home. *This move is going to be okay*, she thought.[7]

The McClanens had a place to stay, but they needed income. Don cashed an insurance policy and signed up to sell World Book encyclopedias. When Don believed in what he was selling, such as FCA, he did well, but World Books failed to spark his imagination. On one of his first door-to-door outings in a suburban neighborhood close to Germantown, he knocked on a screen door and a big dog pushed the door open and bounded out. Don quickly ducked inside and slammed the door. The homeowner checked on the commotion as Don exclaimed, "I'm a World Book encyclopedia salesman. You wouldn't want to buy a set?" "Oh, I've been looking all over for a World Book salesman!" she said. It was the only set Don sold.

Don also checked with the county school system about teaching jobs. But he had no enthusiasm for that either, and after a period of substitute teaching the following school year, he gave that up too. But Don needed an outlet for his pent-up energy, so he and Michael volunteered for grounds-maintenance jobs around the farm. Ralph Talbot, a member of the church, oriented them to the tasks that needed doing. Talbot, a well-paid chemist for Eastman Kodak in Rochester, New York, had retired in the area to be a part of the Church of the Saviour. He served as volunteer caretaker at the farm, with a paid field laborer. In late summer, the laborer quit for a better-paying job, and Don jumped at the chance to take his place. Don was quickly hired at a salary of $66 a week, and the McClanens were allowed to live at the farmhouse rent-free as part of their compensation.

With Talbot's help, Don mastered the fundamentals of operating the farm's two tractors, a grey Ford that Talbot had brought with him from Rochester and an older red Farmall owned by the church. Don spent long days on the tractors mowing 70 acres of fields and 20 acres of lawn around the farmhouse and along the road. During the growing season, Don took two-and-a-half days to mow the natural growth on the 90 acres—just in time to start over and do it all again. He also split firewood, tidied up the retreat and camping areas, removed trash from the lodge and camp after use, performed maintenance on buildings, maintained the farm's well pumps and other equipment, and fed and stabled the farm's horse, two ponies and two burros.

Being a self-described "mechanical moron," Don sought out those who knew something about tractors and other farm machinery. A neighbor, Les Briggs, whose family had owned the Dayspring property years before and who had contracted with the church occasionally to share-crop some of the fields, helped Don with the malfunction of the moment. If he and Briggs could not solve the problem, Don went to a nearby tractor dealership and said, "I've kicked the hell out of this thing; now can you fix it?"

Don and Gloria joined a small group within the Church of the Saviour that met weekly at a home in Rockville, Maryland, a suburb near Germantown. They worshipped, prayed and discussed how the church could be relevant to suburban living. At one point the group studied a book called *Prayer Can Change Your Life*, written by researchers who had performed groundbreaking scientific experiments in 1951 on the power of prayer to heal.[8] With the book came a series of psychological test sheets, which the McClanens and other members filled out and sent off for scoring. Don's results indicated a "strong fear about your deeper emotions, evidently because you have some feelings which you cannot accept."

Don and Gloria began to wonder about the other members of the group. Most notably, one older woman swore like a truck driver. Don and Gloria hadn't heard such language in church settings before. Don called her "General Patton." But aside from her salty language, she became like a grandmother to them, bringing a pound of coffee and a pound of butter to the farmhouse each weekend. Other members of the group appeared to be normal, middle-class suburbanites, but during the weekly gatherings they confessed to all kinds of problems, such as conflict with spouses and children. After a couple of months, Don said to Gloria, "We've really come into a community of sick people." But the moment he said it, Don saw himself and Gloria as the real "basket cases," still grieving Judy's death and Don's departure from FCA, and uneasy about their future. Don also realized that members of previous small groups he and Gloria had started and belonged to had avoided discussing hard things that were happening in their lives. A letter the McClanens received from friends in Kansas City telling of an impending divorce reinforced this observation. The couple had been in a small group with the McClanens for years and had never mentioned marital issues.

Indeed, the McClanens struggled with their own psychological and marital woes. Gloria, lonely and worn out by caring for a one-year-old and "camping out" in a house that wasn't her own, grumbled to other members of the church about how her husband had dragged her to a place she did not want to come for a reason she still did not understand. Don, plagued by a continuing sense of loss about his FCA departure and a sense of futility about his long days of labor, would say to himself, *What the hell am I doing splitting wood?* Unlike his previous life, no welcoming committees waited for him when he showed up at the barn each day and climbed onto the tractor.

One day when Tom Hubers offered to help as Don and Michael dug a hole, Hubers mentioned something about coaches. Don exploded, "What the hell do you know about coaches?" Hubers put down his shovel and silently walked away. On another occasion of farm work, Don became infuriated with a mistake Michael had made. Don's face turned beet red, and he screamed at his son. "How can you continue to do this to me?" Michael pleaded. "There's nobody except Mother who loves you as much as I do." This entreaty blunted Don's anger, but he could not answer his son's question. He shook his head and, without a word, walked away. Don's emotional storms passed quickly, but they were intense and hurtful.

Don's and Gloria's mutual frustration led to tense discussions and occasional yelling matches. At one point, Don declared, "A tribe can only have one chief, and I'm it." He walked out the door, leaving Gloria yelling behind him, "I hate you, Don McClanen." Don sought refuge in Dayspring's camping area to pour out his fear and frustration: "God, God, God, I hate you. What are you trying to say to me? What else do I have to do? You've taken my kids, you've taken my life's work. Now it seems you might be taking my marriage."

During the winter of 1963, Gloria had had enough. "Get us a decent house and a real job," she said. "I can't live this way anymore. If you can't do that in three months, I'm taking the kids and leaving you." Don stared at her in disbelief. Finally he sighed and said, "Honey, I feel God has us here for a reason and, until I know what it is, I can't leave. If you've got to leave, well, it's not what I want, and I'll miss you." It was Gloria's turn to be shocked. She heard Don say that he was willing to give her up, but more importantly, she heard him say he was sure that he was following God's will. And if that was the case, who was she to buck God? In an unexpected way, Don's response reassured her about the future.

The McClanens enrolled in their first course, "Christian Growth," at the School of Christian Living in Washington, an endeavor they enjoyed doing together. It was the first class of six needed to join the church. The other five were "Old Testament," "New Testament," "Christian Doctrine," "Christian Ethics" and "Christian Growth." These courses, taught mostly by Gordon Cosby, Mary Cosby and Mary's sister, Elizabeth-Ann Campagna, were never dry and academic. In "Christian Growth," for instance, students were assigned to choose someone else in the class they were attracted to and someone they were repelled by. Without saying which was which, they met with both to become better acquainted. Gloria would always remember how likeable she found the "repellent" classmate after spending time with him.

Don and Gloria enjoyed the courses, but Don felt he had things to teach as well as to learn. Gordon Cosby received numerous invitations to speak throughout the country–far too many for him to accept. Cosby would be off to San Francisco one week, Atlanta the next. Don, feeling underused and unappreciated as a farm laborer, thought that perhaps Cosby could slip him a few of those speaking invitations. But the possibility did not seem to cross Cosby's mind, and Don did not have the nerve to suggest it to him.

Don did convey to Cosby that he was ready to launch his Wellspring ministry, featuring conferences about the Church of the Saviour and other Christian movements that had started just after World War II. Cosby said that he considered Don's idea to be an authentic call, but he added, "It's not my call." He suggested that Don approach other members of the Church of the Saviour. If no one else felt ready to "give their life" to that ministry, then Don's call was strictly individual and not a corporate call that the church would support. Don described his idea to eight people, and none responded with enthusiasm. Cosby then advised Don to continue working at the farm and let some time go by. To Cosby's amazement, Don followed his advice.[9]

In fact, Cosby recognized the Wellspring idea as an important one. But he followed a key principle in his ministry: that being a committed member of the community was a higher priority than pulling off a project for God. Powerful ministry happens in community with people growing both inwardly and outwardly, Cosby believed. So Cosby wanted Don to take time to solidify the match between himself and the Church of the Saviour. If the two sides survived their "courtship period," ministry would happen.

The church also introduced Don and Gloria to the discipline of silent retreats. All members of the church did an annual weekend retreat with their mission groups, and they were encouraged to make a second retreat individually at some other time of the year. A typical retreat began Friday evening with a "talking" supper at the Lodge of the Carpenter. After supper, the retreat leader announced a meditative theme for the retreat. After a short worship service, members of the group "entered the silence." Talking from then till Sunday normally consisted of one person reading devotional passages for 15 minutes during meals and during a short worship time Saturday evening. Those on retreat otherwise sat together wordlessly in the lodge, wandered the surrounding fields and spent time in their rooms in the adjoining Inn. They wrote in journals, read "lingeringly," prayed and meditated. On Sunday, after a silent breakfast and one last meditative period, the group assembled for final worship and a time of sharing about what God had taught them in the silence. They departed with the admonition to let the experience of silence temper their re-entry into the noise and bustle of their everyday lives.

Don entered his first retreat skeptical that the experience could enhance his spiritual life. But after several, he noticed that his body's metabolism slowed after 24 hours, and his mind stopped racing from one thought to another. He appreciated the peacefulness, but still he was not overwhelmed by any spiritual insight or mystical experience. Then, in 1963, Don attended a retreat led by Douglas Steere. A Quaker, Steere was chairman of the philosophy department at Haverford College near Philadelphia and the author of several acclaimed books on spirituality. In fact, the Church of the Saviour had consulted with Steere when building the retreat Inn.

On Friday evening, 18 people sat in a circle and introduced themselves inside the Lodge of the Carpenter. Steere, looking old-fashioned with high-top shoes and little round glasses, exhibited an air of quiet authority. He explained that each person was invited to contemplate the question, "Lord, what is the next step you would have me take in my spiritual life?" Steere further advised that people not reason or think too much, but simply be aware of seeking direction from God.

Throughout that night and the next morning, Don's mind was a dry well. No significant thoughts or insights surfaced. *What's the next step? How the hell do you find out in silence?* he thought. But on Saturday afternoon, he entered the comfortable, relaxed state previously experienced 24 hours into a retreat. He sat silently on a sofa in the lodge looking through a picture window at the forest. Overhead hung a portrait of a mysterious Jesus figure with a faraway gaze drawn by a previous Jewish visitor, entitled "The Christ I Met at Dayspring." Don was startled by what seemed a clear word spoken to him: *My son, you are on the next step. If you try to take two steps, you will bloody your nose.*

His amazement slowly gave way to quiet exhilaration. Despite his feelings of futility about life at Dayspring, he felt reassured that something important was happening. When he shared his experience with the group, Gloria listened in the circle, grateful for Don's experience of reassurance and hopefulness. Indeed, a decade later when Don ended his tenure as Dayspring manager, he looked back on his ten years of farming as a vital "retooling," a laboratory of servanthood in which he learned the health of subordinating ego to community life. The decade became "the most important 10 years of my life."

Struggles and Silence

One aspect of Don's courage is his willingness to share openly about his struggles. In this book, as in his life, Don lets others into his grittier thoughts and actions, from arguments with his wife to yelling at God in times of anguish. Don's son, Michael, notes that Don's transparency often has been startling to those experiencing it for the first time. (When you think about it, the biblical writers were similarly raw in picturing the failures and foibles of our spiritual forebears.)

Many people, being more astute at public relations, try to make themselves look good by hiding their weaknesses and vulnerabilities. But those who, like Don, are courageously candid about their humanness put themselves in a special place to be used by God. They invite intimacy, allowing others to open up about their weaknesses. Once sources of pain or shame are confessed to another, people often are freed to change what needs to be changed and accept what needs to be accepted.

The Bible makes clear in story after story that God is in the business of using flawed humans to achieve divine purposes. Think of the murderers who became heroes of the faith, such as Moses, David and Paul. Nowadays, many falsely believe that the divine and the human are opposites. As Father William McNamara says, "When one is most fully human, one is most fully divine."

In addition to being openly human, Don is disciplined. When Don and Gloria joined the Church of the Saviour, they each pledged to spend an hour a day in individual Bible study, prayer, reflective silence and journal writing. For many, dedicating that kind of daily time for spiritual disciplines seems unlikely if not impossible. They are far too busy. But by not taking the time, they risk having a stagnant, superficial faith and staying busy doing less-important things that don't satisfy.

Daily devotional time amounts to "hanging out" time with Jesus, a crucial discipline because of the popular culture's bombardment of overt and subtle messages contrary to Jesus' way. Only by hanging out with Jesus do followers really begin to know him, know how he thinks and acts, hear his messages as loudly as they hear the culture's and allow his Spirit to permeate and change them. Anything less than an hour a day jeopardizes the ability to hear Jesus' quiet voice amid the uproar.

Most active Christians spend at least some time reading the Bible and praying, and many write in journals. Through the discipline of silence, less practiced and less understood, Don allows the Holy Spirit room to work in his life. As Thomas Keating says in his book *Intimacy With God*, "Silence is God's first language and ... all other languages are poor translations."[10]

In more recent years, Don has practiced a form of silence called "centering prayer" or "contemplative prayer." This involves sitting in a quiet place with eyes closed and dwelling inwardly on a sacred word such as "Lord," "Jesus," "grace" or "love." When other thoughts interfere, the praying person returns gently to the sacred word. As Cynthia Bourgeault explains in her book *Centering Prayer and Inner Awakening*, "We let go of our self-talk, our interior dialogue, our fears, wants, needs, preferences, daydreams and fantasies"[11]–all the internal chatter that our egos use to defend and inflate themselves. This is the type of prayer St. Paul refers to in Romans 8:26: "For we do not know how to pray as we ought, but that very Spirit intercedes with sighs too deep for words" (NRSV).

Bryan Sirchio, a former ministry colleague of Don's, describes centering prayer as spending time in the "lap" of God, with no agenda other than to rest and trust and feel embraced. It's similar to the way Sirchio's daughter, when she was a toddler, crawled into his lap and said, "Daddy, I need some snuggle time with you." However, more important than any immediate sensation of peace is the deeper faith, greater hope and stronger love that comes from practicing centering prayer at least 20 minutes twice a day.

Don also has found silence a powerful discipline for groups. He often has opened meetings with a short reading from the Bible or other devotional work followed by 15 minutes of silence. He invites members of the group to share what they have experienced in the silence. Such meetings often are more focused and inspired than ones that do not include silence.

Finally, as in his experience with Douglas Steere, Don uses silent retreats as crucial getaway times with God. During such retreats, the Spirit puts him in touch with suppressed emotional issues, guides him in vocational decisions and clarifies his sense of call. People unfamiliar with silent retreats often can find retreat centers within a short distance of their communities that are able to introduce them to this life-enhancing discipline.

5

Treasure in the Field

*"The farmer waits for the land to yield its valuable crop.
... You too, be patient."
–James 5:7-8 (NIV)*

Don's revelation during the Douglas Steere retreat confirmed that he had more to learn at Dayspring. But it also pointed, ironically, to the farm being the right place for Don to develop a ministry to residents of inner-city Washington, D.C. The previous year, in January 1963, Don had happened upon Bishop Marie Reed's storefront church on Seaton Place. Excited by his discovery and casting niceties to the wind, he asked the bishop if he could come to her home once a week for dinner to experience life on her street. Reed graciously agreed.

During the evenings when Don came into the city for a class at the School of Christian Living, he stopped first at the bishop's home–which also served as the church–where she and her husband hosted him at a table set up in the room otherwise used for worship. The Reeds introduced Don to such delicacies as collard greens, black-eyed peas and sweet potato pie. Don offered to help with the cost of the groceries, but the bishop would not hear of it. So Don brought her a few dozen eggs each week, purchased from a chicken farm near Dayspring. Soon he ran an egg concession out of his truck for other residents of the street, selling cartons at cost.

Don learned that Reed belonged to a group of churches in Washington and New York called the Mt. Canaan Spiritual Conference, which had ordained her a bishop. Don and Reed discussed her church work, her efforts to organize the community and her evolving plans, in concert with Don, to offer a summer camp at Dayspring for children of the block. After several weeks, Don asked a new question: "It's one thing to come and eat with you, but I'd also like to live with you. Is there any way I could come and spend the night?" Reed replied that she had access to a bedroom in a house across the street, and he could stay there if he liked.

On his next evening in the city, Don entered the guest house and felt his way up a dark stairway. At the top of the stairs a light bulb hanging on a cord from the ceiling dimly lit the hallway. A small room with no light and only one item of furniture–a bed with a mattress whose center sagged like a hammock–was Don's guest room. When he arose in the middle of the night, Don discovered the bathroom had no light. When he attempted to sit on the toilet, he discovered it had no seat. When he reached for toilet paper, there was none. The faucet yielded only a slow drip. All this filled Don with excitement. *This is wonderful,* he thought. *I've wanted to understand poverty, and here I am in it.*

On February 6, 1963, Don spent one of his nights on Seaton Place. Dressed in his farm clothes, he had brought a nice suit, white shirt, tie and dress shoes in a brown paper bag. The next morning he put on his farm clothes and drove downtown to a fancy hotel. He slipped into a bathroom, changed into his suit and attended the National Prayer Breakfast, where President John F. Kennedy spoke. At the breakfast he chuckled inwardly at the incongruity of having come from one of the city's poorer neighborhoods to have breakfast with the President and a thousand others.

Back at Dayspring, Don identified a small source of income for the farm: selling sod–rolled-up strips of grass–from Dayspring's fields to the county roads department for use on highway roadsides. To cut the strips, Don bought a sod-cutting machine, which looked like a souped-up lawn mower. A blade sliced through the soil about a fourth-inch under ground to create foot-wide strips of grass that jail inmates loaded onto county trucks and hauled away. The business brought in $300 an acre.

In the spring of 1964, the sod business took an unexpected upturn. Brian Finger, a state horticultural extension agent who had previously given Don farming advice, came by to say that he was about to take a job with O.M. Scott and Sons, a leading national lawn-care company. Finger said the company was recruiting farmers to grow premium grass for sale to home builders, golf courses and

other commercial customers. Scott was particularly keen to introduce farmers to its Windsor Bluegrass, a new variety discovered in a
pony pasture at the company president's home in Marysville, Ohio.
It was a naturally occurring mutation with excellent properties: a
dark green color, slow growth rate and good disease resistance.
O.M. Scott would sell Don the seeds and fertilizer and provide him
with technical advice, Finger said. A year after planting, Don would
be able to sell the sod for $1,800 an acre, six times the price of com-
mon field sod.

Don's ears perked up. Here was a way to make Dayspring self-
supporting, and even bring in substantial funds to support the
Church of the Saviour's ministries. He did some calculations. In
addition to seed and fertilizer, he would need a new truck and a new
tractor. An even bigger-ticket item would be excavating a lake to
provide irrigation for his 90 acres of fields. This, plus a pump and
aluminum irrigation pipes, brought the total proposed investment to
$55,000. It was a handsome sum in the mid-1960s–almost twice the
cost of an average house.

Finger arranged for Don to learn more about the Scott program
by visiting the company headquarters in Marysville, near Columbus.
Don flew up and was given VIP treatment, staying overnight in the
Scott House, a company guest residence built from a design by
famed architect Frank Lloyd Wright and surrounded by an acre of
pristine lawn. The next morning Don toured test fields and the Scott
headquarters, then lunched at the home of the company's president,
Paul Williams. Williams, a bald man in his 60s dressed in a suit but
with a down-to-earth manner, became enthused by Don's account
of running a church-owned farm. Williams, Don discovered, was a
devout Christian.

Back in Maryland, Don presented his research to the church
committee that oversaw Dayspring. They agreed the idea had
potential but, aside from the price tag, they had two concerns. The
first was Dayspring's topology. Sod operations are usually located on
flat bottomland. Did Dayspring's rolling hills create the risk that
rainwater would run down and erode the topsoil before the grass
seed could fully germinate? But advisors from the county's soil conservation office had told Don that growing sod would probably
cause less erosion than planting other crops, since sod did not

require frequent plowing. The conservation officials also said they could contour Dayspring's fields, at their expense, by bringing in large earth-moving equipment to scoop intermittent gullies along the face of the hills to divert rainwater from running straight down.

The Dayspring committee's second concern was Don. Would he stick around to see the operation to completion? By this time Don and Gloria had come to an agreement: they wanted to remain in the Washington area and become full members of the Church of the Saviour. With its two concerns met, the committee approved the project.

During the summer, the Dayspring committee took out a bank loan and Don bought the needed equipment. He put in a $10,000 seed and fertilizer order with Scott, and hired an excavating contractor to dig a one-acre bowl that would become the lake. A creek ran across some of Dayspring's fields and into the bowl and would eventually fill the lake, thanks to an earthen dam constructed at one end of the bowl. The soil conservation advisors told Don not to expect the lake to fill completely for a year or more. Indeed, with the dry conditions of that summer, the lake was more like a mud hole. Meanwhile, Don contracted with a local chain of hardware stores to supply Windsor Bluegrass when the sod matured for harvesting in a year.

In the waning weeks of summer, Don worked dawn to dusk, disking the fields for planting with his new Massey Ferguson tractor. By early September, all the seed and fertilizer were in. But the dry weather caused him to fret. Would there be enough rain to germinate the seeds and keep the grass growing? All he could think to do was roll the pump, which was on wheels, into a puddle at the center of the bowl, hook up the irrigation pipes and dribble a little water onto the fields. But it clearly was not enough. He needed rain.

On a Saturday night in mid-September, Don heard the encouraging sound of raindrops on the farmhouse roof. The sound became less encouraging as it gathered force into a major storm that lasted all night. On Sunday morning, Don looked down toward the lake and was amazed to see it filling with water. With the heavy drops pelting him, Don rushed down to the barn and revved up the tractor, then drove across the field to the lake to save the pump from being inundated and lost forever. He backed the tractor into the bowl until water half-covered its rear wheels, and there he hooked the pump onto the back of the Massey Ferguson. The tractor wheels spun on the slippery incline as Don maneuvered the pump to high ground. But now, Don realized, he could lose 30 irrigation pipes under the incoming water.

Don scrambled off the tractor and splashed into chest-deep water. He groped for the pipes with his feet, then reached underwater to grab them, uncouple them and drag them to dry land. As he continued his salvage operation, he noticed the recovered pipes were now in danger of being re-submerged by the continually rising water. Don broke into delirious laughter. *The Lord is going to fill this thing today!* he exclaimed over and over. As he raised his eyes to the fields surrounding the lake, he saw an anguishing sight. The torrent was washing away his grass seed and fertilizer and, indeed, the precious topsoil itself. Weeks of effort and thousands of dollars in supplies were being swept to the bottom of the lake, now 12 feet in depth. Don returned the tractor to the barn and entered the farmhouse drenched and disconsolate. He called Gordon Cosby to give him the bad news. Cosby replied, "Don, the loss of that money is not the issue. The question is, what does that kind of discouragement do to you?"

It was a disaster, but not a total one. O.M. Scott replaced the grass seed and fertilizer at half price. As the soil dried, Don redisked the fields and replanted. He now had plenty of water in the lake to pump through the irrigation pipes. Still, the delay jeopardized his ability to meet his contract with the hardware company. The following summer, the Dayspring fields showed off the uniform rich green of a sod operation, but the grass wasn't mature enough to harvest. So Don drove to Long Island, where sod operations were numerous, and purchased several tractor-trailer loads of turf to fulfill his contracts with the hardware stores. A year into its operation, the Dayspring sod farm had lost money rather than made it.

A turnaround was in the offing. The Windsor Bluegrass, ready for harvest the following spring of 1965, found an eager market, not only from the hardware store chain, but also from home developers. Replanting went smoothly, and a profitable operation had begun. Don's FCA past turned out to be a boon. His old friend, Otto Graham, was named head coach of the Washington Redskins football team in 1966. Graham introduced Don to Joe Mooney, the groundskeeper in charge of the Redskins' home field, D.C. Stadium (renamed Robert F. Kennedy Stadium a few years later). Don provided turf for the stadium's baseball infield, home of the Washington Senators, after the Redskins finished their football season.

Don also sold sod to the Washington Hilton hotel and the Governor's Mansion in Richmond, Virginia. A *Washington Post* article in December 1966 touted the quality of the sod grown at the farm: "Windsor, it is said, can even be grown over asphalt if properly watered and fertilized." Don, the article added, had given up his previous career and, at age 40, had "committed himself to a life of work with the church."[1] Don's commitment, however, was not without continuing inner conflict. Periodically he announced to Gordon Cosby that he was sick of farming and wanted to resign. Cosby listened patiently and, by the end of their conversation, Don withdrew his resignation. Once again, Don realized that he awaited God's next step, that the Church of the Saviour was where he wanted to be and that his farming served that community. He was learning a humbling lesson in patience and obedience.

Likewise, Gloria gradually lost her sense of humiliation at being a farmer's wife. One afternoon she found Don lying on the living-room floor. Assuming he was resting after a hard day, she stepped over him to turn on the TV, then heard him moan, "I think I'm having a heart attack." At the hospital emergency room, an admissions clerk asked Gloria her husband's occupation. In the past, Gloria had described Don as "superintendent of a church-owned farm." But this time she said simply, "He's a farmer." She then thought, *It's okay for him to be a farmer.* Fortunately, her farmer recovered quickly. He had suffered, not a heart attack, but a chest muscle sprain from constant turning that day on his tractor to open and close a fertilizer release lever.

The *Washington Post* article about Don's farming included a photograph of a typical work day at Dayspring. With a pastoral, rolling landscape and the farmhouse in the background, Don filled the foreground, dressed in dark work shirt and pants, maneuvering the sod cutter up a hill. Behind Don, two inner-city youth bent down to roll the cut turf for shipping.[2] Indeed, Don had combined his Dayspring turf business and inner-city outreach. The summer after meeting

Bishop Reed, Don hosted several weeklong camp sessions for kids from Seaton Place. During each session, three to four dozen children of varying ages slept in tents at a Dayspring campsite originally built for families of the Church of the Saviour. College and teenage volunteers from the Church of the Saviour served as counselors. Bishop Reed and mothers from Seaton Place, as well as from the Church of the Saviour, prepared the evening meals.

The activities included baseball, basketball, archery, swimming (after the lake was built), horseback riding, wagon rides, scavenger hunts and rock picking. As for the latter, Don painted several stones white, placed them in a sod field and asked the children to bring all the rocks they found to a wagon. Those bringing the white stones got a prize. The children were amused, and Don had help clearing his fields.

During wagon rides, "Farmer Don," as the children called him, stopped on a hill overlooking a pond, shushed the children and told them to listen to the wind in the trees and the birds and insects and think about the amazing world God created. The inner-city children, being more accustomed to police sirens, fire engines and helicopters, found this idea instructive but comical.[3] Insects did interest the children. They liked to trap daddy longlegs, spiders and grasshoppers and put them together in little boxes to see if they would fight. The campers also experienced some things that they had only read about or seen on TV, such as roasting marshmallows over a campfire and eating "s'mores." By the end of the week, campers frequently cried at the thought of going back to the city.

In 1964 after one summer camp, Don again mixed sod farming and inner-city ministry. He asked Bishop Reed to recommend some Seaton Place teenagers he could mentor while paying them to work on the farm. Reed identified three 13-year-olds: Charles Morgan, Horace "Sportio" Collier and James "Hot Dog" Robinson. Don picked them up on Seaton Place on Friday afternoons after finishing deliveries in his "ton and a half" International Harvester flatbed truck. All four rode to Dayspring bunched up in the cab. Don brought them home on Sunday mornings in his Volkswagen Beetle while on his way to church. The three spent the weekends with the McClanens in the farmhouse, ate meals with the family and slept in bunk beds in an extra second-floor bedroom. Michael McClanen, now a high school student, and Laurie, a preschooler, took the new weekend housemates in stride. After all, living at the farmhouse had always been a fishbowl existence, with church members trooping in and out while participating on Dayspring work crews or attending picnics. Michael became friends with Charles, Sportio and Hot Dog since they were close to his age and he worked alongside them on the farm.

Gloria was preparing dinner the first time Don arrived with the three boys. She remembers Sportio as a "dark black cloud," sullen and withdrawn. But as weeks passed, he became comfortable and the real Sportio emerged: outgoing, opinionated, a natural comic and a hard worker. Hot Dog was a basketball player with a tall, athletic build and a pleasant, serious manner. Charles was tall and lanky and a little shy. He was also, the McClanens soon discovered, highly intelligent. Don kept the boys busy on Saturdays, paying them more than the minimum wage of $1 an hour to help him split wood, rake leaves, set up the irrigation pipes for the turf operation and do other farm chores. Eventually they drove the tractor to mow grass and disk fields.

The teens did not know about small families with two parents, and they had not been exposed to material comfort. In an autobiographical essay Charles wrote several years later, he told about growing up with seven siblings and a single mother, who worked as a domestic. His family heated their rental house with a wood stove, burning chopped-up crates that a nearby machine shop threw away. When the electricity was cut off for nonpayment, the family lit kerosene lamps and candles. One of Charles' older sisters cooked dinner. The family ate together, but there wasn't enough silverware to go around, so children took turns using the forks. To ensure that he ate in the first round, Charles frequently put a fork in his back pocket several hours before dinnertime. The family's landlord, who owned most of the houses on Seaton Place, rarely made needed repairs in a timely manner. One year the roof started leaking over the bathroom and half the ceiling fell in during the 12 months it took the landlord to attend to it. Charles went to sleep listening to chunks of plaster fall between the walls.

Tenants contributed to some of the disrepair, Charles admitted. "We kids would bang on the walls to signal our friends in the house next door. And after all that banging we had holes in the wall. I can remember eating plaster from those holes. ... We liked the chalky taste in our mouths 'cause our diet was mostly starch anyway. ... Things were difficult, but everybody on the street was in the same condition. As a child I thought that was the way everybody lived, even beyond Seaton Place." Charles had fun on the street, too. The children played tackle football on the sidewalk, using half-gallon milk cartons filled with rocks and paper if a regular football wasn't available. They played basketball, horseshoes and "curb ball," in which players earned points when they rebounded the ball back to themselves by hitting the curb on the opposite side of the street.

Charles learned that the white people who came to Seaton Place were "the rent man, an insurance man or the police–so you learned to turn them off." When he reached junior high school, he was allowed to transfer to a better school across town because of his high grades. But, for the first time, classmates who were predominantly white and middle-class black ostracized him. Miserable, Charles intentionally let his grades drop so he could be sent back to his neighborhood junior high. He scraped through high school, and at graduation was happy to be finished with school forever.[4]

When Don first invited Charles and his friends to Dayspring, Charles welcomed the chance to get away from Seaton Place and earn some money. Still, he wondered about Don's intentions. That a white family would treat the boys almost as sons was frankly "mind-blowing" to the three. And there were amusing misunderstandings. The boys helped Don stack firewood at the retreat lodge, but they had a hard time believing what he told them about men and women spending weekends together in silence for spiritual purposes. For instance, why was a gate closed on the entrance road during the retreats to keep other people out? The boys concluded it must be a "treat center" where adults carried on orgies.

But gradually, they learned the difference between treats and retreats, and Charles came to love his personal weekend retreats in the country. "Don became like a father to me. He really cared about me ... and my family. *Really cared*. It wasn't just talk."[5] Eventually Hot Dog, diverted by girls and parties, stopped coming, but Charles and Sportio continued into their senior year of high school. Then the blowup occurred. The boys had experienced Don's occasional fits of anger, such as when they were careless cutting sod and left several inches of grass between the strips to go to waste. Don did not yell at them or use obscenities, but his face would clench and turn red and he would turn and walk away. After a few minutes of walking in circles muttering to himself, Don would return to the boys and the work would continue. Charles and Sportio were not concerned about these infrequent displays, which were tame compared with the drama they witnessed on Seaton Place.

One day, the boys were supposed to help Don load the sod truck for a special delivery. But they also were expected to participate in an activity at Dayspring that Don supported called Leaders of Tomorrow (LOT), whose goal was to build self-esteem and develop leadership skills of inner-city youth. John Williams, a teacher who worshipped at the Church of the Saviour, led a meeting of the group that day on Dayspring's basketball court near the farmhouse. Though Charles and Sportio had indicated to Don that they would slip away to help load the truck, they felt a responsibility to their fellow LOT members as well. Caught in the middle, they made a snap judgment to finish the LOT activity. After all, they reasoned, it was Don who had gotten them involved with LOT.

Twice Don drove up from the fields in his truck past the basketball court, eyeing the boys from his cab with a grim expression. He had a contract deadline worth thousands of dollars, and he couldn't believe they were letting him down. At the end of the day, when the LOT gathering broke up, he took the two aside. Steaming mad, Don told them they had kept him from meeting his order, that he had expected them to make a more responsible choice and that they were to leave the farm and not come back. Don drove them into Washington in total silence and dropped them off at their homes. The rupture seemed total. For months Don had no communication with them. Charles and Sportio were hurt and bewildered. Their banishment, a 180-degree swing from Don's previous affection, seemed far out of proportion to their offense. Finally, Don called the two and said he wanted to take them to lunch. He told them he had been mistaken in banning them and assured them that they would be welcome again at Dayspring. Charles and Sportio were excited to return to their weekend work, although the two continued to be baffled by what had happened.

After high school graduation Charles went to work for the District of Columbia Department of Parks and Recreation, eventually supervising children at a drop-in recreation center. Don was disappointed that Charles settled for a job with such limited prospects. He talked to Charles about a Presbyterian school in western North Carolina named Warren Wilson College, where Don knew the baseball coach, a former Brooklyn Dodgers scout for Branch Rickey. Charles was totally uninterested. He wanted to earn money, he didn't want to move away from his family and friends, and he didn't want to go to the South. Besides, deep down, he lacked confidence that he could succeed in college. Undaunted, Don talked to Charles' mother, who also wanted better opportunities for her son. She feared Charles might follow in the footsteps of Sportio, who had gotten involved with drugs. Just try college for a year, she urged. Charles finally relented.

Warren Wilson, in the foothills of the Blue Ridge Mountains with a student body of 400, had a large contingent of exchange students from all over the world. Each student worked a required 15 hours a week at jobs needed to keep the campus running, such as tending farm animals, serving food and driving athletic buses. Charles struggled his first year. "I was scared to death because I didn't have that much faith in myself," he wrote. "I figured I'd fall flat on my face and fail." The only person in his family to attend college, one of his sisters, had lasted only one year before dropping out. But Charles stuck with it. His second year went much better. His fellow students appreciated his quiet and thoughtful nature, often seeking him out to discuss their problems. He took on jobs that required extra responsibility, such as being a dorm manager. His grades shot up. When he graduated, influenced by the international flavor of the school, he joined the Peace Corps and spent three years in West Africa. He earned a master's degree in agriculture at Tuskegee University and went to work for the U.S. Agency for International Development, taking assignments in Africa, the Middle East and other parts of the world. He eventually rose to become AID's regional executive officer for southern Africa. Without Don's mentoring, his horizons would have been far more limited.[6]

In 1968, the third year that Charles and Sportio worked at the farm, the Church of the Saviour decided to construct a farm manager's house at Dayspring so that the McClanens could have more privacy and so church members could have full use of the farmhouse for events. The church borrowed $32,500 from three church families to build a four-bedroom house on a hillside by a pond, with a picture-window view across Dayspring's fields to the lake. Downstairs a large recreation room was equipped with pool and ping pong tables donated by Otto and Beverly Graham, who were moving away from Washington after Otto's Redskin contract was not renewed. An architect, Claude Ford, who attended the Church of the Saviour, designed the McClanens' house, including ideas furnished by Gloria. Just as Don had clipped articles about Christian athletes, Gloria for years had clipped home floor plans from magazines, dreaming of once again having a home of her own. The loans would be paid back by sod operation income, and the McClanens would live there rent-free as part of Don's caretaker remuneration. As the family loaded their furniture and belongings on the farm truck for the 100-yard drive to the new house, they little realized that this would be their home for the rest of their lives.

A second event in 1968 left Don heartsick. On April 4, the Rev. Martin Luther King Jr. was assassinated on a motel balcony in Memphis, Tennessee, where King had planned to lead a demonstration for the city's low-paid sanitation workers. A great admirer of King, Don had planned to write the leader to offer Dayspring as a meeting place when King and his lieutenants came to Washington the following summer for a Poor People's Campaign. Don had even considered leaving Dayspring and volunteering full-time with King's organization, the Southern Christian Leadership Conference. King's death sparked rioting in more than 100 cities across the country, and Washington, D.C., suffered the worst. In five days of fires and looting, 12 people were killed and 900 businesses were destroyed.[7] The epicenter of the storm, the predominantly black 14th Street business corridor, sat less than 15 blocks from the Church of the Saviour's headquarters.

The day after King's slaying, Don saw in the paper a small announcement about a breakfast meeting at a downtown restaurant, where civic and church leaders would discuss how to respond to King's death and the resulting mayhem. Don joined more than 50 people, who agreed that they should continue gathering on a once-a-week basis. After several weeks, Don proposed to some that they meet weekly for prayer as well.

The Rev. Bill Porter, a former aide to Martin Luther King and the acting director of a downtown Washington YMCA, offered the use of his facilities. Joining him and Don one afternoon each week were eight others, including Fred Harrison, a reformed hustler who directed the D.C. activities of a youth ministry called Young Life; Virgil Keels, an ex-convict who now worked to stem drug abuse; and Bud Hancock, a school teacher from the Virginia suburbs involved with the organizers of the Presidential Prayer Breakfasts. After six weeks of prayer sessions, Don shared a vision with the group. He and his family had just returned from a vacation at the beach town of Lewes, Delaware, adjoining a state park called Cape Henlopen. The park's shoreline overlooked the Atlantic Ocean at the mouth of the Delaware Bay. As Don had walked the pristine beach in solitude, he mulled over the strife and despair of the inner city. A thought came to him: this would be a perfect place to "lift" inner-city children from their tense environment in the summer for a week of fun and esteem-building activities.

The members of Don's prayer group caught his vision, and they began shaping what came to be called the Washington Lift. The project needed money, officers, a board of directors, articles of incorporation and bylaws. It needed paid staff. Fortunately, Don, brimming with excitement, was well-versed in navigating all these start-up issues. Finally, seven years after leaving FCA, he had found another mission worthy of all the eagerness he could give it. To Don, this mission was not simply helping D.C. youth; it was about saving America's inner cities and ending racism.

Don continued sod farming and his work with John Williams on the LOT program as the Washington Lift took shape. Williams had tapped one of his high school graduates, Henry Sampler, to be co-director of LOT. Sampler, a street-wise kid and star basketball player with an Afro haircut and mustache, showed real leadership potential, despite growing up poor in a rough section of the city. On his visits to Dayspring, Sampler noted Don's impressive array of contacts. For instance, Don and Gloria had become panelists on a weekly religion talk show produced by a local TV station and hosted by the Rev. Ed Bauman, a prominent Methodist pastor and friend to

Gordon Cosby and the Church of the Saviour. Don arranged for Sampler to appear on the show. In another arena, Otto Graham dropped by Dayspring one day to chat and throw a football with a few LOT boys. And when the group decided they wanted to open a coffee house, Don drove them to Newtown, Pennsylvania, to visit with Lyman Coleman, author of a book on coffee houses and founder of Serendipity, an organization that pioneered the national small-group movement in churches. Sampler later became a NASA physicist.

Henry's younger brother Howard, tall, wiry and a star pitcher for his high school baseball team, also participated in LOT. Howard loved to escape from the inner city to the farm, where Don allowed him to ride horses, swim in the lake and earn money helping with the sod operation. "It was almost like Disneyland," Howard said. However, one run-in with Don almost brought this to a crashing halt. At a breakfast for the LOT group at the farmhouse, Howard started giggling as Don prayed. Don exploded and told Henry that Howard should be expelled from the program. Henry interceded for his brother, and Don accepted Howard's apology. Don became a father figure to Howard. When Howard and other youth came around, Don stopped his work and invited them into his house for a soda and a chat. He frequently spoke to Howard about commit-ment–to finish what he started and to never give up–and that lesson became a touchstone in Howard's life. Howard, who became a building contractor, considered his LOT years the happiest period of his life, and he continued to visit Don for decades afterward.

By the spring of 1970, Don had completed the incorporation of the Washington Lift and recruited a diverse board of directors. In addition to Don, there were Harrison, Keels and Porter, a youth spe-cialist with the D.C. government, a community counselor from a Methodist church, a personnel specialist with the Atlantic Richfield Oil Co., a community college teacher and the special assistant to the deputy commissioner of the U.S. Food and Drug Administration. With Don as president, the group refined its mission. Lift would offer "leadership laboratories" for young inner-city adults and older teens identified by various agencies as having leadership potential. This "two percent" of the city's youth population would in turn affect the other 98 percent, the board believed. Training labs would take place at Dayspring, Cape Henlopen and other retreat locations. At a later stage, Lift would open the labs to D.C. youth in general.

Lift held its first series of leadership trainings on Saturdays in the late spring of 1970, led by Hancock and Don Morse, the Atlantic Richfield personnel specialist. Twenty-five youth and adults of various socio-economic and ethnic backgrounds participated, most of them associated with a D.C. Department of Recreation program called Roving Leaders. In the sessions, the participants shared their hopes and dreams, a heady exercise. They brought a banner to the last training session that read, "To those who have liberated us: Wow! Saturdays have been more to look forward to than anything else in the world. ... You have made us confident of ourselves with people. ... To grow, to love, to share the thoughts of life, this is the essence of togetherness. And it's here. Thank you, but thank you is not enough."

The Washington Lift was off to a good start, but the money needed to keep it in flight lagged behind. The program needed funds to hire staff, bring in consultants, rent facilities and transport youth. A fund-raising breakfast in January 1970 featuring Otto Graham and Sally McConnell, wife of a former Air Force chief of staff, failed to bring in substantial amounts. Plans for summer training sessions had to be shelved. Using his experience with FCA, Don threw out his lines for bigger fish. In the fall of 1970, he flew to Chicago to talk with H. Rhea Gray, a Baptist minister who directed the W. Clement and Jessie V. Stone Foundation. W. Clement Stone, a Christian who had made a fortune in the insurance business, was interested in religious causes. Also, Don had heard that the Stone Foundation supported attempts to train inner-city leaders in Chicago. Gray, surprised that the Lift process showed success with young men from inner-city Washington, told Don that the foundation's efforts in inner-city Chicago had not reaped such results. In October 1970, the foundation pledged $15,000 to the Washington Lift, its first major gift. With that amount assured, the board hired Bud Hancock as the organization's first paid director.

Don was good at fund-raising, and he enjoyed it. The key, he had learned, was to forge relationships, as people give money to people more than they give to causes and organizations. He easily developed rapport with people, and he was comfortable asking for money. If he did not get it one place, he asked for it in another. A trip to the Kresge Foundation in Troy, Michigan, struck out. Then Don rejoiced over a $10,500 boost from James Rouse, a Maryland developer and national pioneer in the creation of shopping malls. Rouse, who regularly attended services at the Church of the Saviour, was now building a planned city called Columbia just north of Washington, D.C.[8] Rouse agreed to work his acquaintances, writing a solicitation to, among others, Wallace Johnson, founder of the Holiday Inn chain. The Washington Lift "holds tremendous possibilities for positive change in our big cities across the country, starting with the Nation's Capital," Rouse wrote. The letter failed to produce fruit.

Through FCA friends, Don secured an invitation to meet Billy Graham at the evangelist's home in Montreat, North Carolina. Don's 500-mile drive from Washington ended with a steep ascent up a winding mountain road. At the peak, Don came to a chain-link security fence that surrounded the Grahams' large, log-cabin-style home, which offered a majestic view of the surrounding mountains. Dressed casually in a sweater, Graham was gracious in his welcome. Don noted his familiar Southern twang, his trademark large nose and his dark wavy hair combed straight back. In front of a fireplace in the spacious kitchen with a German shepherd at Graham's feet, Don told about Gloria's 1956 conversion at the crusade Graham had led in Oklahoma City and about the events that brought the Fellowship of Christian Athletes into being. Then he described the Washington Lift. Graham afterward sent Don a telegram with a one-paragraph endorsement for Don to use in his solicitations: "I am most enthusiastic about and greatly encouraged by your work with the Washington Lift in our nation's capital. ... My judgment and that of my associates is that this effort has all the vital ingredients to make a large impact across our land."

During the next couple of years, Don landed major grants from foundation relationships he had cultivated during his FCA years: the Irwin-Sweeney-Miller Fund of Columbus, Indiana, which gave $25,000; and the Pew Charitable Trusts of Philadelphia, which donated $15,000. Don's old FCA friend Len LeSourd also helped him line up gifts of $5,000 and $15,000 from a *Guideposts* charitable fund. But Don came upon his largest contributor, a local foundation, almost by accident. A Presbyterian church in Washington invited Don to speak to a Sunday school class about his ministry. Don grudgingly accepted the invitation, not wanting to miss the Church of the Saviour's service that morning. After his talk, Gloria stood in the back of the room when a well-dressed woman in her sixties approached and said, "Does your husband's program ever need money?" Gloria quickly answered yes. The woman, Adelaide Furman, gave Gloria a card and said, "Give him my husband's phone number and have him call."

Furman turned out to be a trustee of the John Edward Fowler Foundation, a local nonprofit founded by the widow of the foundation's namesake. Fowler, involved in banking and real estate in the Virginia suburbs of Washington, secured his fortune with a factory that made, of all things, snow-cone syrups. The factory sat on what became highly valuable land next to a bridge leading over the Potomac River into Washington. The factory eventually was destroyed to make way for a major hotel, from which the Fowlers reaped a large ground rent. Adelaide's husband, Bill Furman, had an office on K Street in Washington, an address known for high-powered law and lobbying firms. Don found Furman abrupt but helpful. When Don asked what format to use for making a proposal, Furman replied, "We don't need a proposal. Just write it on the back of that envelope and give it to me!" In less than a week, Don had a commitment for more than $100,000, which was paid out over a period of four years.

After bringing in only $7,000 in 1970, Don's fund-raising tally rose to $46,000 in 1971. That amount then vaulted to $163,000 in 1972, including $58,000 from the District of Columbia Recreation Department for a contracted series of youth leadership labs.

Over time, Don became indebted to the Stone Foundation for more than money. The foundation underwrote a leadership training program for people of various professions that was offered periodically at a Chicago conference center. The program focused unremittingly on the positive, helping participants identify and build upon their strengths and aspirations rather than identify and try to solve their "problems." The foundation decided to send half a dozen facilitators of the program to Dayspring in the summer of 1970 to see how it worked with inner-city Washington, D.C., youth leaders.

It worked. One of the Stone Foundation facilitators, Dr. Charles Mader, noted how energized the 30 participants were at lunch in the farmhouse dining room as they excitedly exchanged their reactions to the morning's session. However, one participant sitting next to him remained quiet and serious. Mader asked the young man how he liked the training. To Mader's surprise, a tear fell from the man's eye as he confided, "All my life people have told me I was quiet and that was a problem. But now people have told me it is a strength." Mader realized that the program held the potential to change inner-city residents' negative self-perceptions and, indeed, transform their lives.

Mader, a tall, handsome and outgoing education professor from the University of Illinois at Chicago, was an ordained pastor in his small denomination, now called the Community of Christ. After the training team returned to Chicago, he and Don arranged several back-and-forth visits to discuss how Mader could work with Don as an independent contractor. In December, Mader returned to Dayspring to lead a training session for 19 youth leaders and, again, the weekend was a great success. "We're only beginning, but 'I have a dream,'" Mader wrote Don the following month. "My fantasies include training people of the caliber that were at Dayspring to carry these ideas into the black community. Dreams do come true, I understand."

In the spring of 1971, Mader commuted to Dayspring twice a month to lead weekend Lift training labs. "The strengths and resources which can rebuild Washington are already in this city's residents," said a Lift training lab manual that Mader prepared with colleagues. "The next step is to find a disciplined and orderly way of helping youth leaders and youth to discover and express the great power that lies within them."9

In values clarification sessions, Don watched as participants learned how to recognize their own values, recognize the values of others and affirm others' value systems even if different from their own. In three of the exercises, they described the happiest news they could imagine hearing, described a recent turning point in their lives and ranked their top five values out of a "value pack" of 29 qualities. Participants also were introduced to principles such as "all individuals have solid strengths which are often unidentified and unused" and "a group is necessary to encourage and to reinforce exploration and constructive change." These assumptions, not by design but perhaps not by mere coincidence either, mirrored the Church of the Saviour's emphasis on all members realizing their unique gifts and call from God and applying them to service in the community.

In other sessions, participants were asked to draw an individual "coat of arms" with pictures that represented "two things I like to do or do well," "one achievement," "one thing I would die (or live) for," "one thing I hate or am against" and "my goal." Another exercise was to identify four to ten experiences from their past that made them feel good. And in what Don considered the most powerfully affirming exercise of all four weekends, participants completed a "strength bombardment." They each wrote the strengths they experienced in the others on yellow stickies and pasted them on the people to whom the strengths belonged. The participants were made aware of the positive qualities others saw in them, while experiencing empowerment from affirming others.

In conflict management sessions, participants learned to seek win-win solutions rather than striking back or withdrawing. Instead of considering conflict a "problem to be solved," they were encouraged to consider it a chance to develop greater self-awareness, new strengths and new relationships. As an example, in a conflict between a parent and teenager over driving restrictions, both were to consider the others' actions as an expression of a positive value rather than a negative motivation. Instead of considering the parent stifling, the teenager could recognize the parent as loving and concerned. Instead of considering the teenager irresponsible and foolhardy, the parent could recognize the teenager's need to develop independence and self-reliance. To creatively manage the conflict, the two could affirm each other's values. That might mean the teenager would call home several times on evenings out with the car, while the parent would increase opportunities for the teenager to use the car. Mader was struck by how, despite the rough environment of the inner city, the participants were dealing with the same kind of family and neighborhood issues that many middle-class young people faced.

An article in *Faith at Work* magazine described the effect of these techniques on John Wambley, one of the young men attending a

Mader workshop at Dayspring. "He told us his story," the article said. "'You've all heard of the Wambley brothers. We were headed for jail. ... Finally someone has challenged me to be everything I'm capable of being. At 30 years of age I'm just beginning. Why didn't it happen earlier?'"[10] By July 1972, 600 youth workers had participated in at least one of the Mader's Lift training weekends.[11] The program drew national attention, with inquiries coming from such cities as St. Louis, Kansas City, Indianapolis and Lynchburg, Va.

Don also folded his Dayspring summer camp program into the Lift and expanded it to youth from throughout the city. In the summer of 1971, 20 children came for six consecutive weeks and another 400 came for one-day sessions. Don recruited a D.C. school teacher to supervise the camp. The following summer, he set up weeklong sessions at Dayspring and also affiliated day camps at a Baptist church in Washington and a church-related camp in the Maryland suburbs. Attendance at the three locations totaled 720 campers. Then, in September, the Lift took two groups of 50 youth each to Cape Henlopen State Park in Delaware for a weekend of beach fun and lab training sessions. Don button-holed local government officials for help with the activities. "We had the high adventure of the local U.S. Coast Guard station's furnishing a helicopter and Coast Guard cutter to actually demonstrate emergency land-sea operation exercises for us," he noted in a Lift newsletter. "Then, much to our further joy, the local Army Reserve unit took us to sea and made practice landings on the beach in two of their huge 500-ton, $385,000 amphibious landing craft that had recently returned from Vietnam."

In the summer of 1973, the camping program evolved yet again. This time, in a series of three camp sessions, 140 youth spent five days at Dayspring and five days at Cape Henlopen. One of the campers wrote afterwards, "This was the first time in my life that I had been to camp. ... I'm the kind of person that you used to have to just about threaten me to talk or express myself. Now you have to threaten me to be quiet. ... My mother is very happy that I'm not a quiet, babified, little mouse anymore. She's glad that your camp has changed me to a big mouth kid."

Robert Massie, an inner-city high school student who was a counselor, wrote about the camp's impact on him. The staff was given an aptitude test before camp began, and Robert registered high on imagination and persuasion. "I really didn't believe it," he said. Then he had to break up a fight between two campers, a boy named David and a girl named Wanda. David "was real heated and talked about how he was going to punch her lights out. Instead of grabbing him and shaking him like a milkshake, I tried a new approach. ... 'David, it's no use in fighting a girl; you just can't win. If you beat her, so what, you beat a girl. But if she beats you, everybody knows you're a sissy. So it's just no use.' ... (David) said, 'She hit me first.' I said, 'I don't care. The reason she hit you is because she likes you.' ... That little incident showed I did have a talent and I need to use it more often."

One of the people most affected by Lift training was, surprisingly, Gloria McClanen. In 1972, she participated in one of Mader's weekend labs at Dayspring. During a goal-setting exercise, she pondered the question, "What would you do if you could do anything in the world?" Her mind gravitated to the field of nursing. Gloria had wanted to pursue that profession when she completed high school at the age of 16, but was told nursing students had to be 18. She took a job with a telephone company instead. Then came marriage and children, and she forgot about nursing. Until now. At the lab, Gloria asked Frank Cresswell, a physician friend who also participated in the session, "Do you think I'm too old, at 47, to enter nursing?"

"No," he answered. "Lots of older women have gone back to school to start careers."

When Gloria mentioned it to Don, he was excited. Don knew that Gloria's going back to school would require adjustments in their family, especially with 11-year-old Laurie in middle school. (Michael was 24 and married, with a home of his own). But Don was ready to make necessary adjustments. Four years later, a degree in hand, Gloria started work at Suburban Hospital in Bethesda, Maryland, as a post-operative nurse.

Being with the Poor

Materially comfortable Christians generally understand that Jesus calls them to aid the poor. But Dietrich Bonhoeffer, the great 20th century German theologian and opponent of Hitler, once wrote that this relationship cuts both ways. Affluent Christians also need to be evangelized by the poor, he wrote. Knowing the experience of the poor is "of incomparable value. We have for once learnt to see the great events of history from below, from the perspective of the outcasts, the suspects, the maltreated, the powerless, the oppressed, the reviled–in short, from the perspective of those who suffer. The important thing is that we should have come to look with new eyes on matters great and small."[12]

From the early 1960s on, Don fostered relationships with poor people in Washington, D.C., and around the world. The poor became central to his ministries, not just as recipients, but as teachers. Over the years, contact with the poor gave Don:

• A deeper sense of Christ's teachings. In his Sermon on the Mount, Jesus announced that the blessed are the "poor in spirit," "those who mourn," "the meek" and "those who are persecuted" (Matthew 5:3-10 NIV). Being with the poor and powerless puts those who are better off financially in greater touch with the depths of spiritual poverty to which Jesus refers.

• A greater sense of thankfulness. People who compare themselves to those who have more–better grades, more impressive jobs, more money, bigger houses and fancier cars–may feel dissatisfaction and envy. But when they compare themselves to those who have less–which is most of the 6.6 billion people in the world–they gain a deep gratitude for the simple things too often taken for granted. For most in the world, three meals a day, two pairs of shoes and a home with more than one room would be the epitome of luxury.

• A deeper sense of joy. Those who are well off and in control expect things to go their way. Poor people, on the other hand, have learned not to expect the world to accommodate their needs and desires. When something goes right, they are frequently thrilled. This joy is infectious.

• A greater sense of generosity. A widespread American stereotype that poor people are lazy, drug-addicted and violent results in their being walled off in their own neighborhoods and schools. But those who get to know poor people generally find that they are hard-working, hospitable and generous, just as Bishop Reed was with Don. Seeing poor people be generous with what little they have inspires others to be more open-handed.

Gordon Cosby, pastor of the Church of the Saviour, wants followers of Jesus always to have at least one friend who is financially poor. This is not only to learn the lessons and receive the gifts listed above, he says. It is also God's intent for the human family. Cosby and his associate, Kayla McClurg, wrote, "There is a oneness in the human family that we deny at our peril. Being with the suffering poor is not optional. Jesus himself said that whatever we do or fail to do for the hungry or sick or imprisoned or destitute, we do or fail to do for him. Why would Christ use such a measurement? Perhaps because being with those who completely and utterly have no physical means of support causes us to ask life-altering questions: Am I taking God seriously? What difference does God make for a world with such need? What does God wish I would be about in my one brief life? If I really believe that 'God so loved the world' that Jesus was willing to die for it, am I willing to risk my pride, my self-esteem, my security, my comfort in order to immerse myself completely in loving service to this world? Do I care enough about the things that matter most to God?"[13]

6

Spreading the Word

"The water I give him will become in him a
spring of water welling up to eternal life."
–John 4:14 (NIV)

By late 1972, the Dayspring farmhouse on Lift weekends resembled an anthill, with participants sleeping in almost every room and squeezing past each other in the common areas. At a meeting of a Dayspring facilities committee, Don shared his vision for an expanded ministry. He told the group he wanted to move beyond raising $10,000 here and $5,000 there and, instead, raise $1 million to build a real training center and to expand the Washington Lift nationwide. Eyebrows shot up. *Where are we going to get that kind of money?* everyone thought. After getting used to the idea, they agreed their best bet was the Lilly Endowment, the philanthropy in Indianapolis with a particular interest in religion that had supported FCA and the Washington Lift in the past. Don penciled in a plan for almost half his $1 million: to solicit Lilly for $150,000 a year for three years.

At the same time, another vision was unfolding. A decade before, Don tried to interest several Church of the Saviour members in his Wellspring idea. No one had responded to the concept of introducing people to church renewal movements that sprang up after World War II. Now, out of the blue, two members approached him. "What was that idea you were talking about 10 years ago?" asked David Dorsey, a consultant with a Harvard MBA degree whom Don had hired to be a part-time administrator of the Washington Lift. Pat Davis, a nurse who served in a Potter's House mission group with Don, asked the same thing. In the parlance used by Church of the Saviour concerning an individual's sense of call, both Dorsey and Davis said they would "give their lives" to such a

ministry. With that encouragement, Don envisioned Wellspring conferences as well as Lift labs at the new training facility.

But there was a problem. Lilly had just given a $7,000 grant to
the Washington Lift. Don felt awkward about approaching the foundation so soon for a new and much larger gift. Nevertheless, he
called Lilly's vice president for religion, Charles Williams, and said,
"Charles, can we come see you about a new leading of God we
have?" Williams said Lilly was in "a holding pattern" on grants and
a visit would not be advisable. Don persisted. He told Williams he
was planning a trip to Chicago and asked if he could drop by
Indianapolis on his way back. "No," responded Williams, "but I'll be
in Chicago on that date and I'll see you there."

In January 1973, Don, with Mader and Dorsey, met Williams for
dinner in a Chicago hotel. Williams, a quiet, serious man with long
sideburns, dressed in a stylish business suit, listened intently as the
three described their backgrounds. Time passed quickly, and suddenly Don realized they had only 15 minutes left to present their
new grant proposal. He briefly laid out their vision to expand the
Washington Lift nationally, build a facility for it and include the
Wellspring concept. Mader detected that Williams was listening
with interest. Don then announced the dollar amount they were
seeking.

"What's your reaction to that?" Don asked.

"Very positive," Williams responded.

"Positive enough for us to write a proposal?" Don asked.

"You don't have time to write a proposal," Williams said. "I'm
going to take it to my staff on Tuesday."

"When you say positive, does that mean we'll get it?" Don asked
boldly. He explained that Mader was under pressure from his dean
to spend less time consulting. If the grant came through, Mader
would leave his university job and go full-time with the Lift.

"I can't pre-commit my staff, but I think you will get it," Williams
answered.

Don, Mader and Dorsey floated down the hall outside the
restaurant, giddy with excitement. No one had ever offered them
almost a half million dollars. (Later they learned that their timing
was providential; the Internal Revenue Service wanted Lilly and
other major foundations to give away more of their assets.) Don

called Gordon Cosby to tell him the good news. Cosby shot back, "Keep that quiet!" The pastor feared that having a pile of money for a new ministry before inviting others to join might distort the church's call process.

The concepts of personal call and corporate mission were central to the Church of the Saviour. "We mean business!" said a church brochure written in the mid-1960s. "Crew members urgently desired. No passengers." All members were to ardently seek out the work that God desired for them to fulfill. At the same time, the church insisted that members realize their personal call in the company of a small group of fellow "crew members." These members pursued their "inner journey" through shared disciplines of prayer, study, silence and worship, but also pursued their "outer journey" through work together on a specific mission to the larger world. These mission groups consisted of fewer than a dozen people, for the church had learned that groups larger than that tended to leave some of their members thinking their contributions were not crucial.

"In a small group of persons wholly committed to Christ it may be possible, through the Holy Spirit, to recapture the vision and power of the little band that centered around Jesus," the brochure said. "That group was a fellowship, save for its Leader, of ordinary, weak, fallible men. One was a traitor, one a coward; others were crudely ambitious. When the crisis came, they all fled. Yet, obscure as this group was, within 20 years of the death of Jesus it was being said in far-away Macedonia that these people were turning the world upside down."

At that point in the Church of the Saviour's life, a number of the mission groups focused on the Potter's House. Each group operated the coffee house one night a week. Other groups facilitated the church's retreat ministry, or offered art classes, or provided individual and group pastoral counseling. In the middle to late 1960s, spurred by national civil rights demonstrations and the 1968 riots, powerful ministries that addressed problems of racism and poverty emerged. A mission group called For the Love of Children (FLOC) removed abandoned, abused and neglected children from a dreary city facility and placed them with adoptive or foster parents. A Jubilee Housing mission group turned dilapidated apartment buildings into affordable housing for the poor. Later mission groups provided a shelter for the homeless, a haven for AIDS patients, a neighborhood health clinic and job counseling and placement services for the chronically unemployed. A mission group also supported the Washington Lift. Truly, these small groups of highly committed people demonstrated the explosive potential the church brochure described.

In February 1973, Cosby set aside the sermon time on a Sunday morning for Don, Dorsey and Davis to "sound the call" for Wellspring. The three described their common vision. "Wellspring would be a center for ministers, students, lay leaders and others across the country who wish to learn about the Church of the Saviour and live into various aspects of its ministry," Don explained. At the end of the service, the three invited all who sensed a call to this new ministry to meet in a room upstairs. Ten people came, and they were quickly put to the test. Don suggested the group meet at 5 a.m. each Tuesday. This early hour acknowledged everyone's busy calendars, but mostly Don was discouraging half-hearted participation.

Mur Carrington's spirit leaped at the description of Wellspring, and she flew upstairs to the meeting after the service. She was not deterred by the meeting time. She had come to the Church of the Saviour in 1970 during a period of family difficulty, searching for a congregation that knew what it stood for, and had almost completed the courses at the School of Christian Living required for membership. As she excitedly told how she could contribute, Don assessed her attitude as a non-member to be presumptuous, and he rebuked her. "You have an authority problem," he said sternly, pointing his finger at her. Don assumed Carrington to be one of those well-meaning people he frequently had experienced whose enthusiasm for a cause quickly rose and quickly dwindled. Carrington, crushed by Don's chastising, cried her entire drive home. But her sense of call to the ministry only grew. She screwed up her courage and came to the first 5 a.m. meeting. She became a core member of the group and eventually served as "spiritual director" to Don and the others, proving that Don's first impression was mistaken. She and Don became close, lifetime friends.

Myra Thompson, a former elementary school teacher and Don's Dayspring farm secretary, came to the meeting. She had met Don in

Don showing his animation during a meeting in 1983.

Don as a submariner in 1944.

Don in 1950 when he graduated from Oklahoma A&M College (now Oklahoma State University).

The USS Chub, the submarine on which Don served during World War II.

The McClanens, including daughter Judy and son Michael, in their Kansas City home about 1957.

Don expresses displeasure while coaching the Eastern Oklahoma A&M basketball team in a junior-college regional playoff game.

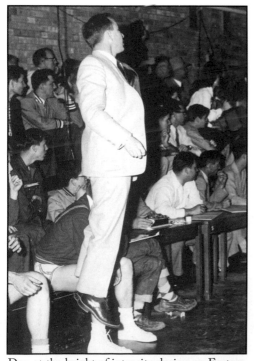

Don at the height of intensity during an Eastern Oklahoma game.

Don speaks at the dedication of the Fellowship of Christian Athletes' headquarters in Kansas City in 1978.

Don in 1955 with three other founding fathers of the Fellowship of Christian Athletes: from left, the Rev. Louis H. Evans Sr., the Rev. Roe Johnston, Don and Branch Rickey.

Don gets acquainted with three residents of Seaton Place in Washington, D.C.

Don harvests turf at Dayspring Farm. © 1996, The Washington Post by Vic Casamento. Reprinted with permission.

Charles Morgan, second from left, and other inner-city youth participate in a Washington Lift exercise in which they place stickies on each other citing strengths they perceive in that person.

Don and "William" pray with Washington Lift youth on an island during an excursion on William's yacht.

Washington Lift youth get under way on "William's" yacht.

Tom White, left, and Millard Fuller, founder of Habitat for Humanity and the Fuller Center for Housing, meet in 2004 after Don has introduced them.

Don and Gloria with Oklahoma State basketball coach Henry Iba, left, and university President Lawrence Boger in 1978, when the campus plaque behind them was dedicated noting the founding of the Fellowship of Christian Athletes.

Don with Tom White, 2nd from right, at a 2004 Harvest Time gathering in Boston. Others include Dr. Paul Farmer, second from left, and Rosemary Feerick, center, a Harvest Time tri-director.

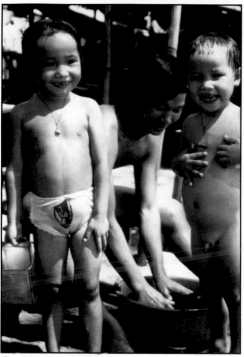

Don's special friends, Ky and No, at the refugee camp for Vietnamese boat people at Songkhla, Thailand.

Don shows Cité Soleil, the Haitian slum, to Nebraska football coach Tom Osborne in 1995.

Language barriers don't stop a Bosnian woman from communicating her gratitude to Don for his group's visit to her village.

Don holds a baby given him by a poor mother in Haiti who asks him to keep the child and provide it a better life.

Don meets with Mother Teresa in Calcutta.

Salma Dormani, educator and social worker in the Mathare Valley slum of Nairobi, Kenya, leads Don and future Ministry of Money board president Frank Butler on a tour in 1983.

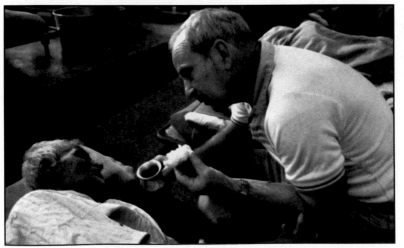

Don feeds a man at Kalighat, the Home of the Destitute and Dying, in Calcutta. Photo by Larry Braak.

Don waves goodbye after playing marbles with children in the City of Joy, a neighborhood in Calcutta.

Don helps deliver supplies to a Kurdish refugee camp in northern Iraq in 1991.

Don talks with members of the Boston Youth Association, a group in the slum of Cité Soleil, Haiti.

Don and his daughter, Laurie, take a beach break during a pilgrimage to Haiti in the mid-1990s.

Don and Michael McClanen visit a monastery in Rama, Bosnia, during a pilgrimage.

Don and Ministry of Money colleague Bryan Sirchio with three Haitian friends who have helped them with security on pilgrimages to Port-au-Prince.

Don with Norman Eddy, second from right, and other participants in a "Cry of the Wealthy" retreat in New York in 1978.

Don with Gordon Cosby, pastor of the Church of the Saviour in Washington, D.C.

Don with former Dallas Cowboys coach Tom Landry and Fellowship of Christian Athletes President Dal Shealy at an FCA event at Estes Park, Colorado, in 1997.

Don visits John Wooden, an acquaintance from Fellowship of Christian Athletes days.

Don and Gloria are honored during a 2001 basketball game at Oklahoma State, where Don first conceived the FCA.

Don with a local merchant and children during a 2001 visit to Kosovo.

1970 in the Potter's House mission group. Thompson was a timid, wounded young woman whose husband had recently left her when their child was six weeks old. She found Don to be fun-loving, but also intimidating in his passionate intensity. Don, acting as the spiritual director of the Potter's House mission group, received a letter from Thompson saying that, as a single mother with a child, she was unable to devote a full hour per day to Bible study and prayer. Expecting a sympathetic reply, she instead got back Don's admonition, "Myra, take yourself by the scruff of the neck and do it!" Thompson later wrote of the experience, "What a gift not to be let off the hook, to find creative ways to carve out the time for the most important activity of each day."

In 1971 Don asked Thompson to relieve Gloria of her hostessing duties for Dayspring campers and groups using the retreat center. Thompson and her daughter, Lisa, moved into a room at the farmhouse and, by the end of the summer, she also became Don's secretary for his sod operation and the Washington Lift. Don and Gloria took Thompson and her daughter under their wing, and Thompson later wrote, "Don was my boss, but it felt more like I was becoming part of his family." The people and the structures of the Church of the Saviour had been such a life-saver to Thompson that she immediately responded to the Wellspring call–the prospect of helping others experience this special community. On Monday evenings Lisa stayed over at the McClanens' under Gloria's care, and the next morning Thompson and Don left Dayspring at 4:15 a.m. It did not take long to get to downtown Washington with the light traffic of the hour and "the way Don drove," Thompson recalled. The gatherings were "magic," she said. "I couldn't wait for those Tuesday mornings to roll around. ... There was excitement. It was this sense that anything could happen, that God was really calling all this into being."

The group spent 30 minutes each meeting in silent prayer and meditation on Scripture readings. The next one-and-a-half hours they discussed their vision for the ministry, sharing about their backgrounds and what they perceived as each other's gifts for ministry. This "gift-evoking," a key to the Church of the Saviour's mission-group structure, uncovered group members' unique interests and talents, enabling the choice of members for group roles, such as mod-

erator and spiritual director. Don was chosen moderator, or overall
leader.

After several weeks, the group switched to evening meeting
times. In the successive months, they hashed over details about the
facility to be built with the Lilly grant. Consensus was elusive, and
tensions often arose. Build the facility on a field near the farmhouse,
or in Dayspring's woods? What does the conference center include,
and what does it look like? Build separate cabins to house Wellspring
guests? If so, are they traditional log cabins or something different?
Would Lilly expect to control Dayspring after giving so much
money to the group? The difficulty making decisions frustrated Don,
and at some meetings he flared with anger. His face reddened, he
used profanity or was at a loss for words. These displays frightened
Thompson and some other members of the group, and they eventually asked Don to seek counseling for anger management.

In fact, Don had been making regular visits to a psychiatrist or
psychologist for the past decade. Unlike many churches, the Church
of the Saviour encouraged psychiatric counseling not just for the
wounded and broken, but for all its members as part of their inward
journey. As Elizabeth O'Connor explained in her book *Journey
Inward, Journey Outward*, spiritual growth inevitably entailed psychological dislocations. "The old land is familiar. We have built over
the years the house we live in. Even if we do not like it, it seems safer
than the unknown. But God would show us a new land and have us
live in a new house, and He churns up the old land and lets the
winds beat and the floods come. ... All the other crises of life that
make for upheaval in our emotions have the same creative potential
for growth and deeper understanding, but the potential for disaster
also exists. It is possible to drown in the undertow if the proper support is not there, and this is where the community must sometimes
draw upon the resources of psychiatry."

O'Connor said that, at the time she wrote the book in 1968, 150
of the church's 250 members had participated in a church-sponsored
group therapy program, and ten percent of the congregation was
involved in depth analysis with psychiatrists outside the community.
She noted that such numbers surely would shock some of her readers. "One of our members who occasionally speaks at other churches always talks about her experience in the therapy program here. ...

The first time the courage came to her was at a coffee klatch of women in the neighborhood. The talk was the light exchange that always characterized these gatherings. When it turned to psychiatry, a lot of glib banter was introduced and the jesting comment–'maybe I should get on the couch.' Into that conversation was dropped the information that she was in therapy. ... Their assurance that she didn't seem a bit unusual was poor comfort, and she left feeling that she had risked her life in the neighborhood. The next day, however, two of the women came to call and another telephoned. They wanted to talk about themselves and the possibility of therapy being helpful to them."[1]

Initially, Don joined therapy groups led by O'Connor and by church-hired psychiatrist Joe Knowles to deal with his anger issues, conflicts with Gloria and wounds from his FCA departure. He later sought individual counseling from private professionals, such as the Rev. Ed Bauman, a prominent Methodist pastor in Washington, a practice he continued for the rest of his life. Some of the sessions focused on his anger and conflicts, but others dealt with his occasional bouts of depression, which began after his breakup with FCA. His spirit sank over his occasional blow-ups and strained relationships; he also felt deep distress over injustices and deprivations he saw taking place in Washington, D.C., and around the world. Don also sought to understand how his strong emotions and passions contributed to or detracted from his spiritual growth. Essentially, he used his counseling as a journey toward discovering his true self.

The Wellspring mission group balanced their tense times with fun times. The first spring they traveled to Martha's Vineyard, Massachusetts, for a weekend retreat of relaxation and prayer at the vacation home of group members Jesse and Marnie Trotter. (Jesse, dean of Virginia Theological Seminary, an Episcopal divinity school in the Washington suburbs, had become involved in the Church of the Saviour.) The group later spent a weekend together each summer at a rented house in Lewes, Delaware, where they enjoyed leisurely meals of seafood and corn on the cob, walked on the beach and prayed together. Don particularly enjoyed their regular outings to a "bumper boats" amusement park, where he and Don Russell, another group member, tried to push each other under a fountain in the middle of the pool.

Final decisions about the Wellspring facilities eventually were delegated to a church-wide committee, since the changes would have a major impact on Dayspring. Don represented the Wellspring mission group on the committee. The committee devised a plan. The conference center, built on a wooded site, would accommodate up to 100 people and would cost no more than $150,000. Three cottages, each holding 15 to 20 people, would house those who came for Lift labs or Wellspring conferences. The plan also called for a cottage adjoining the farmhouse as residence for a Wellspring hostess, and another near the conference center for a facilities caretaker. Finally, the committee decided to purchase a 20-acre parcel adjoining Dayspring to buffer the farm from a planned highway. The Lilly grant would not cover the whole cost, since only $260,000 was approved for facilities; the other $190,000 paid Charles Mader's salary for three years at the Washington Lift and covered other Lift expenses. So Don began to beat the bushes again for additional grants.

Meanwhile, Don oversaw the conference center's construction, which began in October 1973. Architects had devised a "Trinitarian" design that was both modern and rustic. One large pyramid served as a conference room, with picture windows along all three sides looking out to the surrounding woods, a stone fireplace and a cathedral ceiling sheathed in light pine paneling, topped by a skylight. Two smaller pyramids housed an office, kitchen and bathrooms. The contracted cost was $140,000, but the construction firm—run by two of Don's friends, Ralph Hubert and Ed Becraft—donated back their $20,000 profit to lower the cost to $120,000.

Meanwhile, the mission group prepared for their first public event, a weekend "Wellspring Orientation" October 5-7 at the Dayspring farmhouse, designed as a short but intensive immersion into the life of the Church of the Saviour. The group had decided to focus on this one post-World War II ministry rather than numerous ones. Thompson had sent announcements to an extensive mailing list of people who had previously written the church asking for information, generally spurred by reading one of Elizabeth O'Connor's books. Twelve people from across the country signed up for the orientation, the majority of them pastors or pastors' spouses from various denominations.

The mission group, in lieu of a weekend of lectures, planned activities to give the guests an experiential taste of the Church of the Saviour. Before they came, participants submitted spiritual autobiographies and read O'Connor's *Call to Commitment* and three chapters from her *Journey Inward, Journey Outward.* The plan for the weekend included an introduction to the Wellspring concept by Don on Friday evening, followed by a talk on the discipline of silence by Thompson. The participants then would be invited to "enter the Great Silence" at 10 p.m. as they dispersed to their rooms, breaking that silence at an 8 a.m. worship the next morning. On Saturday the participants would discuss their experiences with silence, describe their lives and motivations for coming, discuss the church's concept of inward journey in small groups and travel to Washington to witness some of the church's outward-journey ministries. On Sunday morning the participants would share their reactions to the weekend and end with worship and lunch.

As the mission group awaited the participants' arrivals, Don was restless with excitement at the fruition of a vision he had harbored for more than a decade. Others in the group tempered their excitement with anxiety. A former pastor had revealed in his spiritual autobiography that he was a schizophrenic. What if he got out of control? And what would the other participants think of the weekend? Would it be a success or a failure? Anxieties dissolved as the weekend got underway and mission group members shared openly and honestly about how the Church of the Saviour had helped them with personal struggles. Participants responded with similar openness. The schizophrenic turned out to be an endearing person, and the entire group quickly developed a sense of mutual caring.

The Rev. Jan Linn, a blonde 28-year-old pastor of a Disciples of Christ church in rural southwest Virginia, arrived for the weekend facing a personal crisis. Two years into his first full-time pastorate, Linn lamented the subtle racism and economic divisions taken for granted by the majority of the town's population, as well as the resistance to change in his congregation and the institutional church as a whole. Questioning whether to remain at the church, or in ministry itself, he came along with a friend to the weekend. The discussions at the orientation baffled Linn, since his seminary had not introduced the concepts of spiritual gifts, call, mission groups and silence. When he awoke Saturday morning he launched into a conversation with his friend, who was sharing an upstairs bedroom in the farmhouse. The friend gently reminded him that they were supposed to be in "the Great Silence." Linn, who had grown up in a conservative church, felt anxious about these unusual people from the Church of the Saviour. Were they taking him in a spiritually dangerous direction? Yet he was intrigued by the spirit of the facilitators who, as regular church members rather than trained clergy, exhibited a centeredness, a passion to follow Jesus and a sense of Christian purpose that Linn desperately wanted in his own life. Don impressed Linn with his sense of aliveness and excitement about the Wellspring ministry, as did the others. Later, when Linn discovered that Don was the principal founder of Wellspring, he was surprised at Don's low profile during the weekend.

As the orientation proceeded, Linn realized that "this was the first breath of fresh air that I had found in the institutional church." By Sunday, he had signed up as a three-year "covenant partner," which meant returning several times a year for other Wellspring events and reporting each week to an appointed spiritual advisor on his vow to spend at least 30 minutes a day in prayer, Bible reading and writing a spiritual journal. The weekend and its follow-up reshaped Linn's ministry. He continued the daily disciplines for the next three and a half decades. Each church he led from that time on followed the Church of the Saviour model. At his church in southwestern Virginia, he replaced the congregation's committee structure with mission groups. One group worked on local poverty issues; another started a coffee house, which became the first local eatery where whites and blacks ate together. A black poet packed the coffee house with racially mixed audiences whenever he did readings.

Along the way, Linn marveled at the unleashed power when his church members recognized and followed their sense of call. This approach to ministry contradicted what he had learned at his pastor-centric seminary. During one of his follow-up Wellspring sessions, he mentioned to Elizabeth O'Connor that he needed to leave early so he could preach at his church on Sunday. She burned him with the gentle question, "Oh, you don't believe anyone else in your church can preach?" The next time Linn came to Wellspring, he asked one of his congregants to assume his place in the pulpit. The

sermon, powerful and well-received, was printed in a denominational magazine. For the Wellspring group, the changes Linn made at his
church confirmed their greatest dream: that some of the structures
of the Church of the Saviour could be adopted effectively by a traditional congregation.

"Everything I have done in ministry since 1973 was to try to live
deeper into the idea of church and ministry that I learned from the
Church of the Saviour," Linn said later. He expounded those lessons
in one of his nine books, *Rocking the Church Membership Boat:
Counting Members or Having Members Who Count.*[2] And in 2004 when
he was ambivalent about whether to accept colleagues' urgings to
stand for election as president of his denomination, he fell back upon
the advice of Judith Roark, his former spiritual advisor from
Wellspring. In a phone conversation, Roark told him, "Jan, we've
talked for 30 minutes and I haven't heard you mention the word
'call' once." Linn knew immediately what to do. "I got saved from
the institutional church by the Church of the Saviour," he now
reflects. "I don't think they can ever know what Wellspring has
meant in the lives of people like me."

Inge Hardwick, a native of Germany who had suffered discrim-
ination during World War II for declining to participate in Nazi
Youth rallies, also was deeply affected by the first Wellspring orientation. She had immigrated with her husband to Ontario, Canada,
and worked as a church secretary. An Elizabeth O'Connor book and
an encounter with Mary Cosby at an Ontario retreat center had
introduced her to the Church of the Saviour. Hardwick paid a $60
fare–her monthly salary–for an apprehensive 20-hour bus ride to
Washington. *How can I aspire to rub shoulders with a spiritually enlight-
ened people like this?* she fretted. But her anxieties dissipated after Don
picked her up at the bus station and she met the rest of the group.
"I had never felt so loved and appreciated in all my life," she recalled
later. "I still marvel at it. We were 12 visitors, all crammed into one
big farmhouse, and the whole mission group as well. The weekend
was an indescribably wonderful experience. I remember Myra giving
a short meditation that first evening on our need for 'lap time with
God.' What an image! ... The next day we were taken to some of
their mission projects in downtown Washington. Everywhere I was
deeply impressed with two things: the aliveness and dedication of

the persons involved in these missions and the meticulous attention to the needs of the people served. ... When I returned [home] there were some people within the church who wanted to hear about the Church of the Saviour, but nobody who wanted to use them as a model. For years, I grieved about that. Only much later did I become aware just how many persons went to visit the Church of the Saviour after hearing about it from me. ... Perhaps my mission was to simply spread the news."

Such word of mouth, and O'Connor's books, kept Don and the other Wellspring members busy. They held three weekend orientations in 1974, drawing people from throughout the country. They also held a weeklong workshop for people like Linn who faithfully continued their transformation, which included a two-day silent retreat and time working in various missions of the Church of the Saviour. A November 1974 newsletter noted that other orientation participants had organized a food crisis group in one congregation, created a retreat ministry in another and started a healing mission group at a third.

As the Wellspring conference building was completed in August 1974, Don continued raising money for the three planned cabins and caretaker's house. He received a part-time salary for his Wellspring work, and another part-time salary as president of the Washington Lift. Don also continued with the sod operation, though he gradually turned it over to his son Michael, who had returned to the Germantown area after serving in the Army. It was a busy time in the McClanen household. Gloria had started nursing school. In addition to his three part-time jobs, Don spent time fund-raising for a Poverty Coalition he had helped form that consisted of several ministries at the Church of the Saviour and ministries in Lynchburg, Virginia, that involved Gordon Cosby's brother. Also, Don's aging parents came from Morrisville, Pennsylvania, to live in the downstairs of the McClanens' home. To some, this array of concerns and activities would have been crushing. Don did often feel as if his life careened between non-stop activity and exhaustion. But with his prodigious energy and adventurous spirit, he mostly found life exciting and full.

Don's biggest challenge at the time was from within his own family. As a young girl, his daughter Laurie had loved to ride the

Dayspring tractor on her father's lap and watch TV sports with him, both at times yelling at the set in their excitement. She also loved going to FCA events with her father and meeting sports celebrities such as Tim Foley, a defensive back with the Miami Dolphins. But in 1973, at the age of 12, Laurie was molested by an adult who lived near Dayspring. This triggered depression and a rebellion against her parents' values. She lost interest in school and family activities, and no longer wanted to be involved in the Church of the Saviour. Laurie began hanging out with a wilder group, which cast Don and Gloria into a pit of worry and despair. They sent their daughter to counselors, but she declined to cooperate. When Don and Gloria tried to send Laurie to a private school in Maine that specialized in working with troubled teens, the school denied admission after Laurie declared she would not abide by its rules. Feeling helpless, Don detached from her problems to protect himself from being dragged down by them, unwittingly leaving Gloria to bear the emotional brunt. Don's heavy load of ministry responsibilities, rather than being a burdensome distraction, became an escape from parental woes.

Later in his life, Don looked back at his absentee parenting—prompted first by coaching and FCA travels when his son Michael was young and later by his own emotional detachment from his daughter—as the worst failure of his life. Michael holds warm memories of Don coaching his Cub Scout baseball team in Kansas City. But he acknowledged that his childhood recollections of his father consist mostly of absence and occasional stern discipline. At the age of 15 Michael and his father got in a physical skirmish when Don, reacting to Michael's teasing of Laurie, came at his son in anger. Worried about repercussions, Michael ran away from home. He hitchhiked 50 miles and reached Pennsylvania before deciding to return home. In the later 1970s, when Michael was 30 and had returned to college to complete his undergraduate degree at the University of Nebraska, Don visited while on a Wellspring trip. After an afternoon of talking about family issues, Michael followed a therapist's suggestion and asked his father to embrace him. Don did so, and it was a powerful healing moment for Michael. Afterward, hugging became an integral part of their relationship.

In 1975, the Wellspring calendar filled with more than one event a month. In addition to orientations and workshops at the new Wellspring Center, the mission group took their show on the road–to Linn's church in Tazewell, Virginia, and to churches in Amherst, Massachusetts; South Glenn Falls, New York; Cincinnati, Ohio; and Toronto and Calgary, Canada. They also held special orientation weekends at the Wellspring Center for two churches, one from Pennsylvania and the other from New York, and for an inmate ministry from the Cook County Jail in Chicago.

Don learned of the New York church, Trinity Episcopal on Wall Street, from Charles Williams, the Lilly Endowment executive. Williams flew to Washington in September 1974 for the dedication of the Wellspring Center. As Don drove Williams to the airport afterward, he asked, "Charles, Lilly gives more to religion than all the other foundations put together. Who would be second?" Trinity, Williams responded.

Queen Anne of England had given Trinity a land grant of 215 acres in 1705, seven years after it was founded. Over the next 300 years the church gave away much of that property, including Columbia University's current campus, but kept 15 acres, making it one of the largest landholders in Manhattan. Most of that land sits under 18 prime office buildings, which generate millions in income each year for the parish. The parish dispenses more than $2 million a year in grants for projects around the world.[3]

Don called Trinity's grants director, the Rev. Jack Woodard, saying that Williams had just been to the Wellspring dedication and talked about the commonalities between Trinity and the Church of the Saviour. "Can I come see you?" Don asked. Within a couple of months, he sat in Woodard's office in the 25-story tower that housed the church's staff, describing Wellspring and other Church of the Saviour ministries. Woodard, a forceful, heavyset man in a clerical collar, grew excited at what he heard and called the penthouse office of the church's rector, the Rev. Bob Parks. "I've got someone here from the Church of the Saviour in Washington whom I think you'd like to meet," Woodard told his boss. Don repeated his pitch to Parks, a gregarious man who knew about Don's church, and Parks and Woodard asked Don about a Wellspring event for ten priests from Trinity and other New York parishes associated with it.

Following the event, Trinity sent a $25,000 donation, which paid most of the cost of one cabin.

Adelaide Furman, whose husband, Bill, had helped Don secure the $100,000 Washington Lift grant from the Fowler Foundation, was another contributor. When Bill died in 1974, Adelaide asked Don to help write a funeral service. After the funeral she mailed him a $14,000 donation. Don suggested she might want to let time pass before making any sizable gifts and offered to mail back the check. Adelaide accepted Don's offer but, within two weeks, remailed the check. By 1977, the cabins, each with five to seven bedrooms, and a caretaker's house were completed and paid for.

Don pared down his non-Wellspring activity by removing himself totally from Dayspring farming. Also, the Washington Lift with its own staff and board became increasingly inactive. The Lift's three-year Lilly grant ran out and Charles Mader took a hospital administrator's job in Kansas City. In the meantime, Wellspring's offerings grew. In addition to monthly orientations and annual eight-day workshops, the mission group fulfilled increasing requests from churches, seminaries, colleges and denominational mission boards for special events across the country. The mission group sent out members two by two, much as Jesus had done with his disciples, to lead these out-of-town events. In 1975 Gloria McClanen joined her husband in the mission group, and they jointly led some of the events.

Testimonials flowed in about how Wellspring had changed lives and churches. During an orientation in April 1977, the Rev. Robert Linthicum, a Presbyterian pastor from a large church in the affluent Detroit suburb of Grosse Pointe, Michigan, asked Don about his past association with the Fellowship of Christian Athletes and about his FCA departure. Don opened up about the painfulness of that period and the spiritual wandering that followed, describing his struggles so vividly that Linthicum sensed the freshness of the pain a decade-and-a-half later. This unexpected vulnerability encouraged Linthicum to make an admission of his own—that he often felt spiritually bankrupt. In 1972, while pastoring an inner-city church in Chicago, his spiritual moorings were shaken when his efforts to improve the neighborhood resulted in a death threat from a gang. Now outwardly successful in Grosse Pointe, Linthicum led his church in ministries to the poorest census tract in the nation just across the line in Detroit. But inwardly, Linthicum lacked the spiritual depth to help his affluent parishioners whose lives and families were often falling apart behind the veneer of their wealth. "There was no need for me to play-act anything because Don wasn't play-acting anything," Linthicum recalled. He signed up for Wellspring's three-year program, during which he developed disciplines of daily prayer, silent reflection time and Bible reading that became a spiritual bedrock for his life.

Linthicum's son also was profoundly affected by Don. By the summer of 1980, Bob Jr., a rebellious 16-year-old, hung out with a gang in Detroit and dealt drugs. With hair below his waist, his typical dress was a black leather jacket, bellbottom jeans, boots and a wallet chain. His father had arranged a summer job for him at a Christian camp outside Chicago, but the camp kicked him off the staff. Linthicum, desperate to get his son away from Detroit, called Don for advice. "We have a summer position here at Dayspring," Don said. "Why not have Bob work here?" Bob came and quickly developed a sense of belonging. Unlike at the Chicago camp, Don and others living or working at Dayspring accepted him and his freakish appearance. Bob's sense of self-esteem and competence blossomed with the strenuous work, which included driving a tractor and truck. After Don invited him to a Dayspring worship service, held weekly in the farmhouse, Bob became a regular—partly because of an attraction to the pretty daughter of the worship leader.

Bob fell back into his rebellious ways and gang activity when he returned to Grosse Pointe at the end of the summer, but seeds of change had been planted. They would come to full flower when Bob joined Don and his father on an international trip in 1982.

Like Linthicum, the Rev. Charles Gipson, pastor of a Methodist church in Indiana, experienced a spiritual awakening through a Wellspring encounter. After an orientation in spring 1978, Gipson wrote a distress letter to Don noting that he had let day-to-day pastoral duties crowd out his newfound daily disciplines of prayer and Bible reading. "I do want help, spiritual direction, and continued involvement with Wellspring, and the sooner this begins the better," he said. For the next three years Don, as Gipson's spiritual director, responded every two weeks to Gipson's reports. As the three-year period came to a close, Gipson wrote to Don, "You have encouraged me in the dry spells and loved me in the painful places. ... You have constantly reminded me that I am Somebody, and you have not allowed me to think otherwise. ... In a particularly critical time, you came to see me, slept on the couch in my living room and spent a day sharing with Lois and me. ... You have given me what Elizabeth O'Connor calls 'the greatest gift which we can give one another.' Being authentic with me, you have shared your own journey, incredibly intense, painful, risky, and you have modeled for me the life lived in obedience to vision and call of God."

Later in his pastoral career, Gipson used the Wellspring model to design a "Three-Year Covenant Community for Spiritual Formation" program that shared with more than 1,000 Methodists in Indiana and elsewhere the Church of the Saviour's approach to inward disciplines, outward mission and mutual spiritual support.

In 1975 Don participated in a seven-day silent retreat led by Father Luke Malik, a 59-year-old Dominican priest of Lebanese descent known for building bridges between Christians, Jews and Muslims. His brother was Charles Malik, who had been president of the United Nations General Assembly in 1958.[4] As busy as Don was with his three-ring circus of pursuits, he cleared his schedule for the event, acknowledging a desperate need to recharge his spiritual batteries. He also wanted the extra depth that came from a weeklong, rather than a three-day, descent into silence.

Eighteen people gathered at the Lodge of the Carpenter. Malik, with the dark features of his Middle Eastern heritage and a quiet manner, gave few instructions. He told the participants to sign up for an appointment with him if, during the week, they needed help processing some experience. But he instructed that they first take their questions directly to God. For the rest of the retreat, Malik spoke only once a day, giving a short meditation. Other than occasional gatherings to sing or listen to music, the participants were on their own. Don had read about the third day of a weeklong retreat, a time when participants often felt a panicked impulse to flee the silence. Those riding out that impulse often broke into a deeper plateau of inner awakening. Don experienced otherwise; his initial restlessness, anxiety, doubt, fear and temptation ebbed away and his mind grew steadily clearer and more centered throughout the week. When he sat silently with others in the lodge, he felt deep compassion and camaraderie. At the end of seven days, he felt as if he easily could have stayed in silence for 30 days.

At the final gathering, Don said little. But three months later when Malik returned to Washington to meet again with the participants, Don announced that three subjects had kept returning to his attention during and after the retreat: money, sex and anger. He had found them closely linked in his marriage, where repeated arguments with Gloria over money sparked anger and doomed for that moment any chance of sexual intimacy. Sister Marcella Jordan, a Catholic nun who worked at a Church of the Saviour ministry and participated in the retreat, looked at Don and said, "Do you know what you're doing?"

"No, what do you think I'm doing?"

"You're contemporizing the old monastic vows of poverty, chastity and obedience."

Sister Marcella's insight suggested to Don that he was onto something important. In the arena of money, for instance, he believed that his and Gloria's commitment to tithing early in their marriage became his second most important decision as a Christian, exceeded only by his vow in the Oklahoma City church to surrender his will to Christ. Don researched references to money in the New Testament, and discovered that in the four gospels Jesus spoke of money more often than any subject other than the kingdom of God. Don concluded that if he had not subordinated his material possessions to Jesus, he would not have been able to subordinate other areas of his life. He was grieved that so few were choosing to follow this path, as indicated in national surveys showing that less than five percent of church-goers chose to tithe.[5] As a fund-raiser, he was acutely aware of how the availability or lack of money encouraged or stunted vital ministries to the poor. Fund-raising also had shown him that the wealthy, often trapped by their money rather than freed by it, isolated themselves from others and missed the joy and creativity that accompanies giving.

"My growing awareness and conviction is that to seek funds for the poor, without dealing with the deeper root problem of why more is not readily available, is to continue to nurture the problem— to treat with Band-Aids that which requires major surgery for a healing solution," Don wrote in a paper outlining a "Ministry of Money." He knew he faced fierce headwinds from the culture: the ideas that money remain a personal matter, that it not be discussed outside the family and that being comfortable and secure meant accumulating more. In the paper he noted some dilemmas faced by the church:

"1) While many are saying God is first, money is most often the real security, goal and source of trust.

"2) While agreeing that we should 'feed my sheep,' most Christian people, deep down, do not only not care for the poor, they are often afraid and repulsed by the thought.

"3) Tithing is most frequently thought of as the pinnacle rather than the starting place."

Don recruited the Wellspring mission group to embark on a year-long study of money. The members wrote "money autobiographies" and shared them with each other. They described their thoughts and feelings about material possessions at various stages of their lives and gave a detailed accounting of assets, liabilities and personal giving practices. In most churches, such disclosure would have been unthinkable, but the Church of the Saviour had already conditioned an openness by requiring members to reveal their financial situations. At the end of the study, mission group members called it the most important year they had spent together. They became more free in their openness with each other, more free from anxiety about their financial situations and more free to use their money in creative ways.

Don set out to find expert opinions on Christian approaches to the use of money. He read what books he could find on that subject, which were few. He visited friends in New Jersey, New York, Oklahoma, California and elsewhere to sound them out on the topic and to gather more names of possible advisors. He formed a "steering committee" that included such people as Jack Woodard, the Trinity Episcopal Church grants director, and Robert Greenleaf, a friend of Gordon Cosby and the Church of the Saviour and retired director of management and research for American Telephone & Telegraph (AT&T). A Quaker, Greenleaf had founded an organization that promoted the concept of "servant leadership."[6]

Don organized Wellspring's first Ministry of Money retreat in August 1976. In addition to steering committee members, attending were Gordon Cosby and Elizabeth O'Connor from the Church of the Saviour; Landrum Bolling, president of the Lilly Endowment and former president of Earlham College; James Rouse, nationally prominent urban developer; and Jim Wallis, founder of the Sojourners Christian community in Washington, D.C. The four-day schedule included times to share personal experiences with money; presentations by Don, Woodard, Rouse and others; and a 22-hour period of silence. One participant, Fred Taylor of the Church of the Saviour, noted how engaged the wide range of people became in the topic. *Don has hit a chord*, Taylor thought.

Don followed up with a series of three workshops on the "unholy trinity" of anger, sex and money the following fall and winter. Interest grew—each drew 20 or more participants—and sessions were lively. But Don realized that tackling three loaded topics at once "opened up such gaping holes or wounds in our lives, it was too much to deal with." Considering his experience as a fund-raiser and his relationships with wealthy people, he found the topic of money floating to the top.

Elizabeth O'Connor, who helped lead a money workshop with Don in January 1977, wrote afterward of the complexities of that one issue. "In the course of the weekend participants shared their expectations, hopes and, once in a great while, their fears. We pondered Scriptures on money and used journal exercises to reach back to discover what home and parents had taught us about money. We played games with money to be in touch with more instinctive responses to our handling of it; in pairs we shared our happiest and saddest experience with money, an exercise that I would especially recommend. ... We worked with a financial inventory that would give us an understanding of what our resources were. A few discovered how vague they liked to keep the matter of just how much they had. ... We longed for the freedom of that man in Christ who said: 'I have learned to manage on whatever I have, I know how to be poor and I know how to be rich too. I have been through my initiation and now I am ready for anything anywhere: full stomach or empty stomach, poverty or plenty' (Philippians 4:11-12)."[7]

After two more money workshops in 1977, Don arranged an unusual gathering he called "The Cry of the Wealthy" in August 1978. He convened a group of five people at the small rowhouse of

Norman and Peg Eddy in East Harlem. Norman Eddy had inherited wealth through his family, which had founded the Stanley tool company in the 19th century. Both he and Peg were United Church of Christ pastors, with Norman serving a congregation in East Harlem and Peg teaching at Princeton Theological Seminary in New Jersey. After attending a money workshop the previous year, Peg had invited Don to address one of her seminary classes. The Eddys, another couple and a pastor's wife spent one day in East Harlem, then drove to the Eddys' country home an hour-and-a-half north of the city for the rest of the weekend.

"I have never before had a chance to talk freely about the subject of money with people in situations roughly similar to Peg's and mine," Norman wrote afterwards. "As a group we did some significant sharing and there was an experience of relief and relaxation in being with other wealthy persons." The pastor's wife, named Catherine, also affirmed the experience in a letter to Don. But she added, "We barely scratched the surface in our time together. ... It's heavy going for those who feel a lot of questions in this area. ... It was striking to me that though you kept offering scriptures or concerns, we always returned to a few immediate questions (exactly 'how' to give, whether to give to children, guaranteed income, or such). We avoided Scripture, it seemed to me, probably an indication that it plays no central part in our view of money."

Catherine, in her 30s, had been living in upstate New York where her husband pastored a church when she came to a Wellspring orientation in 1975 and met Don. He mentioned that he was organizing the Poverty Coalition to raise money for inner-city ministries. Catherine privately told him that she had a stock portfolio worth about $30,000 that made her uncomfortable because of how it was invested. "I wanted to sell it or give it away," she later wrote. "But I knew no institution whom I trusted to use it responsibly. ... When the opportunity was given to contribute part of the portfolio to C of S's Poverty Coalition, it was good news. ... As my whole life began to be re-ordered through my relationship with Wellspring, I began to see money as a potential opportunity rather than as burden."

Aiding the needy evolved as a central theme for Don's new Ministry of Money. During a money event in June 1979, Don featured a film about Mother Teresa's work with the poorest of the poor. Participants also paid visits to two low-income families who lived in an apartment building operated by a Church of the Saviour ministry. Don had hit on a powerful way to crack open the financial lives of those seeking to more closely follow God's will: by introducing the well-to-do to the down-and-out.

Mission Groups

Many churches today form small groups for fellowship, Bible study, prayer and mutual support. Many churches also press these groups to take on the work of outward ministry, carrying out needed tasks within the congregation or addressing needs in the broader community. Often, the results are disappointing. The groups do well with their inner focus, but spin their wheels—or simply resist—launching an outward mission.

Don's congregation, the Church of the Saviour, provides a model for how small groups work well on both inward and outward cylinders. As Elizabeth O'Connor describes in her book *Servant Leaders, Servant Structures*, the church's small groups initially ran into the same wheel-spinning as other churches. "Church members met in small fellowship groups committed to worship, tithing, prayer, study and corporate outreach. Not one of them, however, was able to agree on what its outreach would be. ... We were slow to recognize that the very diversity of gifts made it impossible to find a corporate mission. One person would say, 'Let's have a street music group.' The next person would reply, 'I'm tone deaf.' Someone would suggest working with alcoholics, and another person would answer, 'Not for me.' The exploration went on and on, and it seemed there was always someone to put out the fire in another."[8]

The church eventually took the painful step of dissolving its groups, despite the tight bonds that had been forged between members, and reconstructed them on the basis of mission. As with Don's Wellspring call, someone would have a vision for ministry and announce it to the congregation. Others who were excited by the vision answered the call and formed a ministry group. These groups met once a week to carry out their outward ministries while incorporating the inward functions of fellowship, Bible study and prayer.

The groups kept their members accountable by having each report weekly to an appointed "spiritual director" on how they were doing in their individual, daily disciplines of prayer and Scripture reading. Members of the mission groups came together not by social affinity, but by a common desire to make a difference in some small corner of the world. Such mission groups, often more diverse than other small groups, found that their effectiveness depended on their diversity, because each member offered talents and interests that no one else in the group could provide. No one in the group was expendable.

With church members responding to needs on the basis of their passion, rather than from recruitment pressure by a pastor or church leader, remarkable ministries can be birthed. Small groups forming out of the Church of the Saviour have, among other things, sheltered the homeless, taught low-income children, cared for AIDS patients, purchased apartment complexes for the needy and helped the unemployed find jobs. Obviously such a mission-group structure calls for high commitment. But higher callings and strong community often breed such high commitment.

7

Citizen of the World

"The rich and the poor have this in common:
the Lord is the maker of them all."
–Proverbs 22:2 (NRSV)

In January 1979, Don and Gloria embarked on their first pilgrimage to India. They tacked on a visit to Australia, where they led that continent's first Wellspring orientation in Melbourne, organized by an Australian couple who had attended a similar orientation several years before in Maryland. Don reunited with a Perth family that had befriended him during a World War II submarine refitting stop, and Gloria excitedly met dozens of her father's relatives whom she had never seen before.

But when they returned to the United States, it was the experiences in India that crowded Don's mind. Calcutta had been "mind boggling," he wrote in a February 1979 Ministry of Money newsletter. "The extremes of poverty and man's lack of caring, self-centeredness, and dehumanization ... defy description." In the same newsletter Don included a Jean Vanier quote that prophesied Don's money ministry. "Jesus calls me also to hold out my hand to the self-satisfied, to the comfortable. ... Having seen and touched people in distress, they will begin to love, begin to dispossess themselves of their riches, begin to share." Vanier was a Canadian Catholic who founded L'Arche, a movement that organized communities in which the developmentally disabled lived with non-disabled persons, and Don and Gloria had visited a L'Arche house in Calcutta.

In a later newsletter Don mused on related words from Mother Teresa. "I heard her say, 'The poor are the hope of the salvation of mankind.' ... Money and increased amounts of it misplace our trust in the one true security, Jesus Christ." Don believed that well-to-do

Americans experiencing what he had seen in India would be cracked open to a new level of compassion and deeper desire to follow Jesus. In all its brokenness, Don felt drawn to Calcutta, an irresistible catalyst for change. But when he asked others if they might want to share his experience, all said, "Thanks, but no thanks."

In spring 1979, the night before Don was to attend a conference in Atlantic City, New Jersey, the powder keg of emotions he had tried to contain since returning from India exploded. He went to bed early, only to be awakened by a phone call about 9 p.m. Infuriated, he flung his pillow across the room, rose and smashed his arm into the wall. He stalked out the back door of his house and went screaming into an open field. He returned to the house and called an airline. "Has your last flight of the day left for Miami?" he asked, picking a city through which he had frequently flown. Told that it had, he called the Potter's House, where Gordon Cosby was on duty that night. "Gordon," he said, "I feel like I'm going berserk. I probably should be going to St. Elizabeth's," a psychiatric hospital in Washington, D.C. Cosby replied, "Knowing you, I don't think you're going berserk. I think you're just experiencing a deeper level of spiritual impotence." Cosby told Don to meet him in Cosby's office the next morning.

There Cosby elaborated, "You've just come from Calcutta and you're aware that Mother Teresa is just a drop in the bucket in healing the misery of that city. We at the Church of the Saviour are similarly a drop in the bucket here." This realization was a good thing, Cosby said. Don was coming to understand at a new level that he couldn't pull off anything that made a difference—only God could. Don felt his anguish subside as he took in Cosby's diagnosis: "not insane." But he was still too churned up to attend the conference that day, he told Cosby. "Why wouldn't you go?" Cosby replied. "It seems like that's the best place for you to be." Don drove to Atlantic City in a fragile state.

The conference was organized by Evangelicals for Social Action. Its founder, college professor Ron Sider, had written a book called *Rich Christians in an Age of Hunger* and was to lead a money workshop for Don in May. In an auditorium just off the boardwalk with several hundred others, Don listened to a blind singer named Ken Medema play the piano and sing as a warm-up for Sider's talk.

With Medema's first notes, an emotional dam broke and tears streamed down Don's face. He later wandered the boardwalk, feeling cleansed and liberated from the responsibility to fix Calcutta or Washington, giving that burden to God.

During times of emotional turmoil, Don sometimes awakened in the early morning hours with little chance of falling back asleep. Some of these nights he arose, got dressed and drove 19 miles to a truck stop where he ate a middle-of-the-night breakfast and read a devotional book or the sports section of *The Washington Post.* He then returned home and slept for a few hours before beginning his regular daily routine. Gordon Cosby kidded Don about this habit. "Why don't you take that to your truck stop and come back with an answer," Cosby said at meetings where they faced a thorny issue.

As usual, Don's schedule swept him back into hectic activity. Two weeks after the Sider workshop in May, he and Gloria flew to Tucson, Arizona, to lead a Wellspring orientation. That was followed during the summer by two invitation-only workshops for wealthy Christians, one at Wellspring and the other on the West Coast. In September he flew back to the West Coast to lead a money workshop in Santa Barbara, California. In October he held a special workshop for foundation executives at Wellspring led by Landrum Bolling, the former Lilly Endowment executive and now chief executive officer of the national Council on Foundations. In November Don was back on the West Coast, leading a money workshop in Seattle, Washington.

On return trips from the West Coast, Don occasionally made three-day stopovers at the Spiritual Life Institute of America conference center in Sedona, Arizona. The Catholic facility, in the desert 120 miles north of Phoenix, displayed a sign at its entrance saying "No Fuss." Don carried out a solo silent retreat in one of the one-person cabins, scattered around a small adobe-and-cedar administration building, that were named for contemplative figures such as "St. John of the Cross," "Merton" and "Evelyn Underhill." The short sojourns recuperated Don and reconnected him with God in the midst of his busy travel schedule.

Money workshops, offered several times a year, became the backbone of Ministry of Money. The format–presentations, studying and sharing in small groups, silence and a final worship service–

remained constant over the next two decades. Dale Stitt, a Ministry of Money staff member from 1987 to 1994, recalled another long-time staple: Don's telling the group about his life on the first evening. Such stories as Don skipping school to see a game of his favorite baseball team, the Boston Red Sox; his military exploits; and his starting the Fellowship of Christian Athletes set a mood of irre-pressibility and vulnerability for the group. Yet such was Don's hum-bleness and self-doubt that Stitt had to continually re-convince him of the importance of telling his story, and to reassure him afterward when Don felt he had not told it well enough.

The Rev. Karen Johnson described the impact of a workshop led by Don and his son, Michael, in 1983 for her Episcopal church in Gaithersburg, Maryland. "It changed my life. ... At the time I was a single parent with three youngsters ages 9, 12 and 14. We ... were living on my clergy salary, $21,000 a year, plus $600 a month in child support. I had a large seminary debt, car loan payments, rent and the other typical family life expenses. I gave away about five percent. During the morning study and prayer, I began to hear a new word. God's invitation to us to tithe is rooted in God's desire for our com-mon fullness of life! ... At lunch I talked with a friend about some resistances I was feeling. Could I conscientiously ask my children to participate with me in this venture? It would mean significant changes and I worried I was asking too much of them. ... My friend asked me, 'Karen, what legacy do you want to leave to your chil-dren?' I knew in those moments that above everything else, I want-ed to leave them the legacy of God's utterly loving trustworthiness, that the ways of God are not the ways of the world, but they are the best ways! ... I became an instant tither. That night I gathered with my children around the dinner table and told them what I was con-sidering and why. To this day (22 years later) they all consider that one of the more positively shaping experiences of life."

I, the author of this book, have written earlier of my experience at a 1996 workshop that I and my wife, Marilyn, attended at Wellspring. We stayed in the McClanens' home due to an over-enrollment that filled Wellspring's cabins, and were struck by Don's and Gloria's warmth. Don opened the workshop the first evening, but thereafter stayed largely in the background. "That first evening, all 50 of us sat in a large circle and introduced ourselves with a brief explanation of why we were there or with an anecdote from our experiences with money. I was surprised and touched by people's honesty as they expressed their pain and searching. We were all ages and various income levels. About one-fifth were clergy. There were business owners, social workers who were struggling to make ends meet, a White House lawyer, a physician testing a call to mission work in Eastern Europe. My wife and I explained that we were there because my mother had just died, leaving us a lot of money. We wanted to know what God had in mind for it."

"For the next two and a half days, we heard a pastor and six Ministry of Money board members give talks and we met four times with small groups to discuss what we had heard. Each time we gathered as a whole, we sang. After the last talk each evening, we went to our bedrooms in silence to ponder what God was telling us. ... The central theme of the talks and our small-group discussions, for the most part, wasn't money. It was following Christ. Money was always secondary. At the end of the weekend, one participant said he would have signed up for a workshop years before if he had known it centered so little on 'stewardship' and so much on Jesus.

"The speakers were impassioned. Most described their personal journeys in following Christ. Almost all described encounters with the poor in the Third World as formative. Several spoke of economic injustices that resulted in most of the world's population going hungry each day, and we watched a video about the exploitation of teenage garment workers in Central America. But remarkably, the weekend was free of manipulation and inducements to guilt. Though impassioned, the speakers also exuded a gentleness and humility that precluded judgmentalism. More than one speaker expressed the desire that we take from the weekend, above all else, a sense of how much God loves us.

"They also set a tone of astonishing honesty. Several wept as they touched on painful aspects of their lives. Cheryl Broetje, my small-group leader, disclosed financial details of her multi-million-dollar-a-year, 3,000-acre farm in the state of Washington. She then asked us why we couldn't discuss money with Christian brothers and sisters. This jolted us into an openness that deepened throughout the weekend under her gentle prodding. I came to love my fellow group members as I was given privileged glimpses into their struggles. We reached levels of intimacy that I had never experienced before in a 'church' setting.

"The weekend reoriented my life. A talk by Gordon Cosby ... convinced me that the only way to truly follow Christ is to embrace self-sacrifice and suffering. I, like most Christians, had always temporized Christ's call to take up his cross, preferring instead to follow the culture's call to be on top, to be a winner. Cheryl Broetje reinforced this conviction with her tale of making room at her farm for both abused teens and the families of migrant workers, and the suffering this sometimes brought to her and her family, including the pregnancy of one of her daughters. 'You have to be able to choose your ditch, crawl in and be prepared to die there,' she said. She also explained that we would find God calling us to our individual ministries through those places in our lives that were filled with the most pain.

"On the last day of the retreat, an indelible image emerged in my mind: I was on the edge of a walled, hilltop city, looking across a valley at another hill, topped by a cross. My life's journey was towards that other hill, and the valley—my only way there—was a garbage pit. But I also sensed that the path through that pit was the only way I would become truly alive, the only place where I could truly experience the love, peace and joy that Christ promised. ... I have found, to my surprise—and God's amusement—that the garbage pit is not out there, but inside me." The workshop convinced me and Marilyn to raise our giving above the ten percent level and provided us a vision of sacrificial Christian living that slowly took root in our lives.

The ministry bore fruit in other lives, Don noted in a September 1979 newsletter. "From a marketing specialist in the North comes a letter saying, 'Wellspring has changed my life. I can never be the same again. Among other things I now know I must change my vocation, a decision I've been avoiding for some time. Here's a token gift of $100. I'll be at the next money workshop wherever it is, in any part of the country. I feel liberated and energized.'" Tim Foley, a defensive back for the Miami Dolphins, gave $1,000 to Don for ministries to the poor and said he would be working on his fellow players to do the same. A lawyer in the Midwest, infected by "this kind of crazy, exciting way of coming at life," downsized his car from a

Cadillac to a Volkswagen and planned to give a $100,000 investment return to a Christian cause. A West Coast couple with a homebuilding business, "whose marriage three years ago was on the verge of collapse as they prepared to move into a new $200,000 home, said, 'Because of Wellspring and the Ministry of Money ... we have sold the big house to our former partner, moved into a smaller home, and are now enjoying giving away 40 percent plus of our income.'" While Don did not solicit or accept donations to Ministry of Money during workshops, participants frequently responded afterward with gifts, which provided him a salary of $37,500 and paid for a secretary, the costs of travel and other ministry expenses.

Don acknowledged pushbacks and disappointments. "When I read your 'Tithe as Teacher' piece I was angry and resented it," one person wrote. "I have to call and cancel coming to the money workshop, it so threatens my wife," another wrote. Still another said, "Seeing your new logo with a cross in the midst of a dollar sign was so brash ... like being punched in the mouth." Don also observed workshop participants edge toward major changes in their giving, only to draw back to economic safety. Still, he was overjoyed to see an increasing number of small manifestations of the Spirit, the type of conversions that 20 centuries before had turned the earliest Christians into a reckless band of givers.

As Ministry of Money's workshop schedule expanded, Don's newsletter mailing list initially grew to about 100 people. (By 1995 it contained more than 15,000.) His personal correspondence also grew. Since his Fellowship of Christian Athletes days, Don always had maintained a voluminous exchange of letters–to set up events, communicate with people registered for events and follow up with those who had attended, not to mention keeping in steady touch with friends, ministry partners, prospective funding sources and those who sought him out as a mentor. He always signed his letters, "Faithfully, Don." Winnie Rader, his secretary from 1978 to 1979, came to see a multiplicity of meanings in that closing: Don's faithfulness to the person he was writing, his faithfulness to Christ and his faithfulness to God's call on his life.

Don and Rader worked together in a cramped room in the basement of Don's house, where piles of letters, newspaper articles, books, magazines and other written materials covered Don's desk, bookshelves and work table. They also overflowed onto the floor, and Rader had to step carefully. If Don found an article or book interesting, he would inevitably send off copies to those he thought would appreciate it. Rader was repeatedly amazed at how he knew in which pile to search for a document he needed.

Rader admired Don's sense of fun as well as his faithfulness. A snowstorm hit on February 2, 1978, her first day of work, and Don's first assignment was for her to help push cars out of the Wellspring Center parking lot. As they slipped and slid on the snow, "that was my introduction to Don's way of collapsing into uncontrollable laughter in the midst of major difficulty–doubled up, tears streaming down his face, almost unable to talk or breathe," Rader later wrote. At other times Rader found Don's passionate intensity intimidating. She once retreated to the bathroom in tears when Don furiously confronted someone on the phone.

One of Don's angry interactions, which Rader did not hear, was with Frank Underwood, top aide to C. Davis Weyerhaeuser of the Tacoma, Washington, family that owned the huge timber and wood products company. Weyerhaeuser, executive of the Stewardship Foundation that he had created with 10,000 shares of company stock in the 1940s, served as a sponsor for a November 1979 money workshop in Seattle.[1] During a planning meeting in Tacoma, Underwood mentioned to Don that he did not want to hold the workshop at his church because some members might object to the subject. Don responded with a raised voice, "Frank, are you still struggling with a concern about being offensive and unpopular?" After Don had returned home, Underwood called and said, "In light of the anger you showed with me the other day, I'm offering you a $2,900 scholarship to go through an intensive therapy program dealing with your emotions." Underwood explained that the Stewardship Foundation sponsored the three-week program for selected clergy and lay leaders to promote psychological well-being. Don shed tears of thankfulness. Here was a dramatic new opportunity to achieve what had eluded him through so many years of therapy: a greater awareness of his feelings so that he could manage them before they erupted in outbursts of anger. He also anticipated new insights about the high-emotion topics of sex and money.

Don flew to Seattle on Feb. 3, 1980, rented a car and followed a foundation employee to a house overlooking Puget Sound between Seattle and Tacoma. He was instructed to purchase two weeks of groceries and leave the house only for a daily trip to a psychiatrist's home a half-hour drive away. The daily sessions would last an hour. He was not to read any books, watch TV, write letters or talk to anyone on the telephone. Journal writing was allowed as long he shared entries with the psychiatrist. The only break in the three-week program would come after two weeks, when he had a free weekend.

With Don lying on a couch, the psychiatrist opened the first session with, "Tell me about your mother"; the second day, it was, "Tell me about your father." The queries dredged up such vivid memories, Don could see clearly the street of his boyhood home and smell the sweaty, barnyard odor of a Morrisville friend who worked on a farm. But the experience left Don so agitated that he had trouble sleeping. On the third day he asked the psychiatrist for a sleeping pill, but was refused. Don's emotional state went into a tailspin. Swept by waves of anxiety, guilt, panic and terror, he passed his time at the house walking in circles night and day. By the second week, Don alerted the psychiatrist, "I may have to leave. I need to have a breakthrough in my emotions or I'm going to die here." The psychiatrist replied, "You're the first one who has had a problem this serious," and urged Don to give the process more time to work.

After two weeks, Don spent his weekend off visiting a couple in Seattle he had met through Ministry of Money. When Gloria called from Australia, where she was visiting relatives, Don overheard them say they were concerned about his emotional state. But Don steeled himself for a fresh start the third week, determined to push for a breakthrough. In their first session back, the psychiatrist instructed him not to resist his emotions but to let them overwhelm him. By Wednesday, Don was so tormented he fled the house in the middle of the night. He headed for Seattle in his rented car and drove aimlessly through the downtown until 3 a.m., then started back to the house. Returning on a coastal highway encased in fog, Don felt a suicidal impulse. *All I have to do is turn this wheel and head over that cliff,* he thought. At that moment, a sign loomed out of the fog announcing the exit for a hospital. In the emergency room, a nurse's calm, reassuring presence allowed Don to relax a little for the first time in more than two weeks. Alerted by the nurse to Don's condition, the psychiatrist halted the sessions, had an associate give Don a tranquilizing injection and arranged for him to fly back to Washington, D.C.

Don arrived in Maryland a highly medicated zombie. Gloria was still in Australia. Friends from the Church of the Saviour sat up with him for several nights as his insomnia continued. Three weeks later he felt stable enough to lead a money workshop in Chicago with Gloria, who was flying in directly from Australia. But Don discovered he wasn't as in control as he had hoped. When Gloria got off her plane, Don stood at the gate accompanied by two police officers. *Has he killed someone?* Gloria wondered. Don explained that he was walking through the airport when he saw a man carrying a sign jeering actress Jane Fonda for her opposition to the Vietnam War, which had ended five years before. Don, who also had opposed the war, grabbed the protestor's sign, tore it in half and handed it back to the protester, who called airport police. After being booked for destruction of property, Don had just enough time to drive to the workshop before it started.

Returning to Dayspring, Don continued to be encased in a cloud of depression, frequently waking in a panic at 3 or 4 a.m. He walked the family's new cocker spaniel puppy up and down a near-by country road or, at his doctor's advice, climbed in his car and pounded the steering wheel, screaming to vent his anguish. He felt on the verge of a nervous breakdown or even a heart attack. After two months, Gloria pointedly said to him one day, "Tell me what you're feeling!" This unloosed a five-minute stream of profanity, all related to money. With his rage spent, Don's emotional haze lifted. Later, he pieced together what had happened: he had stifled powerful feelings of anger, anxiety and even humiliation evoked by his money ministry. The fund-raising created a particular pressure-cooker—the need to steel himself for rejection with each solicitation, the hours spent walking his office floor thinking about how to respond if a prospective donor said no.

Don's emotional recovery was sufficient for him to continue organizing money workshops at Wellspring and around the country in 1980 and 1981. A workshop at Wellspring drew Roger Staubach, the recently retired Hall of Fame quarterback of the Dallas Cowboys. Staubach had met Don in 1979 when he and Cowboys coach Tom Landry invited Don to speak at a Fellowship of Christian Athletes event at the Dallas Country Club. Don also traveled to Topeka, Kansas, to discuss money issues with Dr. Karl Menninger, one of the nation's best-known psychiatrists. Menninger had co-founded the Menninger Clinic in Topeka in 1925, which pioneered the idea that the mentally ill could be equipped to live in society rather than be warehoused in sanitaria. Menninger also had demys-tified the field of psychiatry to the general public with his popular 1930 book *The Human Mind*.[2] Still active at 87, Menninger agreed with Don that attitudes about money played a key role in a mentally healthy life. Menninger later wrote him, "What you are doing through your Ministry of Money is simply to cure more people than I have in my lifetime. ... Greed is one of the diseases that doesn't get 'well'; it can be incurable. ... Never in the world's history has there been so much money available to the average individual and they keep accumulating and struggling to get still more."

In October 1981, after six years of money workshops under the Wellspring umbrella, Don spun off Ministry of Money into its own corporate entity. In the midst of working toward that separation, Don flew to Thailand in August 1981 to work with war refugees under the auspices of a new ministry of the Church of the Saviour called COSIGN (the Church of the Saviour International Good Neighbors). "COSIGN was an unplanned—perhaps even unwanted—child of the Church of the Saviour communities," Elizabeth O'Connor explained in a newsletter. "We were already too busy when Gordon Cosby preached a sermon on the refugees of Southeast Asia. Nevertheless, a friend in the congregation went home, packed his bag and set out to see for himself. ... COSIGN was our response to his story. ... What the volunteers gain are a heart of wisdom, world citizenship and a new and more compassionate way to be in life."

Don was one of the scores to respond to O'Connor's call. Journal entries convey his excitement: "July 29, 1981: I'm over-whelmed with gratitude as this giant 747 flies over Mt. Fuji, Japan; Hong Kong; and the Gulf of Thailand into Bangkok. What memo-ries this brings back of how as a 19-year-old gunner's mate on a U.S. submarine during WWII, we spent months on end patrolling the coast of China from Japan to Indonesia. On that mission of violence and destruction I never dreamed that such a different kind of mission of mercy and compassion would be mine 37 years later."

The volunteers took a 17-hour train ride from Bangkok down the Thai peninsula to Songkhla, a small city on the Gulf of Thailand near the country's southern border. They passed through picturesque countryside, with rice paddies, water buffalo, palm trees and low mountain ridges covered in tropical growth, and past villages where vendors hawked fresh pineapple and cooking fires filled the air with exotic aromas. In Songkhla, Don checked into a house with ten other COSIGN volunteers. Some shared the two bedrooms, while others camped out on the tile floor of the living room or in hallways. The house's plumbing performed fitfully, and residents often scooped water from a tall pottery jar to bathe after a day in the hot tropical weather.

Seven thousand Vietnamese "boat people" lived in the refugee camp, a barbed-wire enclosure the size of several city blocks. They had fled their country's Communist government on small, motorized craft to escape destitution or political repression. The refugees slept in open-air pavilions with tin roofs and plank flooring elevated on bamboo stilts. They cooked on charcoal fires and relieved themselves in portable toilets arranged in long rows. Refugees erected a row of shanty stands to sell food, soft drinks and other goods on a beach at the edge of the camp. Children, a large segment of the population, played in and around the ocean all day to keep cool. Many of the children's parents had launched them alone into the sea to seek a better life or had been killed in transit by Thai pirates. A Catholic priest named Father Joe, who oversaw a section of the camp for parentless children, had placed a sign at its entrance that announced, "Through These Gates Have Come the Most Courageous Youth in the World." Don worked initially as a carpenter, helping to construct additional buildings. But his skills were limited, and he soon switched to being a physical education teacher, instructing the children in soccer, volleyball, ping-pong and badminton.

Don bonded with two bubbly children, Ky, five, and her younger brother, No. Their mother ran one of the stands at the beach. Ky and No tagged along with Don while he worked, and in his time off he played with them or bought them Sprites from their mother's stand. One day Don gave the mother an old pair of his jeans with rips in the knees that he planned to throw away. The next day, he saw No dressed in astonishing finery—a denim suit that his mother had fashioned from the trousers.

More refugees arrived almost daily, many by truck after landing elsewhere on the peninsula, some on the beach at the camp. One day a COSIGN volunteer noticed a truck unload 50 refugees, none of whom were men. Finding a refugee who could speak English, she learned the group had been attacked by pirates 17 times in their 13-day journey. The final band of pirates, angered at the absence of anything left to steal, stabbed 27 men and boys to death, leaving the sea red with blood. The English-speaking refugee had watched her husband, son and brother die. The following Sunday, Don saw these same women singing in a thatch-roofed pavilion that served as a chapel. "Hearing these people sing praises to God was an experience I will cherish as long as I live," he wrote in his journal. In another entry he wrote, "The predominant word in my life these days is privileged. ... I'm so amazed at the difference in me now, three years after experiencing a similar kind of devastation in Calcutta. ... There I was often frustrated, overwhelmed and blocked. I held the pain at arms' length and couldn't allow it to enter. Now I am able to allow it in more freely." Remarkably, experiencing the suffering of Southeast Asian refugees was healing Don of the emotional pain he had felt since Calcutta.

The dignity and spirit of the refugees helped inspire Don's recovery. Their mood was hopeful, given that their stay in Songkhla was usually short and their eventual destinations would likely be Australia, France, England, Canada or the United States. Buses left regularly with refugees bound for Bangkok and then their new homes. Don wrote on August 14, "Over the past several days, I've wondered what would happen to Muoi, the seven-year-old parentless Mongoloid boy. ... Who would want him? ... This morning I looked up and got my answer, as the first bus load pulled out. There was Muoi, standing on the front seat, smiling and waving to me from in between a beautiful young couple who lost their own child in the crossing. My heart leapt and broke at the same time."

Through his pilgrimages to Calcutta and Thailand, Don was coming to consider himself a citizen of the world. And unlike after his return from Calcutta, more than a dozen people who had told him thanks but no thanks now said they wished to go on a Third World mission trip themselves. Within two months he returned to Thailand and Calcutta to line up permissions and accommodations for a group of 20 to visit in the fall of 1982. Don dubbed the pilgrimage "Frightening Good News."

In a December 1981 newsletter, Don inserted a borrowed metaphor for the world he was starting to know. "If the world were a village of 100 people, 70 would be unable to read, over 50 would be suffering from malnutrition, and over 80 would live in what we call substandard housing. Of the 100 members of the global village, six would be Americans. These six would have one half of the village's entire income and would consume one third of the total energy resources available. Of the U.S. population, less than two percent would own 80 percent of the U.S. corporate wealth."

Despite his focus on Ministry of Money, Don still led some Wellspring orientations. In February 1982, he and Gloria returned to Australia to conduct a Wellspring event—as well as anger, sex and money workshops—in Perth, Melbourne and Sydney. One of the organizers was a witty lawyer and pastor from Perth named Neville Watson. Years later he sent Don a booklet entitled "The Saintly Qualities of Donald McClanen," replete with endorsements on the book jacket noting that the contents were "quite obviously the result of exhaustive research." Inside were 30 totally blank pages. But Watson wasn't joking when he wrote Don a few months after the Australian tour describing an experience that he said would not have happened save for the influence of Wellspring. "About five weeks ago [a friend] wanted someone to transport a group of fringe dwellers (Aborigines, the 'outcasts of Australian society'). ... The next day I picked up a van full of delightful hyperactive Aboriginal kids and set off for Gidgegannup. Within 10 minutes of moving off, one of the children leaned over and said, 'Has your nose always been as big as it is, Neville?' I answered in the affirmative and said I was born with it; to which the nine-year-old commented philosophically that I couldn't be blamed for it, then. ... It was a day in which I received as much love and affection as I can ever remember—and this from a bunch of grotty, snotty-nosed Aboriginal kids who in half a sentence could turn the air bluer than I have ever seen it before. ... The irony of it all struck me—I, who had everything by the world's standards, am receiving so much from this group of people who have nothing. It called to mind the words of Mother Teresa: 'We give nothing to the poor; they give to us.' ... It really was quite simple: Christ walks with the poor, and as we walk with them we have the chance of touching the hem of His garment."

Another Australian, a Roman Catholic dentist, attended an anger, sex and money "trilogy" workshop. "The morning I woke before going to your Trilogy in Melbourne I knew something important was going to happen, and there would be no turning back," she wrote to Don. "I have doubled our tithing to 20 percent of our income, giving the extra ten percent to World Vision and Catholic Relief. By the end of next year when our older sons will be finished college, I hope to increase our giving to 40 percent and with God's help I hope soon after that that we will just retain enough for simple needs."

In November 1982, a group of 18 embarked on Ministry of Money's first Third World pilgrimage to Hong Kong, Thailand and India. "We are largely strangers to each other, coming from Atlanta, Detroit, Little Rock, Great Bend (Kansas), Cleveland, Greenville (South Carolina), Washington, D.C., San Antonio, Rockford (Illinois), Melbourne and Perth (Australia)," Don described in a newsletter. "We are nurses, a lawyer, teachers, administrators, a librarian, editors, priests and pastors, church lay leader and homemakers, a farmer, a dentist and students. ... We are beginners in the faith, we are old warriors, we are conservatives and liberals, we are priests and laity, we are scared, humbled, richly blessed to be chosen of God to reach out to the uttermost parts of this amazing global community." A Bible verse, Habakkuk 1:5, helped Don express the promise of the trip: "Look at the nations and watch—and be utterly amazed. For I am going to do something in your days that you would not believe, even if you were told" (NIV).

Gloria helped Don lead the pilgrimage. Don appointed Robert Linthicum, the Presbyterian pastor from the Detroit area, to lead a daily reflection time for the group and direct a silent retreat at the end. Linthicum's son, Bob, also came, serving as trip photographer. Linthicum admired Don's lack of inhibition on the flight from San Francisco, during which Don lay on the floor under the seats to catch some sleep. The group stopped in Hong Kong for three days, where they visited Kai Tak North, a refugee camp where 6,000 Vietnamese boat people were trapped in disheartening conditions. The refugees lived in corrugated-aluminum boxes that were stacked three high and open in the front. "A given family would have one to three cubicles, according to its size," Linthicum wrote. "In those cubicles, they would live–they would eat, play, sleep, make love, give birth. Their only privacy would be whatever cloth covering they might drape over the mouth of the cubicle, while all their possessions shared space in that cubicle or hung about it. It was unbelievably public, undignified, survival-oriented living conditions." Even after having experienced the deprivation of Calcutta, Don and Gloria were shocked by Kai Tak North's conditions.

In Thailand, the group took a daylong bus trip north of Bangkok to visit Ban Vinai, a huge camp of 33,000 Hmong refugees from the mountains of Laos, who had fought on the losing side of a civil war. Linthicum wrote of how much it differed from Kai Tak North. "The camp struck me more as a large Hmong village than a refugee resettlement camp" and the people seemed "healthy, happy, and well-cared for," he said. Linthicum also observed that Don seemed to be having the time of his life. Wearing a Thai bamboo hat, Don approached the refugees and tried to start conversations with bold hand gesturing. Most had no idea what he was saying, but sensed his interest and returned it with smiles. Don also became a pied piper for the children who, dressed in their traditional, brightly colored robes or in T-shirts and shorts, skipped behind him waiting for him to spin suddenly and say, "Boo."

When the group landed in Calcutta, "the cab drive from the airport to our hotel immediately alerted us to the fact that India was different," Linthicum wrote. "The cab in a battle with every car, bus and truck as it raced pell-mell down the road, cows walking sublimely through city streets, beggars swarming the cab at each intersection, skinny Indians pulling rickshaws up steep hills, dirt and debris and garbage everywhere, buses packed 'to the gills' with kids hanging on the back, people urinating in the streets, masses huddled next to buildings or sleeping on the sidewalks, their blankets wrapped around them while they lived among filth and urine and dirty clothes."

The trip's most highly anticipated event came on November 23: a 45-minute audience with Mother Teresa, who had just arrived in Calcutta from foreign travel and was leaving again shortly for Manila. "She is truly a small, frail lady, her hands broad and gnarled with work, her feet misshapen," Linthicum wrote. "But there is a glow, a power, almost a luminosity about her. One could see her walking through an airport lobby or on a street without her habit, and you would still know you were in the presence of a saint. There is a gentleness and yet a firmness about her, a naiveté and a cunning, an open acceptance of all and yet a high demand for all who would serve the poor. But what most stands out about her is her utter Christ-centeredness. ... Never have I heard the name of Christ more the center of a conversation than it was in that 30 minutes."

For six days the members of the group worked in one of the Missionaries of Charity missions: Shishu Bhavan, an orphanage; Prem Dan, a care center for the paralyzed and non-terminally ill; and Kalighat, the Home for the Destitute and Dying. In the orphanage, which comprised two buildings the size of a small elementary school, 50 children stayed in one large room in long rows of cribs. Gloria spent her time holding them, often two at a time, and mopping the floor and cleaning cribs in an uphill effort to keep conditions sanitary. One morning she, Don and two other nurses assisted at a once-a-week medical clinic the Missionaries of Charity operated at a nearby village, where they dressed wounds and the nurses gave inoculations. Gloria felt heartbroken treating a young mother severely disfigured by burns from a fire, and also by seeing so many who had formed a half-mile line that morning be turned away without treatment when the clinic closed at noon.

Don bathed, fed and shaved residents at Kalighat and at Prem Dan, a converted factory building where those who survived Kalighat were sent, many with little hope of ever recovering enough to leave. One day he led all the pilgrims on a visit to a leprosarium operated by brothers of the Missionaries of Charity order in Titagarh, a village near Calcutta. After riding in a train so crowded that the press of bodies hardly left them space to breathe, they arrived at a former factory building where hundreds of lepers with missing fingers, limbs and noses operated textile looms, grew vegetables and raised poultry and pigs. Don thrilled at seeing the residents derive a sense of worth from their work assignments—even a roomful of blind, deformed lepers whose job was to sing together, "Jesus is my eyes, Jesus is my ears, Jesus is my everything."

Before the pilgrims left Calcutta, Mother Teresa's administrative assistant, Sister Frederick, told them, "I cannot tell you what your presence has meant to us. ... When I first saw 'Ministry of Money' I said, this was another money business. What crazy business! I was tempted to put it aside and have no time for it." Don responded to her, "As your ministry is to the poor, our is to the wealthy. And those two need to be combined and kept in tension. As we go, we have a unique ministry to the wealthy, starting with ourselves, all of us being wealthy."

Don saw profound impacts from Calcutta on many of the travelers. One group member, Pamela Borne, expressed her reaction to Kalighat, the Home for the Destitute and Dying, in poetry:

> "Broken body, broken spirit,
> Cries of pain, of loneliness, of anguish
> That do not stop.
> The ritual of bathing does not prevent
> The smell of human excrement, which
> Pervades this holy place,
> Where disinfectant cannot overcome.
> Tired bodies, wizened breasts
> Showing the secrets of worn out flesh.
> I am overwhelmed by that smell.
> I can resist no longer.
> As I run to the roof for solace
> The scenery confronts me further,
> There is no escape from this poverty,
> Interrupting my life and ripping me apart
> Revealing in myself a microcosm
> Of this city of living hell.
> I feel
> Compassion, anger, selfishness and greed
> And the tears fall from my face
> An outward sign of inner conflict,
> It's out there, and it's inside me too.
> Lord, my life has been touched

With the awful reality of the enormity
Of human poverty.
Show me how
To be responsible,
To love,
To transcend my humanness
And follow you."

Linthicum returned to the United States a different person. Three occurrences during the trip stood out for him. One was being asked directly by Mother Teresa, "Young man, do you love Jesus?" Linthicum answered, "Of course I love Jesus." Mother Teresa then said, "Yes, but do you love him in the distressing disguise of the poor?" That hit Linthicum hard. He realized that he had considered his work with the poor in Detroit a way of doing the work of Jesus, but instead needed to treat it as something deeper and more mystical: a way to be in communion with Jesus.

In the second occurrence, Linthicum steeled himself to volunteer at Shishu Bhavan, the orphanage. He knew it would be an intense experience, for it would dredge up his unpleasant memories of having himself grown up in an orphanage in Philadelphia. For almost his entire adult life Linthicum had shut these memories out until, a year before the trip, he had entered therapy to heal from his past. During his days at Shishu Bhavan, long-repressed feelings surged back: feelings of abandonment, of being vulnerable and unprotected and unloved, of feeling that he had to watch out for himself because no one else would. After the trip, Linthicum's therapy sessions surged to a whole new level of healing. The orphanage experience also created a new dynamic in his sometimes-turbulent relationship with his son. Told by the nuns to play with the children, Linthicum was at a loss until Bob Jr. showed him how to do it. His son sat on the floor, pulled out his camera and let the kids operate it. Linthicum followed suit, with a new sense of respect for his son as the teacher and himself as the student.

The third occurrence was a dream that came Linthicum's last night in India. He was stepping over a poor woman in a sari lying on the ground—replaying a very real scene that the group had experienced walking in predawn Calcutta on the way to a 5:45 a.m. Mass at the Missionaries of Charity Mother House. In his dream, the poor woman rose on one elbow and motioned to him. As he leaned down, she put her hand around the back of his neck, pulled him toward her and kissed him. Linthicum immediately awoke, and immediately knew the meaning of the dream. "I had been kissed by India—by the urban poor of India and by the urban poor of the two-thirds world—and I wasn't going home again."

Physically, he returned to his affluent church in Grosse Pointe, outside Detroit, for three years. But as he described his trip in his sermon the following Sunday, one of the members of his congregation leaned over to his wife and said, "We've lost him." Indeed, Linthicum, with the congregation's blessings, began to spend all his time in the church's outreach to the inner-city poor in Detroit. He knew that God was preparing him for a next step. Three years later, his wife, Marlene, was reading a magazine from World Vision, a Christian relief agency for the poor around the globe, and saw a job advertisement for someone to build the agency's work in urban centers. She tossed him the magazine and said, "It sounds like they're describing you." She was right. Linthicum went on to direct World Vision's urban ministries for 11 years.

As striking as was Linthicum's transformation, that of his son, Bob, was even more dramatic. Even after spending a summer at Dayspring a year and a half before, Bob continued his drug-selling and gang involvement. But that was before he experienced Kalighat. On a day when he and others arrived to volunteer, they found the home packed. "The nuns had been going around picking the dying off the streets, and there were so many people that there were no cots left," he recalled. "Mother walked right in and got down on her knees and started helping people." A nun told her, "'Mother, you're too old, you can't do that.' She said, 'Get away from me; I'm loving the person.'" Don and the others in the group knelt down also and began tending to the sick. Bob, taking photos of the scene, was the only one who remained standing.

"All of a sudden one of the nuns grabbed my arm and said, 'Can you help out?' She handed me an orange and said, 'Feed that person.'" Bob looked down and saw a nine-year-old girl on a cot. Her hair was matted and crawling with insects, her skin was like leather and she was lying in feces. "At first I wanted to throw up," he recalled. "But then my eyes met her eyes, and I just fell to the floor." He picked up her emaciated body and began to cuddle and rock her, stroking her head and feeding her bits of orange. "I could not stop looking at her eyes; how sad she was. She was mumbling something in Indian. I stopped one of the nuns and said, 'What is she saying?' The nun said, 'She thinks she's dead and in heaven, and she thinks you're an angel.'"

Bob, the tough gang member and drug dealer, began to bawl. The nun told him the girl also had said he was the only man she had ever met who didn't hurt her. "My heart gave out and I was crying and crying, tears streaming down my face. I realized I needed to compose myself, because I didn't want to make her sadder. I gave her one more long hug, put her down and went outside to get some fresh air. ... When I came back in the cot was empty, and I said to a nun, 'Where's the little girl?' She said, 'The minute you put her down she died.'" Bob was shown to a nearby room that served as a morgue, with a sign over the door saying, "I'm on My Way to Heaven." There he found the girl's body placed on a stone slab. He stared at her corpse for several minutes and finally prayed, "God, I'm yours. I'll go anywhere and do anything." It wasn't an idle vow. After completing high school the following spring, Bob began a two-and-a-half-decade career in Christian missions in a dozen countries around the world as well as serving as a pastor to gang members in Southern California.

Being 'hilarious' with money

Don points out that money is the second-most recurring theme in the Bible after the kingdom of heaven. The way we handle our possessions is central to how we follow Christ. "For God loves a cheerful giver" (2 Corinthians 9:7 NIV) or, as Don says, "a hilarious giver," since the Greek word translated as "cheerful" is the root word of "hilarious."

Here are suggestions Don has developed for hilarious givers:
• Search seriously through the New Testament for passages about money. Underline or highlight them. Thank God for the clarity and inspiring guidance. Many readers will be surprised how many

references there are, and how deeply they challenge unconscious, cultural attitudes about money.

• Think of the Old Testament tithe–the ten percent owed as an offering to God–as a minimum, not a maximum. Richard Foster points out in his book Freedom of Simplicity that Jesus mentions the tithe twice in the New Testament, both times in a negative context, indicating that he considered it insufficient as a true foundation of giving.3

• Cultivate relationships with poor people to develop a stronger sense of the world's need, which cultivates compassion and generosity.

• Write a money autobiography. Each person coming to a Ministry of Money workshop completed one, which included the roles money and possessions played at various stages of the person's life and what emotions they evoked. Such an exercise can be highly revealing.

• Share your money autobiography and your current financial situation openly and fully with at least one other person who is not your spouse. This violates one of our society's greatest taboos. But leaving your money life shrouded in secrecy often breeds fear, shame and inertia. Confiding your complicated emotions and experiences with money to a trusted friend, spiritual advisor or fellowship group can liberate you to move toward trusting, joyful, hilarious giving.

8

Pilgrims' Progress

"For the Lord ... will regard the prayer of the destitute."
–Psalm 102: 16-17

Delighted with the success of the first group pilgrimage, Don made plans for a second in 1983 that would last a month and include stops in Calcutta, Thailand, Hong Kong and Nairobi, Kenya. The cost was $4,200. Meanwhile, Don consulted Henri Nouwen, one of the leading theologians in the United States, on the challenges and rewards of American Christians traveling to poor countries.

Nouwen, a Catholic priest born in the Netherlands, had moved to South America in 1981 to explore the spiritual interdependence of the two American continents after teaching at Notre Dame University and Yale Divinity School. He described a remarkable spirit of thankfulness he found among the poor in Bolivia and Peru in his 18th book, *Gracias!: A Latin American Journal.* "In many of the families I visited nothing was certain, nothing predictable, nothing totally safe," Nouwen concluded. "Maybe there would be food tomorrow, maybe there would be work tomorrow, maybe there would be peace tomorrow. Maybe, maybe not. But whatever is given—money, food, work, a handshake, a smile, a good word, or an embrace—is a reason to rejoice and say *gracias*. What I claim as a right, my friends in Bolivia and Peru received as a gift."

Don met Nouwen in February 1983 when both spoke at a Chicago conference of the Evangelical Covenant Church, a small denomination founded by Swedish immigrants. Nouwen had returned from South America to teach at Harvard Divinity School. Dressed casually in a crewneck sweater, his longish dark hair a sea of unruly curls behind his receding hairline, he mesmerized the audience as he ambled to and fro across the stage, tossing off extempo-

raneous insights about his new sense of call to connect America's
privileged class at Yale and Harvard with the poor of South America.
Don quickly recognized their common interest. Also, Nouwen, in a
restless search for community, was intrigued by Don's relationship
to the Church of the Saviour, whose reputation he knew. When Don
asked Nouwen to speak the following month to the Ministry of
Money board of directors in Washington, D.C., Nouwen quickly
agreed. At the board meeting, Nouwen spoke of visiting the poor in
foreign countries as "reverse mission," so named by the Maryknoll
organization, an American Catholic missionary society that had
hosted Nouwen in Lima, Peru. The phrase suggested that wealthy
North Americans come to South America not to teach and help and
give, but rather to learn and be helped and receive.[1] This struck Don
and the Ministry of Money board members as a precise description
of what they wanted their Third World trips to be. Don knew from
leading his first international trip that participants "broke open" to a
seismic rearrangement of their priorities. The culture shock–the
panic, pain and disorientation unleashed by being in a destitute environment–fostered a sense of helplessness and dependence on others
for survival. Don soon began referring to his Third World trips as
"pilgrimages of reverse mission."

The term also fit snugly with a description by Elizabeth
O'Connor of the COSIGN mission to Thailand. "I feel that it is not
enough for the churches of America to send some of their highly
motivated, educated and sensitized persons to work in the refugee
camps of the world. Those camps exist because in our world 'compassion has been sent into exile.' Compassion is not born of an educated mind alone. It is born of an educated heart as well. If our civ-
ilization is to survive, we have to begin the work of education of the
emotions."

The next stage of Don's collaboration with Nouwen came quickly. Don, Ministry of Money board member Louis Fischer and the
Rev. Frank Alton flew to Peru for a five-day visit in August 1983,
staying at the Maryknoll Center with Nouwen. Alton was a pastor
at Bel Air Presbyterian, a wealthy church in Los Angeles whose
head pastor was Don's former FCA colleague Donn Moomaw and
whose members included Ronald and Nancy Reagan. Alton was
much more interested in the poor of the Third World than in pow-

erful celebrities, having spent a year working with university students in Bogotá, Colombia, and having married a Costa Rican. Don first met Alton at a Ministry of Money workshop at Wellspring in 1978, and they had stayed in touch. When Alton's wife died, Don provided Alton with writings of Nouwen that he hoped would be comforting. Don then arranged for Alton, who had an intense desire to meet Nouwen, to come along on the trip.

Alton was surprised to find that Nouwen was not at all the way he had pictured him. Instead of being monkish and quietly spiritual, Nouwen was high-strung, impatient and occasionally profane. Put off at first, Alton came to the comforting realization that people with deeply spiritual yearnings could be imperfect and rough-edged like himself. Nouwen took the group on a bus ride to Pamplona Alta, a shantytown on the edge of Lima that rose up the side of a dusty, treeless mountain. The bus dumped them off at the bottom and they hiked up to the home of Sophia and Pablo Ossco-Morena and their three children, with whom Nouwen had lived during his previous stay in Lima.[2] Afterward, Alton and Nouwen discussed a vision that both had conceived separately: a "seminary in the slums" that would bring American theology students to a Latin American squatter settlement like Pamplona Alta to temporarily live and study. Nouwen's attention, however, swung to the situation in Nicaragua, where U.S.-supported *contras* were killing innocent civilians in their fight against the elected Marxist Sandinista government. Nouwen felt compelled to arrange a speaking tour in the United States to denounce U.S. involvement. Three years later, having become a regular correspondent of Nouwen's, Alton fulfilled their vision, living for nine years in a Mexico City squatter community where he hosted visits by seminary students and church groups.

Before leaving Lima, Don agreed to line up speaking engagements for Nouwen. When Nouwen returned to the United States, he came to Dayspring in July 1983 to meet with Don and Bill Price, head of the Church of the Saviour's World Peacemakers mission group. Meanwhile, Don's son, Michael, had returned to Washington, D.C., after four years in Colorado where he had been seriously injured in a construction job. Now divorced, Michael had left his two daughters with their mother and was waiting to embark on a new adventure: a Peace Corps assignment in the small African country of

Swaziland. Michael volunteered to chauffeur Nouwen from Dayspring to the Capitol in Washington to meet with U.S. Senator Mark Hatfield. En route Nouwen asked him, "Why are you going to southern Africa when the action is in Latin America?" That evening, after Michael listened to Nouwen speak at Catholic University in Washington, he wrote a letter canceling his Peace Corps appointment. Two weeks later Michael arrived in Nicaragua's capital, Managua, to stay with a Methodist missionary couple whom Nouwen knew.

Nouwen also flew down to Managua and took Michael on a 10-day tour. They drove north over dirt roads, through tropical jungles and beneath volcanic mountains to an area close to *contra*-Sandinista fighting. Nouwen chatted animatedly in Spanish with villagers, peasant farmers, Catholic bishops and high-ranking Sandinista officials. After Nouwen left, Michael stayed on in Managua. The more he saw, the more enraged he became about U.S. policies. In a tightly wound state of agitation and paranoia, he flew home on October 12, 1983, determined to work against U.S. support for the *contras*. Michael broke down and wept when he saw Don awaiting him at the airport gate. "We are overwhelmed with gratitude for your contribution to Mike's unfolding, true sense of call that you have been instrumental in clarifying," Don wrote to Nouwen. A year later, Michael became a paid Third World pilgrimage director for Ministry of Money.

Don and his second group of pilgrims on reverse mission arrived in Nairobi on November 3, 1983. It was late at night, and several dozen child beggars, some with partial limbs or other deformities, accosted the group outside the airport terminal. Ruth Butler, of a suburb of Boston, was surprised at how sternly Don told the group not to give the beggars any money. (Don had adopted Mother Teresa's advice not to give to beggars because they often were under the control or employ of unscrupulous bosses.) A bus deposited the pilgrims at a YMCA in downtown Nairobi. When Ruth and her husband, Frank, saw their small room with two cots and a dim hanging light bulb, they wondered, *What in the world have we gotten ourselves into?* But the next morning's bright sunlight revealed a beautiful city, with a deep blue sky and lush tropical trees and flowers. Attending a Mass at a Catholic church reinforced that sense of beauty, as

Kenyans in bright robes sang and danced down the aisles to the infectious beat of drums.

Don divided the pilgrims into groups of two or three for mission assignments. The Butlers boarded an overcrowded bus headed for the city of Nakuru, about 100 miles north in the wildlife-profuse Rift Valley. Passengers hung from the windows and perched on top, and some clutched chickens or other animals. The passengers smiled at the Butlers, but no one spoke English. The Butlers' initial anxiety gave way to wonder, though, as the bus climbed a beautiful mountain range studded with bright flowering bushes. They then descended into the Rift Valley, where Lake Nakuru, a sanctuary for pink flamingos, opened before them. At the bus depot, an English-speaking social worker escorted them to a one-story hotel constructed of mud blocks with a hole in the bathroom floor for plumbing and the biggest cockroaches the Butlers had ever seen. They quickly learned to shake out their shoes in the morning.

During their two days in Nakuru, the Butlers witnessed the indomitable spirit of poor African women. Since many of the men sought jobs in the city, the women formed trade cooperatives at home. At one cooperative women hand-rolled fibers from hemp plants into twine and then used the twine to weave baskets. The Butlers had never encountered groups of women so enterprising and so seemingly happy. The women sang and laughed together as they worked. The Butlers reached the same conclusion as Henri Nouwen had in South America: that these Kenyans, though abjectly poor, possessed a secret to joy that eluded most Americans. Just as people in the United States expected things to go as they wanted and expressed frustration when they did not, the Kenyans doubted things would go well and so were thrilled when something did. It was unforgettable proof for the Butlers that money doesn't buy happiness and that, in fact, possessions can distract from relationships and simple pleasures that do provide happiness.

Frank (who later served as president of Ministry of Money's board of directors) added to the women's joyfulness by trying his hand at "women's work." He hoisted his pants legs and attempted fumblingly to roll the hemp fibers into twine on his knees. The women giggled at the sight. The social worker informed Frank that the women wondered if he also could breastfeed their babies. On another occasion the social worker walked with the Butlers down a street carrying a heavy gas can in one hand and a pickax in the other. She declined Frank's repeated offers to carry one of the objects, but finally relented. Soon children gathered to gawk at this strange sight of a man bearing a woman's burdens. Irritated at creating a spectacle, the social worker grabbed the pickax back from Frank.

When they returned to Nairobi, the Butlers joined Don and the rest of the group for a foray into the Mathare Valley, one of the most populous squatter settlements in the world. An estimated half million people were packed into a few acres, living in shanty homes the size of packing crates and constructed of pieces of corrugated tin, scrap wood and cardboard. The pilgrims broke into groups to tour various aid projects in the slum. There was no electricity, no running water and no paved roads. Sewage ran down gulleys in the dirt pathways between the houses. Don's group followed a medical missionary to a mud hut where a physical therapist tended a crippled youth. Soon a barefoot boy appeared at the door of the home holding four Cokes for the guests, who were sweaty in the tropical heat. The mother, who had so little, had sent one of her children to spend a week's earnings to give her guests something to drink.

Don thanked God daily for the results of these reverse mission experiments, including Neville Watson's reaction to the generosity of spirit shown by some of the Mathare Valley's inhabitants. "I picked my way through the maze of deprivation to a hut where three of the Taizé Brothers (of a French Protestant monastic order) live their life of 'presence' within the slum," wrote Watson, the Australian lawyer and pastor. "My apprehension vanished in a moment as about a dozen children emerged in the half light and started leaping in the air. They were all over me and, in a moment of spontaneous childishness, I too jumped up and down and shouted, with kids clinging to my arms and legs and whatever else they could grab. ... Brother Dennis took me to meet some of the people of the slum. ... As people responded to him, and he to them, I had that eerie feeling of what it must have been like to walk with Christ in Palestine." (As with Jesus, Brother Dennis' ministry provoked hostility as well as adoration; some slum-dwellers had set fire to his home on several occasions.)

Watson continued, "We returned to the hut where we engaged

in a sing-song amongst 20 or so raucous kids. The rhythm from the drum was easy to pick up so I joined in the singing, making up my own words, and holding a warm, wet retarded child in my lap. ... Then came the moment which to my dying day I will never forget. There came from the side of the room the quiet, clear voice of Dennis: 'We pray for the people of Australia, for Ned and his family,' and from the group came the equally clear and quiet response, 'Jesus, remember them when you come into your kingdom.' ... I thought of Australia luxuriating on its bed of pleasure, stupefied in the euphoria of the America's Cup and completely oblivious to the existence of the Mathare Valley slums. The incongruity of it all came down on me like a ton of bricks and I thought to myself, 'God, if Australia has any hope at all, it will be because of kids like this.'"

After the group flew to Calcutta, Don arranged for it to visit the various facilities of Mother Teresa's Missionaries of Charities. Ruth Butler observed health practices that disturbed her. "How do you warm shivering bodies by 'drying' them off with same wet towel?" she wrote in her journal. "How do you stem the spread of scabies or tuberculosis when you're forced to use a common cup or lotion?" But she also was inspired by the sisters who poured out their lives for unfixable people. Butler noted that a fellow traveler wrote, "Sitting in the chapel of the Sisters of Charity and witnessing their dedicated service throughout the day, I was again brought to a full awareness of the poverty of my own commitment." Butler added, "We were barely beginning to sift through these feelings ... when we were ushered into the presence of Mother Teresa. All of the paradoxes, all the complaints of inefficiency, all the frustrations with the lack of sanitary precautions melt away before this tiny but incredibly powerful woman. ... 'We can do no great things,' she tells us, 'only small ones with great love.' When we ask her what word she has for us to carry home she does not say she needs money for her work, or more hands but, 'Love one another, as Jesus loves us. The world is hungry for love, more hungry than for bread. ... Any work of love brings a person face to face with God.'"

Another pilgrim, Colet Van Der Ven of the Netherlands, picked a poem by Jean Vanier of L'Arche to describe her experience:

"Everywhere around us we see two worlds

    The world of misery
    The world of those who wait
    The world of those trying to get out
Then the other world
    The world of riches
    The world of those shut up
    In harshness and security
Between these two worlds
    A huge wall
    Which prevents direct contact
    Meeting, communion–
    Sometimes there may be
    Exchanges
    But never any direct contact
The comfortable throw money
    Or things
    Over the wall
    But the last thing
    They want
    Is to see or touch.
They send roses
    They don't give them
    They throw them
    Over the wall ..."[3]

Van Der Ven added her own postscript:

"We didn't have the courage to climb the wall carrying our roses with us but we at least tried to hand them over the wall instead of sending or throwing them.

    The first step in a long journey
    Nothing less
    Nothing more."

The trip reconfirmed for Don that Calcutta would always make a deep impression on his Third World pilgrims. But he realized that few could afford the time and cost of such lengthy travel. Don hit upon Haiti as a closer, more affordable alternative. Mother Teresa had declared Cité Soleil, a slum in the capital of Port-au-Prince, the worst in the world. Don made an exploratory trip that confirmed

Cité Soleil was at least as destitute as the slums of Calcutta. The Missionaries of Charity operated facilities in Port-au-Prince similar to those in Calcutta, including a Home for the Destitute and Dying and an orphanage. Pilgrims could get to Haiti in one day from various parts of the United States for an $800 weeklong trip, a fifth the cost of a month-long pilgrimage. Don arranged for Ministry of Money's third pilgrimage of reverse mission to take place in Haiti from February 10 to 18, 1984.

Don arranged for his son, Michael, to travel to Port-au-Prince in advance and stay a month with three brothers of the Missionaries of Charity order. The brothers lived in a tiny concrete-block house on the edge of Cité Soleil with no electricity and no running water. The brothers used an outhouse for a toilet and showered by pouring a bucket of water over their heads. They lodged Michael behind their house in a six-foot-by-six-foot cement shed with a tin roof that previously had stored charcoal. Michael closed the door each night to keep out insects and sweltered on a reed mat amid the barking of dogs and cackling of chickens. By day he followed the brothers through their daily tasks, helping at the orphanage and the Home for the Destitute and Dying. When the pilgrimage group arrived from the United States, Michael joined them at a missionary guest house, which he found a luxurious change.

As the plane descended over the island, Don pointed out the border of Haiti and the Dominican Republic–the Haitian side largely stripped of vegetation, the Dominican side green with lush growth. The pilgrims found the Port-au-Prince airport small, run-down and chaotic. Riding into Port-au-Prince, they observed women walking along the roadside in blouses and skirts carrying buckets of water, produce or laundry on their heads, and men in T-shirts and jeans pulling carts. Haitians knocked on the van windows at stops, asking in hand motions to be given something to eat.

Don led the group on a tour of Cité Soleil the following day. The slum was built on top of a former garbage dump with no trees, no bushes, no electricity and no running water except the sewage running through ditches dug in the earth. Built of corrugated tin, cardboard and other discarded materials, the homes were so small that some families took turns sleeping for lack of floor space. One toddler, dressed only in a T-shirt, squatted to urinate on the ground outside his home, putting his hands over his eyes to create a sense of privacy. The pilgrims left the slum feeling overwhelmed and depressed.

When the pilgrims chose between various volunteer assignments at Missionaries of Charity facilities, the Rev. Vicky Curtiss of a Presbyterian church in inner-city Cleveland picked San Fil, the Home for the Destitute and Dying. Just as in Calcutta, the plain concrete-block building housed rows of emaciated women on cots. Curtiss joined the volunteers who fed them, rubbed them with lotion and occasionally entertained them with songs. Despite a bias against the rich, Curtiss found herself bonding with "Mary," Don's Christ House benefactor from California who was also a first-time pilgrim, as they tended the women and sang duets of "Frere Jacques." Mary described her experience: "In the poverty of the poorest of the poor I was made the richest of the rich. ... Hands. I never knew what they were for as long as they were covered with rings and lotions. Now, for the first time, I see my hands as being gifts from God because they have been used to heal, to soothe, to bind up [pus-filled], ulcerated feet with the skin ripped off and toes hanging by a few strands of ligament and muscle. Thank God for hands, and thank God for arms, and thank God for lips and eyes–all of which speak one word so sweetly. And that word is love."

Don had invited and paid pilgrimage costs for Lynda Stanback, a resident of one of the Church of the Saviour's subsidized apartment buildings. "I spent many hours watching my neighbors," she wrote later. "Each morning this woman came out of her hut to start the day. First she washed her dishes, then she washed herself, then her children, and then she washed her clothes. She did all this in the same small tub of water. After she was through she gave the water to a neighbor to start the cycle all over again. Just two weeks before the start of this trip, my doctor told me I needed to drink more water; I told her I didn't like the taste of water. Life is so weird. I can drink water whenever I like and I don't–and the poor in Haiti are dying for lack of it. Each night I pray for the people of Haiti."

Vicky Curtiss admired the compassion Don showed for the Haitian poor, as well as his liveliness and laughter. Don's forcefulness also impressed her. Don told the group to leave their cameras in their rooms, both because the Missionaries of Charity generally did not want picture-taking and because Don wanted people to experience the poor directly, not from behind a lens. One group member repeatedly ignored the rule, along with other commitments pilgrims had pledged to uphold, and Don asked Curtiss to be present when he confronted the man. Curtiss was surprised to see Don back the man against a palm tree and ream him out.

During the next 15 years until he reached the age of 74, Don organized, and usually led, more than 90 pilgrimages to Haiti, Thailand, the Philippines, Kenya, Sudan, Mexico, Nicaragua, Egypt, Bosnia, Kosovo, Jordan and Palestine. He loved these experiences Just as in his years following college, his pilgrimage role was as a coach and teacher, imparting hands-on lessons in Christian compassion rather than athletic skills. The adventure of seeing so many exotic places; the excitement of improvising arrangements in countries where telephones, transportation and accommodations often did not work; the deepening that attended working among the poorest of the poor; and the thrill of witnessing growth in so many pilgrims confirmed for Don that this was God's true call for his life.

Pilgrimage co-leaders included his wife, Gloria, whose availability increased after she stopped working as a nurse in 1986; his son, Michael, who became a Ministry of Money staff member in 1985; and a succession of other staff members whom Don hired, along with volunteer pilgrimage veterans like the Butlers. The groups followed a similar daily format for most of the trips, adopted with advice of the Missionaries of Charity, who advised limiting the pilgrims' daily work time with indigents to three hours to prevent physical and emotional exhaustion.

The typical day started with devotions at 7:30 a.m. After breakfast, pilgrims left for their work stations. Three hours later they returned to the YMCA or hotel, dirty, tired and emotionally drained. After lunch and a brief rest, the pilgrims broke into small groups to help each other process what they had experienced in the morning, after which they traveled together to a site that offered perspective on the country's situation, such as an art gallery, U.S. consulate or office of a local government official. Returning mid-afternoon, they relaxed and ate dinner at 6 p.m. At 8 p.m., a local speaker came to offer additional information about the country. In Haiti this would occasionally be Claudette Werleigh, the minister of foreign affairs, whom Don met on an early trip after calling her office for an appointment. Haiti pilgrimages concluded with a day of silence and group sharing, while month-long pilgrimages had a similar wrap-up lasting two days at a retreat facility.

Don scheduled pilgrimages to Calcutta for late November and early December, a time when Mother Teresa was almost always there to hold a retreat with her Calcutta sisters. His relationship with the Missionaries of Charity expanded to include Washington, D.C., where he volunteered once a week in their house for AIDS patients and the homeless. Don also served as an international mailman for thie sisters, carrying medicines, crucifixes, Bibles, personal letters and documents with him to and from India or Haiti.

The sisters in Calcutta and Washington kept Don apprised of Mother Teresa's travel schedule, and he arranged to see her at receptions during her visits to Washington and New York. Once Don took along "Mary," his California benefactor, whom he introduced to Mother as his "wheelbarrow lady"—a reference to Mary's role in rescuing the homeless from the streets of Washington through funding Christ House, just as Mother Teresa had rescued her first indigent person from the streets of Calcutta with a wheelbarrow. Mother looked warmly at Mary and told her, "Just keep on loving, my dear. Just keep on loving." Don later bought Mary a small replica of a wheelbarrow, which she installed on her living room mantle as a favorite keepsake.

More than 900 people went on Don's pilgrimages. Despite their visits to Third World slums and other places of potential danger, none were ever attacked or injured—a remarkable record that Don ascribed to divine mercy. Few of these pilgrims returned unmoved and unchanged. They were all encouraged to keep journals of their experience. Here is what some said in their journals or in interviews.

1983: Kenya-India-Thailand

Mary Hillas, hospice chaplain from Maine: "The pilgrimage has ... helped me see that the diseases of the Third World (the diseases of poverty)—starvation, malnutrition, leprosy, prolapsed uteruses—are related to the diseases of the First World (the diseases of affluence)—hypertension, cancer, coronaries, alienation, loneliness—and that this relationship is of critical importance in the struggle for world peace. Henry Okullu, the Anglican bishop of Kenya, says that there will be no peace while millions in Africa die of hunger and millions in North America die of overeating."

1984: Calcutta

Ken Morton, a college professor from Grosse Pointe Woods, Michigan: "I was feeding a withered, brown old man with a gray stubble beard. He was too weak to sit up and was covered with a blanket. I accidentally spilled a few grains of rice onto his neck. At first I didn't want to retrieve the rice because I didn't want to risk touching him. After some time, however, I realized that the rice was probably uncomfortable for him and that the only thing to do was to remove it with my own fingers. As soon as I touched him, all Heaven broke loose. He began to speak, smile and wiggle his head. ... Though I couldn't understand his words, the body language was unmistakable: he was overwhelmed with the simple joy of a kind human touch. The feeding continued for some time–interspersed with numerous outbursts of joy from him. Somewhere during this time something surprising happened to me. A big, childish irrepressible grin came over my face. I had become infected with his joy. It was a joy so deep that I had almost forgotten that such feelings even existed. ... A worker nearby suggested that ... these people frequently have dry, painful skin (dehydration is, I believe, one of the final stages of starvation) and that they liked to be rubbed with soothing lotion. When I pulled back the blanket from the old man's body to begin rubbing the lotion, I was shocked by the view. His body looked like the pictures of Jews who had been dumped into mass burial trenches in Nazi Germany. As I rubbed his chest, arms and legs he seemed to be in 'seventh heaven.' He began to stroke my arms in return, and I was surprised at how much strength he could muster with the withered muscles. Eventually he was satisfied; he curled up contentedly like a baby and went to sleep. ... I owe him a lot because he reawakened my thirst for Joy."

1985: Mexico, Nicaragua

Michael McClanen and a pilgrimage group that he co-led with Don visited a village in northern Nicaragua near the *contra*-Sandinista war zone. The settlement of 250 people had adobe houses and horses tied up in front of stores. Villagers in cowboy hats greeted the Americans warmly and treated them to a lunch of beans and rice. As the Americans prepared to leave, one villager proposed they play an international game of baseball, the Americans against the Nicaraguans, on the village's sandlot field. The game proceeded amicably until Michael hit a booming fly ball over an outfielder and into the jungle beyond. He ran around the bases whooping in glee until he noticed glum looks on the faces of the Nicaraguan players. Everyone joined the hunt for the ball, but to no avail. Michael had lost the only baseball the villagers possessed.

1985: Sudan, Kenya, India

Sandy Huffaker, a prize-winning cartoonist and illustrator from Princeton, New Jersey, said of visiting a Sudanese camp for refugees who had fled violence in neighboring Chad: "We just played with kids all day. Love and laughter flowing from kids to us and back again. Serious adults became silly little kids! Lots of hugs and hand-holding—I had about 40 hands held at once. I walked on my hands and the kids went nuts—then after, a little boy tugged at me and held out his hand full of change I had dropped. Two others dusted my rear. Love explodes everywhere! ... The World Vision people said we turned the camp 'upside down' including the Muslim help. 'We will never be the same,' said Jen (the head). It was as if these suffering kids were pent up with joy waiting to be released. ... Arnie (World Vision) said we taught him that maybe they had become so toughened by dealing with the 'nuts and bolts' of the camp operation that they may have lost sight of something—joy and mutual humanity. So maybe we did something good in a totally spontaneous, spiritual way. ... In a sense it was unfair of us to receive this joy—the 'nuts and bolts' people earned it. We were just passing through."

Later in Calcutta: "After a few days of being around Mother Teresa, seeing her work and hearing about her from others, I am convinced she is the saint she is supposed to be. She sends herself and her sisters to very dangerous missions, but her feeling is 'so what if they died and go to be with Jesus.' The way she lives her life is almost a literal copy of Christ's life: She refuses dainty morsels at the homes of the rich, rides the crowded public transportation here, won't shut windows to keep out the street noise of Calcutta during Mass, has no financial advisers–keeps everything in her heart and head and calls people at all hours with her inspirations. Again she repeats the oft-told line of 'live for the day–the past is gone and we don't know of the future.' ... She doesn't push anyone to give up everything or do more than they can comfortably do and keeps stressing that our families and loved ones back home are what are most important. She operates like Don McClanen–on instructions from the Spirit as opposed to man-made logic–she moves when she feels moved. She has no real home, and no limousines will meet her in New York next month. She will stay with her sisters, and Air India will fly her free."[4]

1985: Kenya

Leslie Hawke, a New York business executive, described the aftermath of working in a Sudan refugee camp and visiting the Mathare Valley in Nairobi: "Our last two days in Africa were spent at Amboseli Game Park. ... Standing in line to get our room assign-ment I eyed a sumptuous-looking buffet through the double doors of the vaulted dining room. It was a lovely lodge–the traditional porches and stone fireplaces, lots of exposed beams and rows of win-dows overlooking grazing elephants on the savannah and Mount Kilimanjaro beyond. ... The ambiance [of the dining room] was much like a southern American country club–polite, well-groomed [Africans] stood by as animated, well-groomed Caucasians chattered to each other, the sound of silverware on china forming a kind of pleasant background tinkle. ...

"I sat down, ordered a cold beer ... and began to eat–my first fresh vegetables in two weeks. But as I put the first forkfuls in my mouth, I realized I was on the verge of sobbing. 'Don't be a fool,' I told myself and continued eating. My eyes welled up with tears. ... I tried to casually excuse myself from the table and headed toward the outdoors, my face losing its composure along the way. ... It wasn't just all that food. It wasn't even the unconsciousness of it. There was something ugly in that room. There was a power structure embodied in that room that ran the world. I wandered around aimlessly near the edge of the lodge property sobbing. ... And then I laughed, remembering how worried I'd been about getting weepy in a refugee camp. Who'd have thought I'd lose it in a game preserve? It's not poverty and suffering that are hideous–it's the ignorance, self-satisfaction and spiritual poverty of those of us born into the ruling class."

1987: Haiti

Cara Taylor, a mother and community volunteer from Sacramento, California: "In the first ward of dying and destitute people [at San Fil, the Missionaries of Charity facility], I found myself appalled. ... I cringed touching the first thin hand I shook. What kind of germs were on this hand that had touched the filth in the slums year after year until the body could no longer function and they knocked on the Missionaries of Charity door? ... I was counting the minutes until we could complete the tour of their facility and return to the bus. ... How did I come here? How could I have possibly thought I was going to be of help? I must be a glutton for punishment. No one else I knew did this sort of thing. I encouraged [my husband] Paul to come on this trip–it was all my fault we were here!"

Two days later: "I carefully sat down on the foot of a woman's bed. Certainly didn't want to get near the head because everyone was constantly coughing and spitting up from tuberculosis or other dire diseases. Didn't want to sit in the middle of the bed because many couldn't control their bladders. A woman smiled and began talking in Creole. ... I noticed a group of stones on one bed. The woman motioned me to sit down and play a game similar to jacks. Throw one stone up in the air while trying to pick up the other stones. This was fun until I dropped one on the floor. I could now tell why the odor in this room was unbearable. The floor hadn't been cleaned yet."

The next day: "I made my way from bed to bed and was eagerly greeted by smiles and pointing to either finger or toe nails. The smell of the [fingernail polish I had brought] was a welcome relief to the stench in the hot room. Soon I forgot about the odors as I intently focused on each hand and foot. While applying polish I reflected on Christ's hands and feet as he was on the cross. Suddenly dry, cracked feet, some without toes, looked beautiful. ... I was in the manicure/pedicure business for about an hour before a dying woman grabbed my arm as I was about to leave her bed. She wanted me to stay and hold her hand. I was surprised at the strength in her cold hand as she clung tightly to my arm. She pointed to her closely braided hair and motioned to me to get a comb. ... It took me an hour to unwind all the braids as they were so matted. The woman loved it and would close her eyes. When I paused thinking she was asleep, she would reach up and move my hand. I massaged her scalp. ... Two days ago I didn't even want to touch this woman and now she was giving me such joy looking at her contented face."

The next day: "One moaning woman spied my lotion bottle and motioned me to come over. I remembered seeing pictures of starving women in Africa and this woman looked the same. Her leg fit between the circle of my thumb and finger. ... I gathered my courage and gently put the lotion over her body. She took my hand and pressed it deeply into her stomach, motioning me to continue. I was terrified her request would cause some vital organ to be ruptured. However, her smile and whispered words, 'bon, bon,' assured me that it felt good. ... At the end of the massage the woman looked up through her beautiful eyes surrounded by curling eyelashes and whispered, 'Merci.' I said, 'Merci' in reply, for this woman had removed my fear and repulsion of her body and put in place a deep love."

The final day: "I entered the ward with 'Bonjou!' The women that could respond waved and smiled back. Yes, I was greeting friends. ... I had learned among many lessons this week not to plan an agenda but rather go and see what surprises God had in store for me. ... Their goodbye response, waves and smiles, I will always remember."

Outside, "a jeep arrived for its twice-a-week pickup of bodies. I looked up just as two men, one grabbing a nude, dead woman's legs and the other grabbing her arms, threw her onto the bodies in the jeep. I wanted to cry out, 'Stop, handle her gently, she is a very special, beautiful woman,' but then I realized she was with God and that was just her body which would soon decay. ... I believe that 'eye surgery' was performed on me by the numerous people I met during the ten days. Unlike when I arrived, I left Haiti seeing a city of joy and the beauty of creation around me. I now realize that joy is not the absence of pain but rather seeing the presence of God in all persons, places and things."

Before Taylor left Haiti, Don suggested to her that she might hear a new call from God when she returned to the United States. Shortly afterward, a Sacramento nonprofit organization asked Taylor to open and direct a residence for homeless people with AIDS. Following a seven-day silent retreat at Dayspring hosted by Don and Gloria, Taylor accepted the call, realizing that God had used the Haiti trip to remove her fear of sickness and death. Her husband, Paul, later served as a Ministry of Money board president.

1991: Calcutta

Sharon Lukens of Gig Harbor, Washington: "I was convinced ... that the pilgrimage had been designed to match Dante's description of the descent into hell. ... I stepped out of the plane into a dense smog/fog through which orange neon letters glowed, 'Calcutta.' I remember my panic as I thought, *I can't breathe here.* God bless [pilgrimage leader] Dale [Stitt]; he led us through the chaos of the airport and bundled us into two taxis which sped off into the night. I was in the one with Mary Fran and Fletcher, and as we hurtled through the dark fog in the mad ballet of Calcutta traffic, Mary Fran kept shouting at the driver to slow down for God's sake! I was still trying to catch my breath in the sweaty, smoky, thickly scented night when suddenly, out of the dark, popped a glittering, brightly colored shrine of sorts, brilliantly lit with hundreds of white light bulbs. Music blared as we roared by back into the darkness. What was that? The driver was intent on his invisible race and I was left to wonder at the midnight festival we had witnessed in the darkness. Our taxi brushed against the car next to us as we sped and careened wildly from side to side. Mary Fran screamed and Fletcher grabbed onto the seat. Just then, another brilliantly lit scene flashed by the window. Was it the same festival? Another deity being honored? Were we in the city? In the countryside? On the planet earth?

"Thirty nerve-wracking minutes later, Mary Fran's cries had muted into her mumbled conviction that we were being kidnapped, soon to be sold into white slavery. Fletcher had stopped repeating the words, 'Fairlawn Hotel?' and we were now winding through darkened streets, obviously in the city, but at the mercy of our silent, driven driver. I became aware of my exhaustion, of my vulnerability and of my entry into another level of broken-openness for which I no longer had any defense. I slumped into my corner of the back seat, sinking into surrender, when the taxi slowed to a halt. We had come to a dead end, in a courtyard of some sort, and as I cautiously got out of the car, I saw the dim outline of a figure standing in the dark. I heard the familiar 'heh, heh' and followed it into the safety of your welcoming embrace. You [Don], standing there, chuckling in the dark, offering a matter-of-fact welcome in the midst of the deepest unknown, is the image that captures the essence of who you are to me. ... Finding a friend in the dark when utterly lost is theology I understand."

1993: Calcutta

Don Remmey of Meadowbrook, Pennsylvania, owner of a small manufacturing company, recalls Don on pilgrimage as both sensitive and tough. Remmey and other pilgrims struggled with the shock of witnessing humanity in utter deprivation; one pilgrim sobbed throughout an afternoon debriefing session. Don gently encouraged and reassured them. Don also showed his vulnerability by confessing regret over his occasional impatience and lack of understanding toward pilgrims in earlier years, when he had been less secure as a leader in difficult Third World circumstances. Remmey noticed Don's toughness in his dealings with taxi drivers, bargaining down the driver's fare even though to Remmey the driver appeared impoverished and in need of whatever income he could obtain. Don noticed his surprise and, with a chuckle, explained, "Hey, we're in Calcutta; that's what you have to do." The Missionaries of Charity and others had told Don that bargaining was part of Indian culture and foreigners who did not engage in this practice lost respect.

Various Years: Haiti

Bryan Sirchio of Madison, Wisconsin (a singer-songwriter who worked with Don at Ministry of Money in the 1990s and later in Don's Harvest Time ministry): "Don was driving a van full of people and he saw two Haitian guys fighting on the edge of a cliff. One guy was prevailing over the other and he picked up a large rock and was about to crush the guy. Don screeched the van to a halt and ran up behind the guy with the stone and grabbed him in a bear hug so that he couldn't throw it. ... We can talk 'blessed are the peacemakers' till we're blue in the face. He's the one who, like that, stops the van and jumps out. The guy could have easily turned and crushed Don's head. But it was just very clear to him at that moment that someone had to prevent this killing."[5]

Sirchio also recalled: "One time [at San Fil] the nuns asked me to give a haircut to this guy. By that time I had started to speak Creole some, and we were having a conversation. ... I asked him if he thought I was rich. And his response to me was, 'How many times a week do you eat?' It was one of those moments when the world just stops. I didn't say anything and he said, 'Well, you mean you eat every day?' I said, 'Yeah.' He said, 'Oh, well, you're rich.'

1995: Haiti

Rosemary Feerick, a religion teacher at a Catholic high school in Maryland, recalled Don driving her pilgrimage group in a van from Port-au-Prince toward Jacmel, a picturesque beach town on the south coast. The group reached a river where the bridge had washed out. Feerick assumed Don would turn the vehicle around and head back to Port-au-Prince. Instead, Don located a "guide" whom he paid to walk through the river in front of the van to assure they would not hit big rocks or holes. The crossing was successful. "It was classic Don," Feerick said. "Where most people would have turned around, he got creative."

Feerick also recalled Don's cheerful questioning of the pilgrims about their intestinal status. "Anyone loose or stopped up?" he asked after each morning's devotion.

1990s: Haiti

Bob Hadley, an attorney from Dayton, Ohio, became a Ministry of Money board member and frequent pilgrimage co-leader with Don. On one trip Hadley drove with Don to Jacmel in search of an American collector of Haitian art. After they located the collector's French provincial house, Don entered the open back gate and yelled for the man. Soon the collector appeared in his underwear. Don coolly asked if he would mind hosting a group of 11 to look at his art. The man said no, and the pilgrims had a lovely time at the collector's house that evening.

1999: Haiti

Rosemary Williams, director of Ministry of Money's Women's Perspective, an affiliated ministry that offered information, workshops and pilgrimages specially for women, led her first pilgrimage to Haiti for women only. Don, not on the trip, became her touchstone when unplanned difficulties arose. Williams and her small group flew into Cap-Haitien on the north coast, where she had reserved a rental van to drive to another town where they would work at a Catholic orphanage. A clerk at the car rental agency told her no vehicles were left. On a previous pilgrimage to Haiti, Williams had witnessed Don insist that guards at the gate of a government building allow them to enter. The guards, who spoke only Creole, signaled that Don's group should go to another gate, but Don kept saying that they needed to enter there, his hands gesturing more and more furiously. Finally the guards shrugged and allowed the group to enter. In another situation, Don parked a car in an illegal space and when the group returned they found that police had lifted it onto a truck, about to drive away. Don waved furiously and shouted, "You can't take that car; I need that car!" *Is he going to get arrested?* Williams wondered. After a few minutes of stalemate, down came the truck's ramp and off came the car.

Inspired by these memories, Williams demanded to see the rental agency's manager. The manager knew only a few words of English, but Williams kept insisting on her need for a vehicle with frenetic arm-waving. Finally, she went behind his desk, grabbed his arm and told him she was taking him to lunch. After the women and manager had dined together, Williams returned with him to the office and told him she would wait there until he produced a vehicle. By 4 p.m. she had two cars.

"Don has an enormous faith that God will win out in the end, and he has the perseverance and determination to stay with something till it works out," Williams said.

Justice

When Don insists that working for "justice" is a key part of following Jesus, some bristle. They see the term as a cover for political policies that take money from those who have worked hard for it and give it to those who have not. In the true Christian sense, however, justice is not about keeping what is rightfully ours, Michael Gorman points out in his book *Reading Paul.* God's justice, related to the word "justification," is God's granting us what we don't deserve and saving us when we don't merit salvation. If we imitate Jesus, we will practice this kind of self-sacrificing justice rather than a me-centered one.

One strong argument for Christian justice—making the world more "fair" for all people—is the number 26,000. That is how many children under the age of five die each day of largely treatable and preventable causes.[6] Having seen people starving in many of the world's poorest areas, Don feels this number deeply. He believes that Christians are being called to reform the political and economic systems that allow this tsunami of preventable deaths. As Theodore Jennings Jr. writes in his book *Good News to the Poor,* "The earth, reeling as it is, produces more than enough food to feed plentifully every man, woman and child on the planet. There is enough food; yet, our economic system produces murderous scarcity. A few have more than they can consume, so much that garbage disposal is a critical problem, while millions perish in sight of plenty. One nation, containing a tiny fraction of the earth's population (the majority of whom think of themselves as Christians), consumes half the earth's resources, yet it still manages not to feed its own hungry."

Marian Wright Edelman, founder and president of Children's Defense Fund, agonizes over U.S. social disparities in her book *The*

Sea Is So Wide and My Boat is so Small–Charting a Course for the Next Generation. "In the first decade of a new century, our nation and world have veered alarmingly off-track and become less safe, less just, more precarious and Balkanized," she says. She points out that the United States ranks first among the industrialized nations in gross national product and amount of health expenditures, yet ranks 25th in rate of infant mortality and dead last in rate of child poverty. The United States also ranks No. 1 in the number of incarcerated people. Looking more widely, "the net worth of the world's 946 billionaires, most Americans, exceeds the combined gross domestic product of 138 countries with a combined population of nearly two billion people ... Why can't the greedy find a way to ensure a minimal safety net for human beings while earning generous, rather than grossly excessive, profits?"

To reframe the question "Isn't it wonderful what Mother Teresa did?" to "Why are Mother Teresas necessary?" leads American Christians to take a hard look at the lethal poverty issues that affect the majority of the world's citizens. Biblical passages such as the 25th chapter of Matthew (in which Jesus judges people at the end of time according to how they responded to the hungry and destitute) and the 16th chapter of Luke also prompt reflection. The Luke passage describes how a rich man goes to hell because during his life he lived sumptuously while ignoring a hungry, sore-ridden beggar who lay at his gate.

In the face of such need, many Christians respond with charitable contributions through their churches and through relief agencies. The next step is to think about how to change systems to prevent the hunger and destitution in the first place. For example, the United States has offered food aid to countries struggling to feed their people, but has insisted that the food be purchased in America and be shipped to the recipient country. This produces economic benefits for American farmers (and political benefits for their congressional representatives), but undercuts agricultural development in the recipient countries. How can this be altered to become more just? Walter Brueggemann suggests, "Justice is to sort out what belongs to whom, and to return it to them."[7]

Bryan Sirchio, Don's ministry colleague, met a dying man at a Missionaries of Charity home in Haiti. "Tell me, are you a

Christian?" the man said. Sirchio answered, "Yes." The man asked, "Does God love you more than me?" "Of course not," Sirchio answered. Finally the man asked, "Then why am I starving and dying, and you're not?" Sirchio had no answer. But after a week of struggling with that justice question, Sirchio pledged to the man, "I will make my life a response to your question." While the answers to that question are often complex, Don's trips succeeded in prompting many pilgrims to think and respond in new ways.

9

Warn-torn Lands

"Your message is like a fire burning deep within me."
–Jeremiah 20:9

Don planned and led as many as five pilgrimages and six basic money workshops a year during the 1980s and 1990s. Annual events also included "advanced money workshops," led by major Christian thinkers and activists whom Don recruited. Among these were Richard Foster, Walter Brueggemann, Millard Fuller, Jim Wallis and John Haughey.

Don called Foster, a Quaker associate professor of theology and writer in residence at Friends University in Wichita, Kansas, after reading his 1981 book *Freedom of Simplicity*, which dealt with some of the themes central to Ministry of Money. Foster also had written a 1978 book called *Celebration of Discipline* that was on its way to selling more than one million copies and being listed by *Christianity Today* magazine as one of the top ten Christian books of the 20th century.[1] Foster accepted Don's invitation to lead a workshop at Wellspring in May 1982.

Foster had learned about Don's church a decade earlier. A young pastor at the time, Foster was disillusioned by his small, dysfunctional congregation in Southern California and considered leaving ministry altogether. When he and his wife, Carolynn, came to Washington, D.C., for a conference, they stopped by the Potter's House one evening hoping to catch Gordon Cosby, whom they had read about in Elizabeth O'Connor's books. Cosby listened to their tales of woe, including Carolynn's distress over Richard's low salary. Cosby offered only one piece of advice: "You've got to go back and ask your church to double your salary." Foster didn't follow the advice, but Cosby's point made a deep impression on him. He realized that staying in ministry for the long haul would require that he be practical as well as "spiritual." He returned to California with new hope and energy.

At the time of the Ministry of Money workshop, Foster was 40 years old with a close-cropped beard and warm smile. He adroitly drew out participants' individual stories with his empathetic manner and wove from them his central point: that gratitude was the fitting and needful response to what each had been given. He also inspired a sense of lightheartedness, at one point leading the group in a Shaker dance. He brought his 11-year-old son, Joel, with him, and their mutual affection was evident as Foster frequently draped an arm over the child's shoulders.

Impressed with Don's ministry, Foster returned to Wellspring in 1983 to lead another money workshop. He liked Don's approach to helping the wealthy think through their faith-and-money issues, which he did not see taking place elsewhere on the American church landscape. Don also provided Foster with a key concept for a book Foster was formulating on the contemporary relevance of ancient monastic vows. As Foster wrote in the acknowledgements of his 1985 book *The Challenge of the Disciplined Life: Christian Reflections on Money, Sex & Power*, "It was through Don that I first saw the connection between the money-sex-power issue and the monastic vows; I am indebted to him."

After admiring some of Walter Brueggemann's books, Don recruited Brueggemann to lead a workshop in September 1984. Brueggemann, one of the nation's top Old Testament scholars, taught at Eden Theological Seminary in St. Louis and later at Columbia Theological Seminary in Atlanta. Don was drawn to his 1978 book, *The Prophetic Imagination*, in which Brueggemann wrote, "The contemporary American church is so largely enculturated to the American ethos of consumerism that it has little power to believe or to act."[2] In person, Brueggemann was an impassioned speaker. The contortions of his bearded face and intensity of his dark piercing eyes dramatized his biblical call for justice for the poor and oppressed. He was steeped in the Old Testament accounts of the Hebrew slaves' suffering in Egypt and the post-Davidic prophets thundering against the evils of their political and religious establish-

ments, and saw American materialism as a similar cultural degrada-
tion.

Brueggemann wrote to Don after the retreat that he regarded
Ministry of Money "as a distinctive and urgent model for faith
around the questions that are now facing American Christians. ... We
do not know how affluent Christians are to be obedient, or we do
know yet shrink from it. I know of no other place where those questions are being raised and faced with such discipline and honesty as
they are in this ministry."

Don kept up a steady correspondence with Brueggemann thereafter, and recruited him to lead three more workshops, including one
in London when Brueggemann was there on sabbatical in 1991.
Their friendship grew from athletics as well as theology.
Brueggemann, like Don, was a sports fan. He was born in Nebraska,
and he and Don both cheered for the University of Nebraska football team coached by Tom Osborne, a friend of Don's from
Fellowship of Christian Athletes days. Also, as a St. Louis resident,
Brueggemann loved the Cardinals baseball team. Don's friendship
with former Cardinals executive Branch Rickey gave Don a special
distinction in Brueggemann's eyes. Books on sports figures of mutual interest often accompanied Don's letters to Brueggemann.

In January 1989, Don lined up Millard Fuller, who later founded
Habitat for Humanity, to lead an advanced workshop on
"Simplification of Life." Don had met Fuller at a Faith at Work conference in New York in 1966. Fuller, a tall, thin, congenial man with
an Alabama drawl, told his remarkable story at the conference. He
had made a fortune from a mail-order business he started in college
with a friend, but his affluent lifestyle pulled him away from the values of his church upbringing. In 1965, his wife, Linda, announced
she did not love him anymore and was leaving. He followed her to
New York and they decided to try a new start by selling everything
they had, giving away the proceeds and committing their lives to
whatever God had in mind for them. Millard took a job for two
years as a development officer for Tougaloo College, a historically
black school in Mississippi.

In 1967, the Fullers moved to Koinonia Farms near Americus,
Georgia, a communal experiment in racial integration in the still-
segregated South.[3] The families at Koinonia persisted in the face of

unrelenting hostility from neighbors, which included firebombs, shootings, death threats, vandalism, excommunication from churches and economic boycotts.[4] Millard visited Don at Dayspring in 1968, shortly after Martin Luther King's assassination, bringing with him an African-American friend from Koinonia. They spoke to a local race-relations group in which Don participated.

Millard then invited Don and Gloria to visit Koinonia. Don walked into a gas station in Americus, Georgia, near the farm and asked a white attendant for directions. The man responded, "Yeah, I'll tell you how to get to Koinonia." He walked over to a window ledge, picked up a baseball bat and walked menacingly toward Don. As Don backed out the door and toward the car, Gloria saw what was happening and yelled, "What do you think you're doing? You ought to be ashamed of yourself!" The attendant sheepishly lowered his bat and the McClanens drove off quickly. At Koinonia, they slept in a cottage whose bedroom still displayed bullet holes from a drive-by attack. Gloria had trouble sleeping, but no disturbance occurred during their one-night stay. They left with a deep appreciation for the Fullers' work on behalf of social justice.

Don and Millard–united by their faith, commitment to racial reconciliation and conviction that money attitudes were key to Christian growth–continued a friendly correspondence from that time on. The Fullers moved to Africa for three years, then moved back to Koinonia Farms in 1976, where they started Habitat for Humanity. The organization, using volunteer labor to construct dwellings for low-income people, is now one of the largest builders of homes in the world, with more than 250,000 completed in more than 90 countries.[5] In 2005, Millard left Habitat and founded the Fuller Center for Housing.

Don recruited Jim Wallis, co-founder of the Sojourners community and magazine in Washington, D.C., to lead a "Money and Justice" workshop in October 1989. Sojourners had existed since 1971, when Wallis, Joe Roos and other seminary students at Trinity Evangelical Divinity School in Deerfield, Illinois, were prompted by the Vietnam War to create a Christian magazine advocating peace and social justice. In 1975, Wallis and others felt called to move into an inner-city neighborhood in Washington, D.C.[6] In the following decades the movement broadened into a national network of progressive Christians opposing war and advocating for the poor, and Wallis became a well-known speaker and a best-selling book author.

Don crossed paths with Wallis frequently, especially since Gordon Cosby was Wallis's spiritual director. At one point Cosby mentioned to Don that Wallis needed a place to get away and do some writing. Don called a wealthy friend and arranged for Wallis to use a cottage behind her house. Later Don introduced Wallis to another friend, Mary Ann Richardson, who hosted Wallis numerous times at her beachfront hotel in Daytona Beach, Florida, for free writing sojourns. During some of those stays, Don and Gloria were also at the hotel, since Richardson gave them a free room during the McClanens' annual December vacation in south Florida, where both had siblings. Don and Wallis occasionally played golf together on a course where alligators lurked in the ponds. On the first hole when Don prepared to tee off Wallis routinely joked, "Look, Don, all the alligators are moving to the center of the fairway; it's the only place they know they'll be safe."

Wallis, with a hockey-player build and reddish-brown hair, enjoyed being around Don's infectious faith and enthusiasm. He also admired Don's commitment to tackle "the hardest gospel issue of all" through Ministry of Money. At the 1989 workshop, Wallis spoke with impassioned eloquence in calling for Christians to involve themselves in issues of poverty and violence.

Don's most often-used advanced workshop leader, along with Brueggemann, was Father John Haughey, a Jesuit college professor of theology and ethics. Don met Haughey when they both spoke at a conference in 1983 in Washington, D.C. Haughey was working with the topic of money at the time and approached Don afterward to express appreciation for what he had said. Haughey later completed a book titled *The Holy Use of Money: Personal Finances in Light of Christian Faith.*

Don recruited Haughey for four advanced workshops beginning in 1991, designed specifically for people of unusual wealth. Despite his soft-spoken, reflective manner, Haughey could be hard-hitting about the demands of the gospel. Since God is the true owner of all that we possess, the concept of "my money" is " a lie hot from hell," he said. He identified the spirit of the age as *pleonexia*, a Greek word meaning "a passion for more, an insatiability for more. ... an itch that is never relieved. ... When a critical mass of the citizenry is incited to pleonexia, you have a sick culture."[7] He said when Jesus spoke of the impossibility of serving both God and mammon, he left people with two choices: to administer their money by asking how God wanted it used, or to give all their money away so they would not have a split allegiance. Haughey later used his advanced workshop talks as the basis of a book, *Virtue and Affluence: The Challenge of Wealth.*

Haughey enjoyed Don's "childlikeness": his playfulness, good humor and lack of ego. However, Haughey noted that the topic of money brought out a serious and, indeed, determined side of Don. He thought Don seemed more sure than he did about the rightness of pressing people to "fork over" money to ministry causes as proof of genuine discipleship.

If Don was guilty of any type of pleonexia, it was his passion for jumping into new ministries. When he made his 1985 annual pilgrimage to the Missionaries of Charity Mother House in Calcutta, Mother Teresa was eager to see him. She told Don that residents of New York City's Greenwich Village were fighting her plan to open a house there to shelter AIDS patients. The disease, at that time always fatal and largely associated with gay men, had unleashed hysteria in the general population. AIDS was only discovered in 1981, the HIV virus that caused it was only identified in 1984 and no drugs had been developed yet to fight it.[8] Mother Teresa considered AIDS patients to be contemporary "lepers" who belonged to her flock of the poorest of the poor because of their terminal condition, stigma and social isolation. She asked Don if he would come to the opening of the New York AIDS house, Gift of Love, the following month and bring other supporters. Don and several from the Church of the Saviour felt privileged to meet with Mother Teresa for a short time before the ceremonial opening.

Afterward, Don and Gloria drove south from Washington on their annual vacation to Florida. They stopped for a meal at a Howard Johnson restaurant in North Carolina, where Don read in a newspaper that Mother Teresa had visited New York's maximum-security Sing Sing prison to show her concern for inmates with AIDS. Throughout his vacation he pondered whether God was calling him to a similar show of concern. By the end, he had decided.

Two members of the Church of the Saviour told Don they also

were interested in ministering to AIDS patients. One was Dixcy Bosley, a vivacious 24-year-old nurse who worked on an AIDS ward at a hospital in Washington. Bosley had taken that assignment against her will, and she was fearful of the dying, emaciated patients whose disease required her to wear a "moon suit" for protection. The aversion turned to horror on July 10, 1985 when she stuck herself with a contaminated needle. Bosley rushed to confer with her superiors, who told her she could do nothing but wait to see if she were infected. Later that day, still immersed in a cloud of fear and anger, she returned to the room of the patient where the stick had occurred. As she carried out her duties, three people came to the door. To Bosley the figures appeared shadowy because of the darkened room and the backlighting from the hall. One of them, a small woman, walked straight to the patient's bed and, with ungloved hand, stroked him and told him that he was loved. With amazement Bosley realized from the woman's familiar, wrinkled face and white-and-blue sari that she was Mother Teresa, who had come to Washington to visit her sisters and plan for an AIDS hospice in the city. Mother Teresa stared directly at Bosley with a quiet and kindly look, as if to say, "Watch how I love him; don't be afraid." Then she left the room. The visit set off in Bosley a spiritual earthquake that converted her fear into compassion.

In February 1986, Don, Bosley and a third person, Helen Cary, issued a call during a Church of the Saviour service for an AIDS mission group. No one responded immediately to the call, but the three forged ahead. They befriended AIDS patients on Bosley's ward and offered their supportive presences in the midst of tangled family situations, as parents struggled to come to terms with their sons' homosexuality even as their children were dying. In due course Cary left and three other young women joined, giving rise to the joke that the mission group was "Don's harem." Hospital visitations expanded into courses on AIDS at the Church of the Saviour's School of Christian Living and AIDS coffee-house nights at the Potter's House. Don pushed wheelchair-bound friends in annual AIDS marches in Washington, D.C., and the group created a square for the national AIDS Memorial Quilt on the Washington Mall.

During the mission group's four years together, Don's example inspired in Bosley a sense that God could use her to accomplish significant things. She cemented her dedication to working with those who suffered when she accompanied Don on a 1986 pilgrimage to Calcutta. When Bosley married in 1989, she picked Don to be her "maid of honor."

The wedding occurred shortly after Don had gone through one of his periods of discouragement. One morning in November 1988, he awakened about 5 a.m., "terribly agitated and quite distraught," he wrote in a newsletter. "Quite providentially, I now see in retrospect, my wife, Gloria, was out of town. Our house was deserted, except for our cocker spaniel, Dusty, and myself. I had the freedom to literally cry out and shout at God. 'What in the hell else would you have me do, Lord. I've tried to be obedient. I've tried to listen and hear. Tell me what you want and I will do it!'

His angst came, once again, from a sense of impotence to affect America's materialistic culture. "The USA election of a new president and other political leaders was at hand. And it seemed to me the dominant theme of both parties was 'vote your pocketbook and shop 'til you drop.' ... I was sobered by the truth that this ministry, which I perceive to be so needed, is but a drop in the vast ocean of North American life. ... *Forbes* and *Fortune* magazines were extolling the virtues of the 'rich and famous.' And we were facing a serious shortage of available cash to cover our operating expenses. ... In the midst of my crying out and shouting, ... the words that then came out of my mouth were, 'I feel like my bones are on fire.'"

Don called Gordon Cosby's house early that morning and reached Mary Cosby. When he described his experience, she responded to his surprise, "What you are experiencing is a most profound presence of the Lord." She pointed Don to Jeremiah 20:9: "If I say, 'I will not mention him, or speak any more in his name,' then within me there is something like a burning fire shut up in my bones" (NRSV).

A similar emotion occurred on April 10, 1991. Don watched a TV news report in his living room showing thousands of Kurdish refugees fleeing into the mountains along the Iraq-Turkey border at the end of the first Persian Gulf War, fearing Iraqi army reprisals. As Don watched the images of suffering, he began to weep silently. His three-year-old granddaughter, Ashley, saw his tears and said, "Why don't they come to our house, Pop Pop? We would take care of them." The suggestion stirred in Don a sense that he should go and be with the Kurds, and explore whether to lead a future pilgrimage there.

Nine days later Don flew to the Mediterranean island of Cyprus to consult with the staff of the Middle East Council of Churches. They gave him the name and address of a Mennonite worker in Istanbul who coordinated humanitarian shipments into northern Iraq. Don then flew to Athens, expecting to catch a connecting flight to Istanbul. But an airline strike had grounded all flights between the cities, and ticket agents told him a boat was his only option. From that point on, Don adopted an "anything to get closer" approach. He found a non-strike airline that could fly him to the Greek city nearest the Turkish border, Alexandroupolis, which lies 160 miles from Istanbul. He sat next to an elderly Greek man who spoke no English. Don took an airline map out of the seatback pocket, pointed to Istanbul and indicated that he was trying to get there. When they landed, the old man gestured for Don to follow him. They took a taxi to the man's village about 25 miles outside Alexandroupolis.

At the village's bus station, a ticket agent, who spoke some English, told Don an overnight bus would take him to a Turkish city halfway to Istanbul, where he could catch a train. The bus, filled with peasant farmers, made frequent stops and took six hours to go about 100 miles. When the bus finally dumped its passengers at the train station, Don learned that the next departure for Istanbul was not for six hours. *I'm not going to wait around here for six hours; a war is going on*, Don thought. He decided to hitchhike. At the edge of town Don flagged down a peasant driving a horse-drawn wagon. Bumping down the road sitting on the empty bed of the wagon, Don had a strange thought: *I'm having the time of my life!* His risk-taking spirit exulted in the adventure.

A few more hitch-hiked rides brought Don to Istanbul, where he located the office of Mennonite aid worker Melvin Wittler. A heavyset man in his mid-50s, Wittler listened with interest to Don's tale of adventure. Wittler told Don he would need to fly 200 miles to Ankara, the Turkish capital, and then catch a 400-mile flight to Diyarbakir in southeastern Turkey. There an 80-mile taxi ride would get Don to Mor Gabriel, a Syriac Orthodox monastery that was a transfer point for church-donated supplies going to Kurdish refugee camps.[9] A day later, Don's taxi approached Mor Gabriel, one of the oldest monasteries in the world dating back to 395 A.D., which rose from a barren plateau beside a range of low mountains. The monastery, a fortress-like complex surrounded by limestone walls, with a domed church, rare mosaics, cloisters, terraces and towers, housed a Syriac Orthodox bishop and a dozen nuns and monks, as well as several seminarians and a handful of visitors.[10]

Don was surprised to find among the visitors a Presbyterian minister from Seattle, Washington, named Dale Johnson, who was spending a sabbatical there. Johnson, with a beard, light hair, T-shirt and deep red sunburn, told Don he had made previous aid deliveries in northern Iraq and could take Don the next day. They loaded food and medical supplies in the back of the monastery's red, German-built pickup truck and drove 50 miles to the Iraq border. As they approached the checkpoint, Johnson told Don, "Do what I do." They held up their passports to the window and, when Turkish border officials waved for them to stop, they kept going, motioning toward the medical supplies in the truck bed.

Johnson and Don continued 20 miles on a paved highway through dry, barren terrain, passing anti-aircraft gun emplacements along the road. They pulled up to a refugee camp with long rows of brown tents pitched in the sand and lines of laundry strung between the tents. The refugees appeared healthy and adequately clothed. The U.S. Army had moved in to protect the camp, and its helicopters buzzed overhead. Don helped to pass out round loaves of bread to some of the camp's inhabitants and posed for pictures requested by the refugees. Then he and Johnson headed for Mosul, Iraq's third largest city, 50 miles away. They dropped off their last supplies at a church and drove back to Turkey.

After three days at the monastery, Don rode a taxi back to the Diyarbakir airport to return to Istanbul via Ankara. He saw only one plane on the tarmac. Inside the terminal, the concourse appeared deserted. Don headed for a light shining from an office in a far corner and asked the woman inside about his flight. "That flight has gone," she said in English.

"It's gone!" Don exclaimed. He handed her his ticket.

"Your ticket was made out wrong. That flight left two hours ago."

Don asked about the plane he had seen on the tarmac. The woman walked to a window and, reacting with surprise, said it was, indeed, the plane that Don was supposed to be on. They hurried to the gate, which was closed. "That's my flight; here's my ticket," Don said, frantically waving his arms. The woman protested that the plane's door was closed and the rollaway steps had been moved to the other side of the airport. "Well, go get them!" Don demanded. "I've got to get on that plane." He looked up and noticed the pilot eyeing his antics with an amused expression through the plane's cockpit window. Don pointed urgently to his ticket and then to the plane. The pilot laughed. A few moments later a small escape-hatch door opened beneath the plane and a small fold-down ladder descended. Don scurried out of the terminal and was halfway across the tarmac when he remembered his bag sitting at the gate. He ran back, grabbed the bag and dashed back to the plane. A rope dropped from the hatch, and Don tied his bag to it. Someone hoisted it up. Don, adrenalin pumping, scrambled up the ladder despite his 66 years of age. When he reached the top, sapped of strength, an attendant grabbed his jacket collar and pulled him into the plane. He had not brought any refugees with him, as his granddaughter Ashley had suggested, but felt deeply privileged for being able to complete his mission of mercy. Don planned a pilgrimage to Iraq the following year, but ultimately the Iraqi government prohibited entrance into the country. Instead the pilgrims traveled to Amman, Jordan, to work in Palestinian refugee camps. Through contacts in Jordan Don succeeded in funneling $10,000 in aid to the Missionaries of Charity in Iraq and $25,000 to various Iraqi relief projects.

Don and Gloria were in Florida at the end of 1991 when a brief news item in *USA Today* grabbed Don's attention. Mother Teresa had suffered congestive heart failure and was hospitalized in La Jolla, California. Don flew to join a group of Missionaries of Charity sisters holding a prayer vigil outside her room at the hospital. Shortly after his arrival, Don saw two men in physician's garb leave the room without speaking. The next morning a hospital administrator told Don about the two doctors. As they examined Mother Teresa, she asked them about their religious background. "We're both

Jewish," one said sheepishly. "Isn't that wonderful–just like my Jesus," Mother Teresa had responded.

Don stayed two days as Mother Teresa stabilized. Before he left, a Missionaries of Charity priest invited him to visit a training center for the order's brothers that the priest supervised less than an hour away in Tijuana, Mexico. A month later, Don arrived in Los Angeles a day before a money workshop at the Crystal Cathedral and drove to the Mexican border. Leaving his car on the American side, he took a taxi to the training center, where he found local indigents lined up to receive a meal at a soup kitchen the brothers operated. Don quietly took off his jacket to help serve. A few minutes later, Sister Sylvia, whom Don knew well as a key leader of the Missionaries of Charity in North America, saw Don and did a double take. "What are you doing here?" she asked. Without awaiting his answer, she added, "Come, follow me." Don hustled to keep pace as they quickly walked to a nearby building and into a small room that was empty except for a table and two straightback chairs.

"Sit down and wait," Sister Sylvia said, then disappeared. A few minutes later she returned with Mother Teresa, barely able to walk, clinging to her arm. Mother painfully lowered herself into a chair and Sister Sylvia left. "Mother, what a privilege this is to be with you," Don said, pulling his chair close to hers. In this unexpected and holy moment, he quietly told Mother how inspiring it had been for him to bring so many pilgrims to visit her and to work with her sisters around the world. He expressed his love and gratitude. Mother Teresa, in her weakened condition, replied with similar sentiments. After a few minutes, Don helped Mother walk toward the door as she leaned toward him and rested her head against his shoulder. No further words were spoken or necessary. Sister Sylvia met them at the doorway and escorted Mother Teresa back to her room. It was the last time Don saw Mother Teresa before she died in 1997. Don recalled that, on an earlier visit to Calcutta, he was so inspired by her presence that he mistakenly attempted to hug her. She raised her hands and drew back, wordlessly commanding that he keep his distance. Now, 12 years later, no such distance existed between these friends.

Back in Washington, D.C., Don agreed to help Jim Wallis raise money for the Sojourners movement, which faced a financial crisis.

Don already had committed to raise money for the Church of the Saviour's new theology institute, called the Festival Center/Servant Leadership School, and ministries to low-income children and the homeless. Near the end of 1991, Don also received a call from Henri Nouwen, who had left Harvard to serve as chaplain of a L'Arche community in Toronto where mentally handicapped residents lived with non-handicapped. Nouwen said he wanted Don's help to celebrate his 60th birthday the following year by raising $1 million to build a conference and retreat center at L'Arche. "I'm honored that you would ask me and I would love to do it, but I need this like I need a hole in the head," Don responded. He promised to pray about the request and discuss it with Gordon Cosby.

Cosby estimated Nouwen would actually need $2 million, and that Wallis also needed $2 million to put Sojourners on sound footing. Ever attracted to bold challenges, Don proposed that he lead an effort to raise $5 million, with the extra $1 million going to the Church of the Saviour's ministries. It was a tall order, but Don was confident God could lead them to do it. After all, he had obtained the $2.5 million in 1983 for Christ House, the church's residence for the homeless, and had obtained a $1 million gift to start construction of a building for the Festival Center/Servant Leadership School. Don previously had met wealthy people through Ministry of Money workshops and pilgrimages who had given gifts of $10,000 or more to ministries brought to their attention. Nouwen and Wallis gratefully signed on to what they called the Triad Initiative.

When Don asked for lists of their wealthy donors, Nouwen was clueless and Joe Roos, a Sojourners co-founder and business manager, could name only a few. Wallis and Nouwen agreed to Don's idea that they, Gordon Cosby and Elizabeth O'Connor jointly lead three spirituality retreats during 1992 and in March 1993, and that they invite wealthy potential donors. A $10,000 contribution would be required before attendance at one of the weekends. Don sent invitations to 46 people, almost all previous Ministry of Money donors. A total of 14 attended the three events, plus staff members from each organization. Participant feedback was positive. "The Triad event was a tremendous experience which I am so glad I did not miss," wrote a woman from Pennsylvania. "I was amazed at the depth of trust and sharing that we had created in such a short time. ... I left feeling very well informed and excited about the Triad projects, primarily because of the leaders' single-minded dedication to their clear visions." Another participant, after pledging a $250,000 gift, said in a letter to Don, "It has been a real joy for me to give this money ... because it has loosened up in me a streak that wanted to be generous and now seems to be getting so much pleasure out of it (I guess because I feel I'm doing what God wants me to do). ... Somehow my eyes seem to have been opened to people in need around me, and I find myself e.g., giving a surprise check to a young woman. ... She does housekeeping, ... and has a disabled husband and four young children, works two jobs to support them all, and (of course) is always behind in her bills."

In the end, Triad drew $500,000 in donations, plus pledges for future giving. Nouwen and Wallis pronounced themselves happy with the result, declaring it was a good start and they had learned important lessons about fund-raising. Wallis was struck by Don's willingness to invite his own donors to contribute to Wallis's and Nouwen's organizations. Instead of viewing giving as a zero-sum game in which the other ministries' gains might be his loss, Don instead believed they all benefited from growing more generous givers. Wallis also discovered that he actually enjoyed the interchange with wealthy people he met through Triad, something he had viewed beforehand as a necessary chore. The experience "converted" him to a new interest in developing direct relationships with wealthy potential donors.

Likewise, Nouwen came away with a new attitude toward fund-raising. He expounded on some of his learnings in a September 1992 presentation to a foundation. "Fund-raising is precisely the opposite of begging," Nouwen said. "When we seek to raise funds we are not saying, 'Please, could you help us out because lately it's been hard.' Rather, we are declaring, 'We have a vision that is amazing and exciting. We are inviting you to invest yourself through the resources God had given you–your energy, your prayers, and your money–in this work to which God has called us.'"[11]

Unlike Wallis and Nouwen, Don saw the Triad results as disappointing. "If we cannot raise this money from people we have been in relationship with for years, who are sitting on $3 million to $20 million, especially when we exposed them to Henri, Jim and key leaders of the Church of the Saviour community, we must recognize the nature of the challenge before us as we invite people to live gospel values," he said in an April 1993 post-Triad evaluation. "Only three gave significantly beyond the initial $10,000, even though they [all] agreed to reconsider their estate in light of their learning."

Don also noted that one of the participants had questioned Ministry of Money's role in Triad. She wrote in her evaluation that the "heavy-duty fund-raising" conflicted with Ministry of Money's "sacred, even fragile, purpose ... to minister to the affluent. As I shared with Don, it felt a little like going to a psychiatrist for help with relationship problems and having the doctor ask me out for a date!" Ministry of Money's board had debated the ministry's involvement in fund-raising across the years, and Don had argued strongly that a fund-raising role was appropriate under certain circumstances. "It could be that we are unwittingly contributing to the denial, greed and idolatry we are seeking to help people to address ... if we do not risk by inviting people to give," he said at a Triad meeting in July 1993. Gordon Cosby backed Don and swayed the board. "Unless education eventuates in action, it is not education," Cosby declared.[12]

In the spring of 1993, Don went to a golf course near his home to play a stress-relieving nine holes and met three strangers on the first tee. As they chatted, one noted that all three were retirees and asked Don if he was also. "Heck, no," Don responded. "I'm having the time of my life working with Mother Teresa and her sisters around the world, and taking others with me."

"Have you been to Bosnia yet?" one of them asked. As Don hit his drive down the fairway, he made a flip response, "No, but I probably will go by the end of the month." In actuality, Don had been looking for new pilgrimage destinations because political unrest in Haiti had made travel there impossible.

At the time, Bosnia-Herzegovina, one of the states resulting from the breakup of the former Yugoslavia, was engulfed in a brutal war pitting its minority Serbian population (Orthodox Christians), backed by the neighboring state of Serbia, against its majority Bosnian (Muslim) and minority Croat (Catholic) populations. United Nations peacekeeping forces had intervened, but too tentatively to stop a genocidal campaign of "ethnic cleansing" by the

Serbs in some of the cities they captured. As Don played his nine holes, he couldn't take his mind off the possibility of a Bosnian pilgrimage. He went straight to his office, called his travel agent and asked, "What is the best routing to get to Bosnia?" Within ten days Don flew to Croatia, a country bordering Bosnia, and arranged with a Franciscan order to visit one of their monasteries in mountainous central Bosnia. The Franciscan brothers even lent Don a car to drive to the monastery. His hopes of arranging a pilgrimage vanished when, 20 miles past the Bosnian border, a United Nations roadblock turned him back. Don returned to the United States totally deflated.

In the following days he read in *The Washington Post* that a congressman, Frank McCloskey of Indiana, had just returned from a fact-finding trip to Bosnia that included a visit to Rama, where the Franciscan monastery was located. Don visited McCloskey, who gave him a letter of introduction to facilitate travel in the Balkans. In June 1993, Don flew back to Croatia, learned from the Franciscan brothers that the road to the monastery had reopened and was driven there by one of the brothers. The monastery's head Franciscan, or "guardian," greeted Don with warmth and serviceable English. Rather than the doddering old monk that Don had expected, Father Mijo Dzolan turned out to be vibrant and youthful in street clothes with light hair, blue eyes and fine features. He agreed to receive a pilgrimage of American Christians, but said the number would be restricted to ten. The monastery's facilities were limited and in ill repair.

In August 1994, with a tense Bosnian cease-fire in place, Don led two back-to-back pilgrimages of eight people each. The groups flew into Split, Croatia, on the Adriatic Sea, whose palm-lined streets, deep-blue water and boat-filled marinas rivaled the beauty of the French Riviera. From there the groups traveled by rental van (after paying a $28,000 deposit because war had eliminated insurance coverages) into the mountains of Bosnia. They bounced along a two-lane gravel road built hastily by United Nations forces. The lush mountains and picturesque valleys reminded Jean Mathews, Don's long-time Ministry of Money administrative assistant, of Switzerland, but with the sobering addition of occasional bombed-out homes and upended, burned-up vehicles. Five hours into the trip, the pilgrims looked down on a breathtakingly beautiful valley of small farms, meadows dotted with grazing sheep, houses with orange tile roofs and, covering much of the valley floor, an azure lake. The Franciscan stone monastery and its steepled church seemed to rise out of the lake from its island location. This pastoral landscape, with women working in fields wearing long dresses and aprons, made the reality of a nearby genocidal war all the more sur-real.

The pilgrims drove across a causeway to the monastery. Father Mijo greeted them at the gate, prompting some heart flutters among Mathews and the other women in the group. They soon realized that the priest was struggling under a cloud of depression caused by the ravages of the war. During the group's visit to a nearby valley where Muslims aided by Serbs had massacred 41 Croats–half of them old people and children locked in a house that was set on fire[13]– Father Mijo leaned against the wall of a church where survivors had been treated and covered his face with his arm. Father Mijo's mood, however, was brightened by the Americans' visit. Bryan Sirchio, a guitar-playing member of the first group, convinced Father Mijo to pick up the instrument for the first time in four years. When Don came back with the second group, Father Mijo sat with them in the evenings on a balcony overlooking the moonlit lake and played and sang folk songs. Don could see the weight of war roll off him.

The pilgrimage's most dramatic moments came in a visit to Mostar, one of Bosnia's largest cities that lay 100 miles of partly damaged highway south of Rama. Most of the city's apartment and commercial buildings were ghost-like shells, their windows blown out and bullet-riddled walls blackened by fire. A European Union official whom the group met at a hotel that escaped destruction explained the complexity of the local fighting. Initially Serbs attacked the city, and then Croats attacked the Muslim refugees who poured in from outlying areas. All the city's bridges over the Neretva River were destroyed, including a famous 400-year-old arch that had survived a shelling in World War II.

When Don walked the pilgrims to the site of the bridge, he found a narrow pedestrian bridge temporarily erected in its place 100 feet over the water, with ropes for handrails. Don impulsively started across, the others following. He had gone only a short distance before he felt the bridge sway. He looked at the churning river below and felt fear rise within him. *This is not a good idea*, Don thought. But reversing the line of pilgrims did not seem an option. Halfway across, Don met a short man coming in the opposite direction, and Don spread his legs to let the man crawl between them. The other pilgrims followed suit, assuming that Don knew what he was doing. When the group was safely over, Don breathed a prayer of gratitude and began to lead them over a low barricade that blocked a street. Soldiers ran up to warn them that the street might be mined.

Dark clouds gathered overhead, followed by a strong wind and pelting rain. The group took shelter in the ruined shell of a bank as the wind blew large pieces of metal off bombed buildings around them. Don dashed off as the others waited out the storm. A United Nations tank rumbled down the cobblestone street with lights flashing, making group members feel as if they were in a *Star Wars* movie. As the rain stopped, Don reappeared with a young Muslim soldier he had recruited. Their new guide walked them to a city park that had been converted to a cemetery. The storm had blown down large tree limbs, and people emerged from destroyed buildings where the pilgrims could not imagine anyone still living. The Americans joined residents in cleaning the debris and restoring up-ended vases of flowers on the graves, thankful for the opportunity to show a small gesture of friendship. As the pilgrims drove out of the city and back into the mountains toward Rama, they saw a rainbow over the ruins of Mostar–a sign to Mathews that God was at work bringing reconciliation and rebirth to a tormented land.[14]

On one of their last nights together, the pilgrims talked about Bosnia's vast needs: the destroyed cities and homes; the schools that had been closed for years; the makeshift hospital in Rama that, despite its primitive equipment, was the only health facility for 35,000 people in the region. The group decided that, when they returned to the United States, they would launch a "Rama Project" to raise money to repair schools and hire teachers. Don initially declined to be involved in the Rama Project, saying the pilgrimages of reverse mission were not about fund-raising. One of the first things the group did was to pay for Father Mijo to fly to America the following fall to visit and recover from the sadness of his land. As Don's relationship with Father Mijo grew during five subsequent pilgrimages to Bosnia, he decided fund-raising was appropriate.

Don already had raised money for humanitarian projects in Haiti. He had developed friendships with priests, aid workers and ordinary Haitians during his numerous trips there, and their ongoing dire need fired his sense of compassion. He raised tens of thousands of dollars each year for Haiti causes through a once-a-year Ministry of Money solicitation and by approaching wealthy alumni of workshops and pilgrimages. The money supported St. Martial College, a Catholic high school in Port-au-Prince educating low-income students whose buildings had been destroyed during political turmoil (the students there labelled Don "the lay samaritan priest"); Fonkoze, a non-profit peasant bank and micro-lending agency; and Fondwa, a peasant community outside Port-au-Prince with job-training programs and a school.

During Don's first group pilgrimage to Haiti in the mid-1980s, young men followed the group around Cité Soleil. The men seemed particularly interested in Don's Boston Red Sox cap. A representative of the group shoved a piece of paper into Don's hand offering the group's services as guides. The document said they belonged to the Boston Youth Association (neighborhoods in Cité Soleil included Boston and Brooklyn, American destinations to which many Haitian immigrants had fled.) Don agreed to use their services, figuring they could provide security as well as directions. On Don's next visit the men gave him another written proposal: they wanted money to form a soccer team, build a school and store, and create jobs. Don began bringing up to $2,000 in cash on each visit to finance such projects and provide the men with survival money. Some of the money purchased shovels and wheelbarrows and paid the men to keep the sewage canals cleared. Over the years Don expanded the amounts he distributed as his trust in the association's leaders grew and his awareness of individual needs increased.

In his Haiti fund-raising efforts, Don branched out to friends from his Fellowship of Christian Athletes days, Dean Smith and Tom Osborne. Smith of the University of North Carolina and Osborne of the University of Nebraska ranked among the top college coaches in the nation.

Don had met Smith at an FCA event in the 1950s when Smith was a young basketball coach. They later crossed paths in the early 1970s at the Church of the Saviour, where Smith attended a service, after which they began a decades-long correspondence about sports and faith. Smith's Baptist congregation in Chapel Hill, North Carolina, had adopted some of the Church of the Saviour's approaches to ministry, and Don quickly found he and Smith shared common theological beliefs about social justice issues such as racism and poverty. Smith became a contributor to the Ministry of Money.

In 1995, as Smith neared the end of his 36-year basketball career at North Carolina, Don asked him for help to secure athletic gear for Haitian youth. Smith arranged for the Nike sporting goods company, a supplier to North Carolina's basketball team, to donate equipment for distribution in Haiti and also Bosnia. Don approached Nike directly the following year and came up empty. When Don told Smith, the coach again arranged for Don to receive free goods. Don invited Smith to accompany him on a trip to Haiti but Smith declined, saying he considered his mission field to be in the United States rather than abroad.

Tom Osborne had been a 19-year-old quarterback from Hastings College in Nebraska when he met Don at the second FCA conference at Estes Park in 1957. They reconnected in the mid-1970s when Osborne attended a Wellspring conference led by Don and Gloria at a church in Lincoln, Nebraska. Don began corresponding with Osborne, who was the new head coach of the University of Nebraska football team. The connection with Osborne helped Don's son, Michael, obtain an assistant coaching position at Nebraska in the late 1970s as Michael finished his undergraduate studies at the university.

Osborne became the nation's winningest active college football coach in the 1990s (his final won-loss record was 255-49-3), but a national title eluded him. His teams lost seven straight post-season bowl games, most frequently the Orange Bowl in Miami. Since Don and Gloria vacationed in Florida during that time of year, they regularly attended the game with tickets supplied by Osborne. As Osborne recounts in the foreword of this book, Don and Gloria were once again at the Orange Bowl on January 1, 1995, hoping against history for a Nebraska victory over the University of Miami.

Nebraska fell behind early in the game, 10-0, and still faced a 17-9 deficit midway through the fourth quarter. The prospect of another final-game loss batted down Don's normal aversion to praying for athletic outcomes. *God, I'm calling on you to help us,* he prayed. *This is unjust, this is unfair. Lord, we need a victory.* Nebraska tied the game, 17-17, on a touchdown and two-point conversion pass with 7:38 remaining and, with the clock ticking down, scored another touchdown to take its first lead. Miami had one more possession, but Nebraska's defenders sacked the quarterback twice, giving Nebraska the ball and Osborne his first national championship. (Osborne would win two more national titles before retiring at the end of the 1997 season.)

Don drove Gloria back to his brother's house 30 miles away in Fort Lauderdale, then returned to Osborne's hotel at 2:30 a.m. Don sneaked by hotel security to reach Osborne's room, where he found Osborne in his pajamas. After congratulating the coach on his victory, Don put a question to Osborne that he had asked repeatedly during the past two years: would Osborne go with Don to Haiti to see its poverty firsthand? Osborne gave Don what he considered a positive but noncommittal response. Two weeks later Osborne gulped when he opened a letter from Don saying the airline tickets had been purchased, and they would have a great time.

In February 1995, shortly after being named college football Coach of the Year, Osborne arrived with Don in Port-au-Prince. A conversation with a Missionaries of Charity sister from Canada impressed him most. The nun "explained how she went through nine years of apprenticeship before taking her final vows to become a full-fledged [Missionary of Charity], during which time she worked in a hospital for the dying. The patients, almost all under the age of two, rarely recovered from their illnesses, many of them infected with AIDS or addicted to drugs because of their mothers' addictions. The sister worked many hours, seven days a week with few breaks, able to visit her family only once every 10 years." Osborne asked her how she could endure such grueling work and the loss of so many children. The sister explained that each member of the order spent four hours each day in devotions. "It was that [time] spent in prayer and meditation that gave her the strength to serve under such stressful conditions," Osborne concluded. The conversation reinforced Osborne's determination to dedicate more time each day for Bible reading and prayer.[15]

Osborne's Haiti trip received only a short notice in the *Miami Herald's* sports section. But Osborne followed up by arranging for Adidas, the sports equipment company that held an endorsement deal with Nebraska, to donate more than $17,000 in equipment to Haitian organizations they had visited. He also expressed an openness to traveling with Don to Bosnia at some future time.

Three years later, on Jan. 3, 1998, Don was again at an Orange Bowl game, cheering Nebraska on to victory. Again, Don knocked on Osborne's hotel door in the wee hours after the game to congratulate him on winning his third national title in four years. Don also asked Osborne to accompany him on a Bosnia trip. Osborne, again in his pajamas, told Don he had a full schedule of other commitments but would reflect and pray about it. "I've learned that, with Don, you don't want to commit even casually," Osborne said later.

Fund-raising

Many times individual Christians sense a call to address some issue around them—be it the plight of the poor, the needs of youth or the elderly, or the march of society in some destructive direction—but quickly turn away, overwhelmed by the prospect of marshaling the needed people and resources. Don's life illustrates that God's calls to him often brought a need to raise money. As Gordon Cosby said, "The authentic church is mission. No mission—no church. But there's an inextricable connection between mission and money—no money, frustrated mission."

Elizabeth O'Connor pointed out the dilemma when she described a new "Sarah's Circle" mission group of the Church of the Saviour that set out to buy an apartment building for low-income elderly in Washington, D.C. "It became apparent to us that if Sarah's Circle was to have an incarnational life we would have to raise thousands upon thousands of dollars. A new roof alone would cost $40,000, an elevator $100,000, a new boiler $30,000, and on and on. In the past most of us had not felt too kindly toward fund-raisers. Now we found that we ourselves had to become the organizers and architects of a gigantic fund-raising effort. ... It was no small horror to think that we might be fund-raisers for the rest of our lives when we had had it in mind to be poets, prophets and healers."

Cosby told the group that fund-raising constitutes a positive aspect of mission. For one thing, it facilitates education. "In interpreting the dream, you are helping people to redefine the way they relate to the poor and the old, as well as to redefine the way they relate to their own aging," Cosby said. "Money ... makes possible hundreds of wonderful conversations. Because your mission needs money you will be motivated to get out there and speak in the ordinary course of events." Cosby also noted that fund-raising spurs prayer. "The resources will come through your efforts, but they are not rooted in your efforts. The power to create the new comes only through God."[16]

Henri Nouwen gave similar advice in his pamphlet *The Spirituality of Fund-raising*. Noting that he had learned from Don that "fund-raising is first and foremost a form of ministry," he said, "In fund-raising as ministry, we are inviting people into a new way of relating to their resources. By giving people a spiritual vision, we want them to experience that they will in fact benefit by making their resources available to us." Nouwen also noted that, as Don had helped teach him, fund-raising can help free the wealthy from their isolation. He recounted how a banker who had read his books approached him to offer financial support. The banker did become a supporter, but also entered an enriching friendship with Nouwen.

Nouwen said fund-raising is ultimately a chance for both the petitioner and the giver to be converted. "Fund-raising as ministry invites those with money to a new relationship with their wealth. It also calls us to be converted in relation to our needs. ... Are we willing to be converted from our fear of asking, our anxiety about being rejected or feeling humiliated, our depression when someone says, 'No, I'm not going to get involved in your project'? When we have gained the freedom to ask without fear, to love fund-raising as a form of ministry, then fund-raising will be good for our spiritual life."

10
High-Tension Wire

"It is easier for a camel to go through the eye of a needle than
for a rich man to enter the kingdom of God."
–Matthew 19:24 (NIV)

Don may have been discouraged by his Triad Initiative in the
early 1990s, but he was not defeated. In 1996, at the age of 71, he
launched another bold drive, this time to raise $2 million. He was
moved by "the increasingly desperate needs and opportunities our
pilgrims have experienced in Bosnia and Haiti," as well as continuing needs of the Church of the Saviour ministries, he said in a May
1996 memo. Also, he had seen how Triad, while falling short of its
goal, served as a successful launch pad for Henri Nouwen and Jim
Wallis to later reach their L'Arche and Sojourners fund-raising tar-
gets.

Don believed the rich needed his new effort as much as the poor.
"The Global Outreach Initiative anticipates raising these funds by
contacting approximately 25 individuals of considerable wealth," he
said. "While this effort will be made primarily for the poor, it will be
made out of an equal sense of call and urgency to free and challenge
the rich." Don took quite literally such Bible verses as Matthew 6:24,
"You cannot serve both God and Money" (NIV); he had concluded
most people wanted to do both.

Don knew he was pushing the envelope. As his Jesuit friend John
Haughey had quipped, "We read the gospel as if we have no money,
and we spend our money as if we know nothing of the gospel."[1] Don
wrote in his memo, "This effort is fraught with such impossibilities
that only Scripture can adequately define it as Jesus describes watching the rich young ruler in Matthew 19:24-26," referring to the story
of the man who turned away sorrowful after Jesus told him to sell all

that he had and give the proceeds to the poor. Don clung to his source of hope: the continuation of the rich young ruler story, where Jesus tells his disciples that it is easier for a camel to go through the eye of a needle than for a rich man to enter the kingdom of God. "Who then can be saved?" his disciples ask. "'No chance at all if you think you can pull it off yourself,' Jesus responds. 'Every chance in the world if you trust God to do it'" (*The Message*).

In that trust, Don approached wealthy alumni of Ministry of Money. The first gift of $9,000 came in August 1999 from "Katie" [not her real name], a marital and family therapist from New Mexico whom Don had met when she attended a Wellspring orientation led by Gloria McClanen in 1982. After Katie mentioned at the orientation that she was an adopted child of wealthy parents and struggled with her wealth, Gloria asked Don to talk with her. Katie explained that she wanted to give more generously but did not know where to begin, since her family had never discussed money and her assets were tied up in complicated trusts. Don put her in touch with a helpful attorney in Chicago, where Katie lived at the time, and Don himself became a gentle, encouraging sounding board on her money issues. Katie enlisted Gloria as her spiritual advisor for two years, and returned annually to Washington, D.C., for Ministry of Money workshops. She later accompanied Don on a pilgrimage to Calcutta and co-led one with him to Haiti, also attended by Laurie McClanen. As a fellow adopted child, Katie felt a special bond with Laurie.

Through Don's introduction, Katie became friends with Elizabeth O'Connor at the Church of the Saviour and gave generously to Sarah's Circle, a residence for low-income seniors that O'Connor helped create. Don solicited Katie regularly for his own causes and she frequently responded. In 1993, Katie and her husband hosted a Ministry of Money weekend for wealthy people at their adobe house in a New Mexico desert. Don called it the "Lighthouse Keepers" retreat, referring to his unsuccessful attempt to convince a wealthy Ministry of Money participant to buy a lighthouse and lighthouse keeper's cottage on the coast of Maine where he and Gloria had vacationed the previous year. Don envisioned the property, on sale for only $1.2 million, as a "halfway house for the wealthy"–a retreat center for those with lots of money who wanted to work on wealth-addiction issues. At the New Mexico retreat, participants agreed that people with wealth often suffer from a special insecurity–wondering if those who befriend them are interested in them as people, or are attracted only by their money.

By the end of 1996, three donors had contributed $100,000 or more. One was "Mary," Don's Christ House benefactor from California. Another was "Anne Marie" [not her real name], a 51-year-old former school teacher, also from California. A slender, stylishly dressed woman with short light hair, angular face and striking smile, Anne Marie had grown up lonely as the only child of wealthy and detached parents. They left her millions that her father had amassed through a mortgage company he founded, but Anne Marie experienced her wealth as a painful source of separation from those around her and left the money largely sitting in fund accounts. When laid off from her elementary-school teaching job after 13 years, she earned a counseling degree but decided not to work in that field. She pursued various forms of non-Christian spirituality, but found none truly fulfilling. She described herself as "the walking dead," with little purpose and little hope.

In 1991 a friend invited her to attend a "Women, Money and Spirituality" workshop in nearby Santa Barbara, sponsored by the Women's Perspective of Ministry of Money. After the workshop Anne Marie wrote, "I arrived feeling guilty and shameful about having inherited money and left with a new sense of what I can do with my money that will make a difference in the world. What a gift for me and the world! I know this will result in more self-esteem and a happier future for me and others." In gratitude, she sent a $2,000 contribution to Ministry of Money, which prompted a phone call from Don. Unimpressed by the voice on the other end of the line, perceiving it as formal and businesslike, she pictured Don as a thin man in a dark suit who looked like a mortician. He offered to visit her in California and urged her to attend a regular money workshop, but Anne Marie declined.

In 1994 Anne Marie converted to Christianity as she rebounded from the disintegration of a cult-like New Age group in which she had been active. Two months later, she registered for a Ministry of Money workshop at Wellspring. Her first sight of Don shocked her, for he was the opposite of what she had imagined. Dressed in jeans and a plaid shirt, Don greeted her warmly, and she was struck by his infectious laugh and the twinkle in his eye. After the workshop, Anne Marie told Don that she wanted to make a substantial gift to Ministry of Money. "I don't want you to give money," Don replied. "I want you to get your Christian legs under you first." This gave Anne Marie a reassuring sense of Don's integrity.

During the next year, Anne Marie returned to Wellspring for three more money workshops. Each time she stayed with the McClanens, and began to feel like their surrogate daughter. On one of the trips Don took Anne Marie to downtown Washington to see ministries of the Church of the Saviour, including Christ House. Anne Marie feared that the homeless men would detect that she was rich and shun her. Instead they greeted her so warmly that Anne Marie felt a kinship with them—that they reflected a brokenness on the outside that she felt on the inside. She talked to Don about where to give her money, and he had an uncanny ability to affirm her choices while stretching her vision of what was possible. Anne Marie's giving infused her with a joy she had never experienced before; she felt she was fulfilling God's purpose for her life as she distributed "God's money." Back home, she volunteered as a tutor to substance-abusers at a recovery program.

Anne Marie's growth process was not without moments of terror. She hyperventilated the first time she considered writing a $50,000 check. *No way!* she told God. *You've got to be kidding.* Days later, she decided God wasn't kidding. She developed a decision process for such large donations: after an amount entered her mind, she ran it by the Holy Spirit.

How about I give half of that? she would ask.

No.

How about three-quarters of it?

No.

How about all of it?

Yes, all of it.

In 1996, the first year of Don's Global Outreach Initiative, Anne Marie accompanied him on pilgrimages to Haiti and Bosnia. The Haiti trip was the toughest experience of her life. Her work station, the Missionaries of Charity orphanage, overwhelmed her with its chaotic desperation, as sick babies cried in their cribs and reached out for her affection. The sight reawakened in her the loneliness of her childhood, when she had longed for her parents to pick her up and hold her. By the end of the trip Anne Marie had contracted a parasite whose effects plagued her for two years. The Bosnia trip, however, was more hopeful. Despite the destruction and poverty, she saw new life sprouting up, emblemized by her visit to a flower shop that had just opened.

For several years thereafter, Anne Marie invited Don to California in January to help her draw up an annual giving plan. She initiated the numbers, and Don gave reactions. Much of what she gave went to the Global Outreach Initiative. In Haiti, recipients included causes that Don had supported for years, including St. Martial College, the Fonkoze peasant bank, the Fondwa peasant community and the Boston Youth Association. In Bosnia, she supported a project to renovate the oldest building of the Franciscan monastery in Rama into a "House of Peace" retreat center. Don, Father Mijo Dzolan and others envisioned a facility that would provide counseling services for traumatized war victims and hold reconciliation workshops for Bosnians of all ethnic groups. The initiative also funded Sarajevo Phoenix, an embroidering micro-business for refugee women in the nation's capital, and other projects. In Washington, recipients included the Church of the Saviour ministries to the homeless and chronically unemployed. Later, money also went to support a school in the Palestinian Territories.

Don recruited his son Michael to oversee the distribution of funds abroad. Michael had served as Ministry of Money pilgrimage director until 1990 and worked for five years as an organic farmer before returning to team with his father. Beginning in 1996, Michael stayed three to four months a year in Haiti, Bosnia and the Palestinian Territories, working with the local recipients of the funds. Given Don's intensity and Michael's more relaxed approach, this arrangement proved more satisfactory than being side by side in the same office, which by the 1980s was a small house at Dayspring. Sarajevo Phoenix, the embroidery collective, was Michael's creation. In 1999, he moved to Bosnia full-time and, before returning in 2002, met and married a Bosnian doctor, Amra Slokovic.

In the summer of 1998, Don sought to bring attention to the plight of the homeless in Washington, D.C., one of the Global Outreach Initiative's beneficiary groups, in an unusual way.

Bestselling author John Grisham had just written *The Street Lawyer*, and Elizabeth O'Connor suggested that Don secure Grisham for a book-signing at the Potter's House since the book dealt with homelessness in Washington. A *Newsweek* magazine article further piqued Don's interest by describing Grisham crying at the plight of a young mother and her three famished children while doing research for the book at a D.C. shelter.[2] *Perhaps Grisham and the Church of the Saviour can work together,* Don thought.

After a little detective work, Don discovered that the writer lived on a 200-acre farm in the foothills of the Blue Ridge Mountains near Charlottesville, Virginia. Coincidentally, Don passed near the farm each week while driving 150 miles to Lynchburg, Virginia, where he taught a class at the church of close friend Beverly Cosby, Gordon Cosby's brother. Don stopped at a lavish sports complex of six baseball fields Grisham had built for the youth of his county and found Grisham's secretary working in an office there. She told Don he could send a letter to Grisham in care of the complex. Don wrote, but received no reply. He stopped several more times at the complex—enough times to learn the precise location of Grisham's farm.

One Sunday after leaving Beverly Cosby's church, Don decided he and Gloria would stop by Grisham's house. A teenager appeared at the door and said his father was out by the barn. Don walked to the back of the house, surprising a man with patrician features dressed in casual clothes. It was Grisham. Don quickly explained that he wanted to thank him for writing the book, since Don's church worked with street people in Washington. Grisham, his face clouded by irritation, replied, "Normally I am a very nice person, but I moved here to get away from such visits." Don apologized and walked back to his car. The next day he mailed Grisham a packet of materials about the Ministry of Money and Don's FCA past. Grisham responded curtly in a three-sentence letter: "Your materials have been received. The intrusion is forgiven. Now, please leave me alone."

Grisham's rebuff became one of Don's favorite stories to tell on himself. He giggled at his social impropriety, acknowledging that he sometimes went "too far" when the poor might benefit. One of his friends congratulated him on his boldness. Bart Harvey, chairman of the Enterprise Foundation, founded by developer James Rouse to rehabilitate inner-city areas of America's major cities, wrote, "Of course, John Grisham has a right to privacy—but so too does Don's appeal for the homeless [have a rightness]. The truth doesn't go off to hide unless you cut and run from it."

Don concluded the Global Outreach Initiative in February 1999. It fell short of his $2 million goal, but not by much. Nine donors contributed $1.7 million. Anne Marie's share of that was $550,000. One other donor, Ralph Doudera of Virginia Beach, Virginia, also gave more than $500,000. Handsome and athletic with a hobby of driving race cars, Doudera had resolved at a young age to make a lot of money. By 40 he had achieved his goal by selling life insurance and investing his earnings, then developing an investment counseling business. As he tells in his book *Wealth Conundrum*, Doudera struggled with the intense stress of trying to outguess volatile markets. He also had his hand tightly gripped around his money. Depressed by the market crash of 1987, he was ready to give up his business until he sensed a divine voice during a hike in the West Virginia mountains telling him instead to turn his finances over to God.[3]

Doudera met Don at a Ministry of Money workshop in the early 1990s, then accompanied him on a pilgrimage to Calcutta in 1993. Meeting Mother Teresa and seeing her love for the destitute affected Doudera deeply. "You can't go home the same when you take a mission trip like this," he wrote. "Something snapped inside me on that trip. I wasn't so demanding. I wasn't so fussy. I was much more grateful about just about everything. I didn't get upset about small things the way I had before. I didn't need as much stuff. I had a new desire to give."[4] With Mother Teresa's comment, "Anything that is not given is lost," ringing in his ear, Doudera gave away 50 percent of his annual income through a family foundation. In January 1996 he wrote Don, "My thanks to the Ministry of Money to help me get 'off my butt' and stop talking about giving and actually do it. As a result I was able to distribute more than $1 million to worthy organizations last year. Giving it was definitely more fun than making it!"

As with Anne Marie, Don gave Doudera firsthand exposure to ministries that could use his money, especially during a trip to Haiti in December 1997. They toured a children's hospital, the Missionaries of Charity Wound Clinic, St. Martial College, Cité Soleil and other places of great need. "It seems like everybody knows and loves Don," Doudera observed. "As Don and I had dinner together, we read many personal letters [that Haitian friends handed Don on the day of arrival] that asked him for help. Many are desperate. I'm glad they are addressed to him and not to me. I want to run home and pretend like I don't see this." In the end, Doudera, sufficiently moved by the needs and by Don's example of compassion, gave generously for two years. But he and Don parted ways afterward because of a difference in viewing the solution to poverty. While they agreed on reaching out to the poor, Doudera believed that business development and wealth accumulation were justified as long as business owners then used a portion of their wealth altruistically. Don, instead, believed the wealthy should de-accumulate. When Doudera proposed setting up a fund to generate annual returns for Don's projects, Don, not opposed to endowments in special cases, said most of the contribution needed to be distributed right away because people faced immediate life-and-death situations.

Near the end of the Global Outreach Initiative, Don, at age 74, sensed a new call that would end his 25 years of leading Ministry of Money. Instead of educating people of all income levels to seek God's purposes for their money, Don wanted to work strictly with those whose assets and income reached $1 million or more, raising large amounts of money to alleviate the suffering of the poor. Don hoped a ministry colleague, Bryan Sirchio, would succeed him as head of Ministry of Money. Sirchio, a bearded former pastor and now a Christian singer-songwriter, met Don in 1991 on a pilgrimage to Haiti when Sirchio was 32. They shared an intense commitment to follow Jesus and to work for justice for the poor. Within two years Sirchio, as a part-time Ministry of Money staff member, co-led pilgrimages and emceed workshops. For a decade they spoke in person or on the phone almost daily, Don acting as Sirchio's mentor and Sirchio serving as Don's confidante. Sirchio described their relationship as similar to that of the biblical characters David (the musician) to Saul, or Timothy (the traveling companion) to Paul.

Sirchio appreciated Don's ability to link biblical faith and economic justice, and at the same time love wealthy people. Sirchio remembered being surrounded in seminary by fellow students who criticized the wealthy. It was not a safe environment for Sirchio to work through money issues as a person who grew up in a culture of wealth. At the age of 18, Sirchio had gained access to a family trust fund of about $150,000, which felt to him like a treasure unattainable to his peers. Biblical passages left him uneasy about keeping the money for himself, yet he knew that giving it away would distress his mother. While Don did not suggest that Sirchio liquidate his trust fund, Don's influence along with others' eventually prompted Sirchio to distribute most of his holdings, with much of it going to Ministry of Money.

Despite his closeness to Don, Sirchio did not feel called to succeed him at Ministry of Money. His music ministry continued to be his priority. Don sounded out other Ministry of Money veterans, including Joe Roos, who had been Ministry of Money business manager and previously a co-founder of Sojourners; Rosemary Williams, director of the Women's Perspective; and Bob Hadley, a lawyer from Dayton, Ohio, who served on the board of directors and also acted as a volunteer staff member leading retreats and pilgrimages. None felt called, and the board opened a search for a successor. Don's exit soon grew bumpy and painful, as is often the case with individuals who have founded an organization and led it for decades. Don and the board disagreed on transition issues. The board viewed Don as reluctant to give up control and as oversensitive to any action that could be construed as forcing him out—as if his departure from the Fellowship of Christian Athletes still haunted him. Despite the difficulties, the board honored Don's 25 years of leadership with an album of testimonials, a $6,000 check and a $10,500 pilgrimage scholarship fund created in his name.

Don named his new ministry Harvest Time. In a newsletter, he described its potential with a quote from Richard Parker, a senior fellow at the Kennedy School of Government at Harvard University: "The wealthiest 400 Americans, as identified by *Forbes* magazine, are together worth nearly $800 billion. Out of the one-year (1998) increase in wealth alone (not their total wealth), according to the U.N. Human Development Report, those 400 Americans could have funded the cost of universal education for all children, reproductive health care for all women, and adequate food, safe water and sanitation for the entire developing world."[5] Compared with such numbers, Don's proposed budget was modest: $25 million to be raised over a five-year period and to be distributed to projects in Bosnia, Haiti, Iraq, the Gaza Strip and West Bank, and the United States. He later, with anguish, trimmed this goal to $10 million.

Don viewed Harvest Time as the culmination of his years working with money, a harvesting of the seeds that he had planted. The name also evoked several biblical passages, including Mark 4:29, "As soon as the grain is ripe, [the farmer] puts the sickle to it, because the harvest has come" (NIV), and Matthew 9:37-38: "The harvest is plentiful, but the laborers are few; therefore ask the Lord of the harvest to send out laborers into his harvest" (NRSV). Don sought a time of harvest from a small group of the wealthy who would hear the cries of the poor and lead others in redistributing their possessions. They would ask God not "How much do you want me to give away?" but rather "Since it's all yours, how much do you want me to keep?" In an article about his new ministry in *Barron's*, the business magazine, he explained, "Charity and philanthropy are good, but the gospel demands justice, ... an equitable distribution of wealth. The beauty of Harvest Time is that it will free the wealthy from their wealth as it frees the poor from their poverty."[6]

Don had worked with and discipled a small number of wealthy people for decades, but how to help them move from philanthropy to "discipleship"—a dedication to continue redistributing their wealth until everyone had enough—remained an open question. He consulted theologians and social-justice activists such as John Haughey; Ched Myers, a California-based writer and teacher on Christian justice issues; and the Rev. Lee Van Ham, a California-based Presbyterian pastor who earlier had hosted Wellspring and money workshops at his church. Don also hired Joe Roos as business manager. At a meeting in Chicago in March 2000, these advisors pushed Don to be bold. Would Harvest Time encourage wealthy people to divest all their possessions, as Jesus had told the rich young ruler? Would it view the accumulation of wealth as an addiction, much like alcoholism, and develop a twelve-step program to combat it? Would it urge groups of wealthy people to pool their money and make community decisions about how to distribute it? Don responded that in all his years with Ministry of Money he knew of only a few people ready for such radical steps. The discussion left him distressed over the utter impossibility of what he had set out to do, he said, but also with a paradoxical sense of peace.

When the meeting adjourned, Ched Myers told Don as they walked out of the room, "The one word for you is Sabbath." Don knew immediately the import of Myers' prescription—that he had disregarded the essential rhythm between work and rest and that his workaholic tendencies were threatening him harm.[7] During the following year Don participated in almost one weekend silent retreat a month. The fruit was a greater sense of peace and patience as he opened himself to the Lord's leading.

In June 2000, Don hosted an "exploratory gathering" at the Church of the Saviour with Gordon Cosby, Bryan Sirchio and members of a new Harvest Time mission group. Don also invited Bill Rouse of Lexington, Kentucky, a real estate developer. Rouse and his wife Erin, a Presbyterian seminary student, had come to Washington a few weeks before to attend a "Come and See" open house at the Church of the Saviour's Servant Leadership School. When someone mentioned that Don was a member of the church and had founded the Fellowship of Christian Athletes, Bill recalled his introduction to Jesus at an FCA summer camp when he was 15. He had stopped the smoking, drinking and sex he was involved in at the time, but his resolution crumbled after a few months. Despite attending three more FCA summer camps, Bill succumbed to drug use and alcoholism as a young adult. Despite struggling with his addictions, his company prospered. At age 28, Bill entered a twelve-step program that led him back to Jesus, sobriety and involvement with FCA.

After the Rouses' visit to the Church of the Saviour, Bill called Don to thank him for starting FCA. As they chatted, Don mentioned his new ministry and his current challenge of raising money for Haiti. "I'm sitting here writing someone about a need for $50,000," he said. Bill mentioned the joy he had felt from recently giving a large donation, and Don responded, "How would you feel about giving $50,000 to a desperate need?" To Don's surprise, Bill said, "Let me pray about that and talk to Erin." Bill also accepted Don's impromptu invitation to the exploratory gathering even though it was only a few days away. After the gathering, when Don dropped Bill off at the airport, Bill handed Don a check for $50,000 as he opened the car door.

In October 2000, the Rouses accompanied Don on a six-day trip to Haiti. "It broke us open," Bill said. Erin sobbed after visits to Cité Soleil and the Missionaries of Charity orphanage, overwhelmed by the destitution. Bill's heart cracked when he rocked a cute, desperately ill child at the orphanage and asked the sisters where the girl would go when she grew older. The child will not live long enough to leave the orphanage, the sisters told him. Before the trip Bill had always compared himself to "the next bigger dog" rather than to those less fortunate. The Haiti experiences swept away all possibility that Bill could continue to deny that he was rich. Bill returned to Haiti the following year with Bryan Sirchio, who had become a part-time Harvest Time staff member, and became a major investor in the Fonkoze micro-lending bank. Bill returned a third time at the request of Fonkoze officials to testify before top Haitian officials on behalf of the bank's application for a new charter. The Rouses gave generously to a variety of organizations, including Harvest Time.

In November 2000, Don convened a gathering in Walla Walla, Washington, which included Anne Marie of California and several other Ministry of Money veterans. The gathering took place at a stucco-and-red-tile retreat house built by Cheryl and Ralph Broetje on their 6,000-acre apple farm. Cheryl had met Don in the mid-1980s at a Ministry of Money workshop in the Seattle area when she was wrestling with whether she and Ralph should sell the farm and pursue mission work overseas. She appreciated Don's passion for social justice. She especially welcomed his calming reassurance that major changes in her life might take seven years to fully materialize. Don invited Cheryl to Washington, D.C., where he introduced her to Gordon Cosby and others at the Church of the Saviour. This opened Cheryl's eyes to new possibilities of how a church or business could serve the poor. She also profited from books and other materials Don frequently sent her and adopted a similar approach of sharing resources in her correspondence with others.

The Broetjes decided to keep their farm, with its annual multi-million-dollar revenue, and funnel much of the money into ministry projects. They built a 100-house village for their Hispanic workers to create community and provide a model for proper treatment of agricultural employees. In 1986 Cheryl founded a non-profit organization, the Center for Sharing, to distribute seed money for groups with a vision for serving the poor and marginalized. Recipient organizations provided recreation for youth, clothing for women on welfare to wear at job interviews, transitional housing for the needy and a place for Third World artisans to sell their goods. In 1995, the Center for Sharing launched a local Servant Leadership School, modeled on the one at the Church of the Saviour, that taught courses on spiritual development, servant leadership and ways to change social and economic structures to benefit the disadvantaged. The Center for Sharing later offered courses internationally in such places as Mexico, the Philippines and Kenya. Cheryl and Ralph traveled to India on a pilgrimage with Don, and Cheryl went numerous times on her own, adopting six Indian children off the streets of Calcutta and Bombay to join their three biological daughters.

Cheryl served on the board of Ministry of Money, to which the Broetjes donated $235,000 from 1991 to 2001. When Don started Harvest Time, they gave a $10,000 start-up gift, and eventually contributed a total of $205,000 to that ministry. At the Walla Walla gathering, Don asked how generous givers like the Broetjes could mentor other wealthy people toward deeper Christian discipleship. Cheryl said she was focused on those without money rather than those with. She described, for instance, how she and her husband had given their farm employees the power to disperse up to $900,000 annually in farm income to charitable causes. Others stated hesitations about their readiness. "Who is going to mentor us?" Anne Marie asked. Rosemary Feerick, a former Maryland school teacher who was now a theology student from Berkeley, California, said, "I'm seeking people to mentor me. My portfolio is a mess. I can't mentor anyone."

Sharon Lukens of Gig Harbor, Washington, who had met Don in 1977 at a Ministry of Money workshop, said in an e-mail to the others afterward, "I see Harvest Time as a combination lighting rod, cattle prod and shepherd's staff carried in the hands of a faithful steward. It can be used to empower, jolt and comfort, sometimes all at once, through writings, one-on-one contacts and gatherings of pilgrims eager for an oasis of community along the narrow path."

In May 2001, many of the same people gathered again at a spiritual retreat center in the Los Angeles area. Don's "cattle prod" agenda focused on "jubilee economics," based on an Old Testament concept for wealth redistribution. The participants found the discussion unhelpful and, at one point, one suggested simply sitting silently for 15 minutes. When the silence ended, Feerick said, "All I know is, I'm ready to love you in the mess." The group, eventually naming itself the Beloved Community, decided to meet twice a year to share the status of their financial lives and offer each other spiritual companionship. Members launched various experiments in pooling resources, such as buying a condominium as a retreat location for group members as well as non-members; working with partners from other organizations to turn a member-owned farm in Mississippi into a center for racial reconciliation and healing; and giving jointly to projects in Haiti and elsewhere. Don dropped out of the group by the end of 2002, believing that his call lay elsewhere.

In September 2001, Don read an article in *Time* magazine entitled "America's Best Philanthropist" about Tom White, an 81-year-old who had headed a large construction company in Boston. The article noted that White had given away more than $50 million during his lifetime to charities helping the poor, and was down to his last few million.[8] Don had heard of White previously from Dr. Paul Farmer, a young doctor Don had met through their mutual involvement in Haiti. Farmer was creating a private health system to serve more than a million of Haiti's peasant farmers, and White had given Farmer $30 million to make that possible.[9] "You need to meet Tom White," Farmer had told Don.

The *Time* article mentioned that White also supported Bread for the World, a nonprofit that lobbied the U.S. government to provide greater food aid to the poor both at home and abroad. Don knew Art Simon, Bread's founder, and David Beckmann, Bread's president, whom he had once recruited to speak to his Ministry of Money board of directors. Don asked if Beckmann could put him in touch with White. "I'll do you one better," Beckmann responded, saying Bread's directors planned to honor White the following month in Boston and Don should come and meet him face-to-face.

When Don introduced himself, White, a regular contributor to the Fellowship of Christian Athletes, said he had already heard of Don. As they chatted, White appreciated Don's concern for the poor, especially in Haiti, and recognized a shared desire for the rich to become more generous. The two began to correspond, and Don visited White several times at his vacation home in Tequesta, Florida. In April 2003, Don and Bryan Sirchio interviewed White for a Harvest Time newsletter.

In the interview, White told of having been a friend of President John F. Kennedy, for whom he had raised campaign money in Boston, and General Maxwell Taylor, a chairman of the military's Joint Chiefs of Staff for whom White had served as an aide during World War II. White also revealed the rigors of his childhood growing up in an emotionally cold, alcoholic household, which fostered in him an empathy for underdogs. "People ask me why I do what I do, and I say, 'Well, I happen to have two gifts. I have the gift of compassion, and I have the gift of being able to make money.' ... I don't understand why people don't do more to help those who are hurting. ... What does anybody need $10 million, $20 million or $1 billion for? I've made checks out for $100,000 or $500,000. You don't miss it."

White talked of the joy he received from giving spontaneously. "I gave a $20 bill to a gal who was cleaning the toilets at McDonald's. My wife Lois said, 'You can't go to McDonald's to get a Diet Coke without it costing you 20 bucks.' ... Most of these people who are cleaning toilets at McDonald's barely speak English. They're getting the minimum wage. ... If you give somebody something like that, they look at it and say, 'What's this?' And I get to say, 'It's for you.' 'For me? Why?' And I say, 'Just because, it's a little gift.' Well, their eyes light up."

White met Natalie, a woman in her 60s, during his frequent walks through Harvard Square. "Natalie was never begging. She went around and picked up cans and bottles and put them in her supermarket push cart. ... She'd be sitting on the wall taking a rest. I'd sit down and give her $20. She'd say, 'You can't afford that. What are *you* going to do?' I'd say, 'Don't worry about it, Natalie. I'm doing okay.' One time I came along and she was sitting there looking a little down, and I said, 'Hey, Natalie, how's it going?' 'Well, not too good,' she said. 'I guess I'll always be a street person.' But then her face brightened up and she said, 'But I'm saving up for a red wagon, ... the kind you had when you were a kid.' ... That night I called Sears, and the next morning there I was pulling a red wagon up through Harvard Square. ... As I pulled up her eyes opened wide and she said,

'Oh, my goodness! What did you do?' I said, 'Well, I found this one.' I told a couple of people this story and they said, 'She must have been thrilled.' And I said, 'Hey, who do you think was really thrilled?' I was."

White modeled the wealthy Christian disciple that Don had been seeking. And for White, Don joined the few people he had met who really understood White's outlook on life. As White learned more about Don's work in Haiti, he made several gifts to Harvest Time totaling more than $100,000. Don "was doing good things in Haiti," White said. "By the time I met Don I didn't have much left. Anytime Don asked me to do something, I would try to do it. I trusted him. If I left my wallet in the middle of the street, I would trust that I would get it back, with Don."

In the summer of 2003, Don and Harvest Time business manager Joe Roos agreed that Don, now 78, should diminish his role in the ministry and make room for potential successors. With the board's approval, Bryan Sirchio and Rosemary Feerick came aboard as tri-directors. Don mentioned that, after hearing him recount his adventures, people had told him he should write a book about his life. Sirchio agreed, and he helped Don gather information for a biography and look for an author.

Meanwhile, the tri-directors clashed over expectations and interests. Sirchio and Feerick, responding to requests from some of the ministry's donors that they not be solicited so frequently, sought to systematize the fund-raising for Harvest Time's administrative budget. They set out to recruit ten donors to each pay one-tenth of the annual cost. Don considered the idea misguided, providing some of the ministry's best givers a reason to reduce their donations rather than to increase them. The three spent hours in painful and inconclusive meetings and conference calls, Don from Dayspring, Sirchio from his home in Madison, Wisconsin, and Feerick from her home in Northern California.

As the three struggled to work out their differences, Gloria found Don fumbling in a strange way with his breakfast preparations one morning in April 2004. "Are you all right?" she asked. Don babbled incoherently. Doctors at a nearby hospital diagnosed a stroke. Don's recovery was rapid and without loss of speech or movement, but the doctors directed that, at age 79, Don reduce his activity level.

As Don bounced back, ignoring the doctors' orders, he gained a new appreciation for the preciousness and fragility of life.

In March 2005, Don told the Harvest Time board he would relinquish most of his responsibilities to concentrate on his biography. The board named him director emeritus. In six years, Harvest Time had raised more than $2.5 million directly, and influenced another $1 million in indirect contributions. In February 2006, at the age of 81, Don submitted his resignation from all Harvest Time activities.

As Don reflected on his decades of working with money, he saw the truth of a statement by Archbishop Oscar Romero of El Salvador, who was assassinated for advocating the interests of the poor: that the idolizing of wealth was a "high tension wire" and "woe to him who touches the high tension wire; he will burn his fingers."[10] Gordon Cosby similarly described working with faith and money as "handling live ammunition." One aspect of the high tension for Don was moving back and forth between the poor and the wealthy. He might be with a family of ten in Port-au-Prince one day, confined to a one-room shack with too little food and no access to health care. Back in the United States, Don might spend a weekend with people who owned several million-dollar homes, belonged to exclusive yacht clubs and country clubs, kept live-in domestic helpers and spent the average Haitian's annual salary on a nice dinner out.

These brutally contrasting experiences often encouraged Don to be relentless in approaching his donors for more, even when this made them uncomfortable or angry. Better to go over the line, he believed, than to fall short of it. "If people aren't getting angry," he told Sirchio, "they're not getting it." He could not fathom why his wealthy friends would keep millions that they did not need to live a comfortable life when others struggled to simply survive.

An early experience of singed fingers came in the mid-1970s. Don visited an elderly friend with a vast fortune who had given generously to one of Don's ministries. With the friend's health rapidly deteriorating, Don said to him, "I love you too much not to ask you to give $1 million to the ministry that has affected your life so positively." The bold question prodded his friend to agree that he would include such a bequest in his will. When the friend died, his will made no mention of this exchange. Don approached his friend's widow, whom he knew well, about making good on her husband's pledge. In response, the widow's lawyer wrote Don requesting no further contact with her. Don wrote her one final plea. "Let's face it," he said. "The reason you're bothered by me now is that I keep raising the question of the million dollars. ... I'm convicted, right or wrong, this is the message God has been giving me to share with you. ... In light of your wealth, I feel God is asking for an increased proportion—especially in your will—directly to the Christian cause ... [through which] God gave His greatest love to you and [your husband]." The plea was not heeded.

Don experienced similar disappointment in a relationship with "William" [not his real name], son of the founder of a major national company. In 1968 a former FCA associate told Don that William, who lived in a coastal town in the Northeast, had an interest in race relations and might support Don's work with inner-city youth. Don contacted William's lawyer, who arranged donations totaling $10,000 to the Washington Lift over a period of three years. Casting for a bigger catch, Don called William directly in 1973 and arranged to meet at an airport near William's home. As they sat in the restaurant, William told Don, "I need to let you know something about me. I'm a wealthy man who was born with a golden spoon in my mouth—and you're not going to take it out."

Despite that shot across the bow, William pledged $15,000 after hearing Don's description of the Washington Lift. A long-time friendship emerged. Don and Gloria dined with William and his wife in January 1974 while both couples vacationed in Florida. The following summer, William visited Don in Washington, D.C., to witness Lift activities and visit the homes of Lift youth. Don also introduced him to some of the Church of the Saviour's ministries. In 1975, Don made the first of many visits to William's home, where William entertained Don with his extensive model train set in a second house devoted strictly to that hobby. William also took Don out on the yacht he had personally designed, prompting Don's suggestion that William should take Lift youth to sea sometime. "William, that's just what you've been talking about doing!" his wife exclaimed.

For several summers Don drove a vanful of boys to William's

home. William took them to a restaurant for the first lobster dinner of their lives before taking them out for two days on the sea, where they docked overnight at a nearby island. William, knowing Don and the boys planned to hold morning devotions on a seaside bluff, asked Don if he could join them. An irregular church-goer who described himself as a "cynic," William stood in front of the youth and told them with tears in his eyes, "You fellows have made God real in my life—you are a tremendous inspiration to me and I love you." William became an annual contributor of $10,000 or more, shifting the gifts to the Church of the Saviour's ministries when the Washington Lift ceased its activities.

Don visited William in early December 1983 after returning from his annual India pilgrimage. William kidded him about his Third World travels, saying, "McClanen, what do you have to share from this foolishness?" Don said, "William, why don't you make a really serious commitment to the poor of a million dollars?" William responded as if it were a joke, but Don persisted, calling it a life-or-death issue for the poor—and for William. "Okay, I'll do it," William said finally.

"Are you serious?" Don replied.

"Yes."

"That being the case, you know what the first step is," Don said, pointing to a phone. "Unless you tell your lawyer you want to do it, it won't get done." William made the call and they drove to the lawyer's office, where William directed that the amount be entered in his will. When Don and William drove to the airport afterward, they stopped by the roadside to pray, as was their practice, and thanked God for the miracle of grace that had occurred that day.

William died in 1992, a year after his longtime lawyer's death. Don learned that a new lawyer had changed William's will the previous year, reducing the $1 million gift to $400,000. Don told William's widow of his dismay, and asked her to consider contributions to the ministries her husband had supported. He later received a letter from her lawyer: "You and your organization are not to solicit [William's widow] in the future for any further donations. There was some indication that you intend to contact [her] on your way north to Maine in August or September. Please do not attempt to contact her." Don later reestablished contact, but the topic of giving remained off the table.

Even Don's very best supporters found Don aggressive at times in his fund-raising. Mary, his Christ House benefactor, laughingly told Don he was a "lovable pain in the neck." When he called her periodically to ask if he could visit, she knew what to expect. "We'd play tennis for a while, and then he would sit me down and try to get a lot of money out of me." At one point, Mary became so aggravated that she cut off contact. But a year later she initiated a reconciliation, aware that Don provided a richness to her life that money could not buy. "He gave birth to my spiritual life, nursed it and disciplined it," she said. "He introduced me to Mother Teresa, and to the poor of Washington, D.C., and Haiti, with whom I fell in love. He gave me far more than I gave to him."

Anne Marie also reported ups and downs in her relationship with Don. She bristled when she called him in February 2000 to wish him a happy 75th birthday and Don changed the subject to the plight of someone he knew who needed money. The shift caused Anne Marie to feel as if their friendship was secondary to her money, and she asked him to keep personal and business calls separate. In June 2001, she traveled with Don to Bosnia to celebrate the dedication of the remodeled Rama monastery building as a new House of Peace, to which she had contributed a significant amount of the $800,000 cost. She was excited to see the results, both in the beautifully restored structure and the hopefulness of its reconciliation programs. The Franciscans welcomed her warmly, the dedication drew large crowds, Croatian dancers performed in their native costumes and Don and Anne Marie were interviewed by a Sarajevo TV station. However, when the Franciscans spoke of their desire to purchase an abandoned factory next to the monastery to prevent an incompatible development, Anne Marie felt targeted by their comments. *Wait*, she thought, *I'm not an unending source of funds.*

Don visited Anne Marie and Mary at Mary's California home a month later. While there, he took a two-day side trip to visit a wealthy stockbroker who had contacted Don after reading the *Barron's* magazine article about Harvest Time. Don returned to Maryland in an agitated state, feeling that the stockbroker and his

wife, like many of the wealthy people Don had worked with, hope-
lessly deceived themselves about what it takes to follow Jesus
authentically. Don awoke in the early morning in a furious mood,
called both Mary and Anne Marie and ranted into their message
machines about how he was sick of dealing with wealthy people,
including "you rich women in your big houses." Mary took the call
in stride, phoning Gloria to see if Don was all right. But Anne Marie,
having given $100,000 to Harvest Time just two months earlier, was
incensed

Don later apologized, and their relationship resumed—though
not the same as before. Anne Marie felt forced to push back against
Don's assertiveness, much like a teenager learning to differentiate
from parents. Her autonomy grew further in late 2005, when one of
the Church of the Saviour ministries she had supported suggested
that it might go under unless it received a substantial gift. Under
pressure and feeling like an ATM machine, Anne Marie could not
rally herself to respond. In fact, she felt nauseous at the thought of
giving to any charitable cause, and halted almost all her donations,
fearing she might never want to give again. A year later she resumed
with a new promise to herself: she would make contributions only
when they caused her to feel joyful, rather than guilty or manipulat-
ed.

Despite the ups and downs of her relationship with Don, Anne
Marie remained deeply grateful for his influence. Without meeting
him, she never would have traveled to Bosnia, Haiti, Africa and
Gaza; never have met people who became some of her best friends;
and never have been blessed with the satisfaction of knowing
Bosnian babies were being saved because of incubators she bought
and Haitians had access to clean water because of wells she paid for.
"None of it—zero—would have happened without Don," she said. "I
would never have wanted to live my life without him."

Being Real

"Am I supposed to be reading this?" a reader might ask about
details in this chapter, surprised at the disclosures of people's individual money details. Discussing personal finances is perhaps the
strongest taboo in our society today. In Ministry of Money and

Harvest Time, Don flung open the windows and allowed many to confront the issue directly, discuss hopes and anxieties with others and be freed to make changes.

Honest, intimate sharing in all areas has a power to encourage, unite and change. Don's disarming ability to be transparent in his difficulties as well as his triumphs has allowed others to reciprocate with honesty about the real issues in their lives. Deep has called to deep. As Eugene Peterson says in his book *Run With the Horses*, "What a waste it would be to take these short, precious, eternity-charged years that we are given and squander them in cocktail chatter."

There are risks in opening up to others. Some people do not understand the sacred trust of confidentiality, and use what others tell them as gossip. (In the first chapter of Romans, Saint Paul lumps such behavior with sins as serious as murder and sexual immorality.) In other cases, people store in their memories what is told them, later throwing it back in the face of the teller in an attempt to demean or manipulate. Don advises discretion in telling our innermost thoughts to others.

Conflict often accompanies openness. Honesty reveals heartfelt convictions about religion, politics or ethics that some do not appreciate. Openness may involve confronting people lovingly and directly to invite them to reexamine some closely held belief. Jesus wanted his followers to love each other and be one, but he did not advocate a cautious co-existence by avoiding difficult topics. Jesus meant loving each other through open differences rather than hiding behind false-smile facades. A common critique of churches is that they are gatherings of hypocrites, who pretend everything is upright in their lives on Sunday morning but on Sunday afternoon are back trying to deal alone with their dysfunctional families, addictions, temptations and senses of failure. Christians being real and deeply sharing personal struggles can unlock the power of praying for each other, comforting each other and offering practical help to each other.

To be real with each other, to risk authentic relationships, requires forgiveness. This means listening to one another, experiencing hurt and anger and still coming back for more, trusting that the Holy Spirit uses conflict to mature and knit relationships even more closely together. That is why the centerpiece of Jesus's prayer is, "Forgive us our debts as we also have forgiven our debtors" (Matthew 6:12 NIV). In committing to be real, open and honest, we can be risk-takers, like Don, in the cause of Christ and God's kingdom.

11

Author's Epilogue

"Grow up. You're kingdom subjects. Now live like it."
—Matthew 5:48 (The Message)

When Don first looked for someone to write his biography, one prospective author declined after spending five days with him. "If I wrote your book, I would have to change," she told him. It's true. Don's forceful personality catalyzes change. People cannot spend time with him and not be affected.

My first experience with Don at a 1996 Ministry of Money workshop altered my approach to money and, indeed, to all of Christian discipleship. Don and other Ministry of Money leaders took Jesus's Sermon on the Mount literally and actually tried to live self-sacrificial lives. It was a revelation to me that this type of life was a real possibility rather than a beautiful but unattainable ideal. I was freed to respond to the needs of those around me in new ways, despite inconvenience, hardship or embarrassment. In the realm of finances, my wife, Marilyn, and I decided to give away a third of the annual dividends we received from a stock we had just inherited following my mother's death, in addition to our regular church tithe.

Don's influence on my life intensified after I started writing this book. I now practice daily centering prayer (and can hardly imagine how I survived without it). I went on my first silent retreat (at times difficult but ultimately a wonderful experience, which I have resolved to repeat annually). I have recruited a friend to be a spiritual director (whose weekly feedback I value for its affirmation and its prodding). I have taken steps to make myself more financially open and accountable by sharing numbers and donation patterns with my sister and brother-in-law, and have reassessed my level of financial discipleship as Don sensitized me to the desperate needs of the world's poor. For all these changes, I am grateful.

Don also has been my model as I have worked with others in my community to create a non-profit organization to support our local public schools. Don's entrepreneurial energy and his belief in fund-raising as ministry embolden me to believe this project will make a difference and that I can solicit money without apology, contrary to my natural reticence. Gordon Cosby says that few members of the Church of the Saviour community know the full extent to which Don's willingness to ask for money has enabled the church's ministries. As a small example, a windstorm in the summer of 2008 downed dozens of large trees at Dayspring, and the cleanup cost was estimated to be at least $10,000. When others expressed their discomfort at approaching a likely donor for the money, Don took on the task. The donor quickly agreed to send $25,000. When the check came three days later, it was made out for $50,000. An accompanying note said, "Please call whenever Dayspring faces financial issues." Through one bold laborer, the harvest was plentiful.

Don's approach to money has amused as well as inspired me. The first day I interviewed him at Dayspring, we talked right through lunch. At 3:30 p.m., just as I packed up for an hour drive home, he suggested we buy some food at Taco Bell and he would treat. Would it be okay if we split an order of nachos and cheese, he asked me at the counter. Just before paying the 99 cents, he said to the clerk, "And give me two cups of water." Perhaps such thrift befits someone who has never drawn a salary of more than $37,500 from his ministries (not counting a rent-free house constructed with sod-farming profits for which he and Gloria pay utilities and maintenance costs). But it seems incongruous with Don's friendships with millionaires, his fund-raising of millions of dollars and his penchant for buying plane tickets at the drop of a hat to destinations all over the world.

It also runs counter to his and Gloria's generosity. Don has pushed people hard to grow in financial discipleship and continually increase their giving. The boldness of some of his written solicitations, as well as one overheard phone conversation, amazed me. But he and Gloria have walked the talk. Among a list of 39 donors to Harvest Time from 2000 to 2003, many of them millionaires, the McClanens ranked 13th in the size of their personal contributions to the ministry–$16,000 during that four-year period. This giving probably exceeded all others' as a percentage of income and assets. In 2007 the McClanens gave away almost 40 percent of their $50,000 income (most of the income coming from Social Security, an annuity and renting out the bottom floor of their house). Their generosity also showed in May 2008 when Don received distress calls from some of his former Haitian associates and asked wealthy friends to contribute toward a $6,000 relief fund. When the money was slow in coming in, Gloria told Don they should give $3,000. "I don't think I could live with myself unless I was a generous giver," she told me. Don quotes Marcel Mauss, a French philosopher. "We should come out of ourselves and regard the duty of giving as a liberty, for in it there lies no risk."

Don has said repeatedly that he would have been dead long ago without Gloria. It is certainly true that without a strong and loyal partner, Don could never have achieved what he did. Being married to Don McClanen is no small assignment. Gloria has endured financial insecurity, emotional storms and other trials of living with an impulsive, passionate visionary who has been engulfed in his work and frequently absent on travels. She had to be staunchly devoted and yet exceedingly flexible. "I don't think many wives would have followed him in all his activities without a deep commitment," she said.

Writing this book has given me, among other things, the gift of observing Don and Gloria together in their seventh decade of marriage. I learned early the mistake of trying to interview them together. Their strong wills butted in disagreements over details of events. Gloria's voice rose in a pitch of exasperation, while Don maintained his counter-position in a softer, but no less determined, tone. But mostly I saw a mutual tenderness. At times when Don and I worked at the dining room table in the morning and his "Glory" appeared after sleeping late, he demanded his daily greeting of three kisses. He boasted of how wonderful she was, and she waved off the compliments with a laugh and a semi-ironic, "Yeah, yeah, you're lucky to have me, Don McClanen." Gloria likewise talked about her husband's achievements with great pride.

One of the crosses Gloria bore in living with Don during the book project was the conversion of their house into an archival repository. Throughout my year of visiting them, books, magazines, pamphlets, letters and photos covered the dining-room table, as well as a sofa and fireplace hearth in the living room. I only saw the dining-room table clear of Don's stuff once, in preparation for a dinner with extended family. This prompted a small crisis, as Don tried to convince Gloria it was all right to leave the mounds of material in boxes lining the dining-room wall. "Have you ever thrown a piece of paper away?" she asked. I joked to Gloria that Don's hoarding was a biographer's dream and a wife's nightmare.

Among the books that lie about Don's home and office are a dozen that have been particularly formative. In addition to the Bible, these include Thomas Kelly's *A Testament of Devotion*; Henri Nouwen's *Life of the Beloved* and *Gracias! A Latin American Journal* (among others); Walter Brueggemann's *The Prophetic Imagination*; James Finley's *Merton's Palace of Nowhere* (a life-saver for Don during one of his periods of deep distress); Richard Foster's *Celebration of Discipline* and *Freedom of Simplicity*; Elton Trueblood's *The Company of the Committed*; Ron Sider's *Rich Christians in an Age of Hunger*; Wayne Muller's *Sabbath*; Gerald May's *Dark Night of the Soul*; Thomas Keating's *Open Mind, Open Heart* and *Invitation to Love*; and Cynthia Bourgeault's *Centering Prayer and Inner Awakening*.

No one can enter the McClanens' modest two-story house without realizing their devotion to Jesus. A poster by the kitchen table shows a loaf of home-baked bread and glass of wine with the words, "Jesus of Nazareth requests the honor of your presence at a dinner to be given in his honor." In the living room, devotional books by Henri Nouwen and other authors sit in stacks on a table beside Don's reading chair. Above the fireplace mantle is a reproduction of Heinrich Hofmann's 19th century painting, "Christ and the Rich Young Ruler." Just below the painting is a miniature of the 12-foot cross that stands outside the Franciscan monastery in Rama, Bosnia. (Also on the mantle is a framed cartoon showing two boys with backpacks walking along a sidewalk, one saying to the other, "When I grow up, I want to work with the affluent.")

In addition to Christian objects, the McClanens' walls, tables and bookcases bear dozens of photos of family: their parents and grandparents, themselves at various stages of their lives, their children, their six grandchildren and their six great-grandchildren. There also is artwork from Haiti, Africa and Asia, as well as mementos and awards. In the front hall, for instance, sits a small bronze sculpture of a boy in a track uniform reading a Bible, presented to Don by the Fellowship of Christian Athletes at the organization's 40th anniversary in 1994. Don has received numerous such honors.

In 1978, Oklahoma State University erected a plaque at its football stadium honoring Don as the alumnus who founded FCA.

In 1981, the FCA "huddle," or chapter, of his hometown of Morrisville, Pennsylvania, threw a "Don McClanen Night" and presented Don with a painted caricature of himself signed by 20 professional sports figures from Philadelphia and Dallas.

In 1998, Oklahoma State honored Don again as a "treasured" alumnus during the halftime of a basketball game, at which he was invited to address the crowd.

In 2006, Don was featured at a 50th anniversary reunion of those who attended FCA's first summer conference at the YMCA of the Rockies in Estes Park, Colorado.

In 2009, a new $8 million Oklahoma Sports Hall of Fame and Jim Thorpe Museum is opening that includes a Don McClanen-Don Moyers Chapel. Moyers, a prominent Tulsa attorney who died in 1995, was a friend of Don's and strong supporter of FCA.

At the same time, Eastern Oklahoma State University is dedicating a bust of Don to be placed in the entrance of its new student center. A plaque will note Don's position as athletic director and basketball coach at the school when he founded FCA.

An undated award, of which Don is particularly fond, sits on a shelf in his office. The small, inexpensive trophy says, "Thank you, Farmer Don," and was given him by children from inner-city Washington, D.C., after they attended a summer camp at Dayspring.

Don was nominated for two significant awards that he did not win. In 1980 and 1981, Dick Armstrong, Don's FCA friend and former board member, nominated him for the Templeton Prize, an international award honoring people who have made exceptional contributions in the field of religion. Winners have included Mother Teresa and Billy Graham. Also, in 1959, the Kansas City Jaycees nominated Don for the organization's national Ten Outstanding Young Men Award.

While Don appreciates the tributes, nothing has meant more to him than the commendation of his spiritual mentor and good friend,

Gordon Cosby. "God has 'graced' me through you," Cosby wrote in a 1976 letter. "You remind me of Abram. ... Your divine restlessness helps to keep me from settling. ... So many of us are the recipients of your faithfulness. Dayspring breathes your very life. The Washington Lift has sent many youth in new directions. Wellspring is an artesian well for the nourishing of the Church of Jesus Christ. Your vision of money and its meaning will bring freedom to many who have it and the relief of suffering to many who are poor. ... I just want to say thank you both for the priceless gift you have been to Mary and me and for the inestimable help you have been in building the corporate life of the Church of the Saviour."

Cosby, still preaching almost every Sunday at the age of 91, has said on occasion, "Don't talk to me about retirement because it's not a Christian concept. If you're called, you're not just called to age 65." Don has adopted the same approach. At the age of 83, despite a stroke in 2004 and coping with prostate cancer and an incurable neurological disorder called restless legs syndrome, he is exploring the possibility of a new mission called "Second Journey." In keeping with Meister Eckhart's observation, "There are plenty to follow our Lord halfway, but not the other half," Don hears a call to pursue a new level of obedience, a new depth of dying to self and of opening to God. Susan Bell, a retired clinical social worker and a member of the Church of the Saviour who has explored the call with Don, suggests that first-journey Christians may not even be aware of the possibility of a deeper, second-journey spirituality. Don sees Gerald G. May's book *The Dark Night of the Soul* offering hints of this second journey—"an ongoing spiritual process in which we are liberated from attachments and compulsions and empowered to live and love more freely." May writes that this entrance into the second journey must come through a "dark night" because "if we really knew what we were called to relinquish on this journey, our defenses would never allow us to take the first step. ... To guide us toward the love that we most desire, we must be *taken* where we could not and would not go on our own."[1]

Don's ideas for the new mission also stem from the writings of Rufus Jones, a Quaker philosopher and social reformer in the first half of the 20th century who envisioned a "remnant" of spiritual leaders who would lead the way for others in their vision and commitment to follow Christ against the grain of the popular culture.

Don sees his three decades of work with money as an important base from which to search for greater depth, both for himself and others. His experience and the Bible convince him that money is the No. 1 stumbling block encountered by people seeking to fully dedicate their lives to Jesus. He also sees the completion of his biography as part of this new ministry–a way to teach serious discipleship through the example of his life.

Praying with Don gave me an inspiring window into his spiritual depth. When I arrived for my weekly interview sessions, Don greeted me with a grandfatherly smile and hug, often wearing a plaid shirt and jeans and his beloved Boston Red Sox cap. Before we went to work on the book, we spent 15 minutes in prayer, during which his praise and compassion flowed out. "Oh Jesus, we love you, we love you, we love you," he prayed. "Lord, we pray for all those who go without food and other necessities this day, and also for those who have so much food and other possessions that they don't even know the poor exist." Don's prayers for justice, sometimes edged with impatience, were never self-righteous, as he always included himself among those who needed to repent: "Thank you for the anger, thank you for the guilt, thank you for awakening me."

Don has experienced life as a dramatic, possibility-filled gift, and he has thrown caution to the wind in loving and following the Giver. Ultimately, his world is painted, not in shades of grey or muted yellows and browns, but in bold swashes of vivid green, deep blue and bright red. Like many others, I consider knowing him to be one of the great privileges of my life. Bob Hadley, a longtime Ministry of Money board member, said of Don, "He took me to places I never would have gone." While I have not been with Don to Calcutta or Port-au-Prince, he has taken me to places, and given me glimpses, of a daring, single-minded obedience that leads to bold adventure. Once you have seen the mountains, it's hard to settle back into life on the flatlands.

Ministries
Founded by Don McClanen

Fellowship of Christian Athletes
8701 Leeds Road
Kansas City, MO 64129
816-921-0909 or 1-800-289-0909
fca@fca.org
www.fca.org

Wellspring
11411 Neelsville Church Road
Germantown, MD 20876
301-428-3373
missionwel@aol.com
www.wellspringministry.org

Ministry of Money
1640 Columbia Road, N.W.
Washington, DC 20009
202-737-7692
office@ministryofmoney.org
www.ministryofmoney.org

Harvest Time
c/o Rosemary Feerick
207 Washington Boulevard
Half Moon Bay, CA 94019
650-560-9631
rfeerick2002@yahoo.com
www.harvesttime.cc

NOTES

Introduction

[1] As quoted in Thomas Kelly, *A Testament of Devotion*, (New York: Harper and Row, Publishers, 1941), p. 52.

Chapter Two

[1] Catherine Marshall, *A Man Called Peter: The Story of Peter Marshall,* (New York: McGraw-Hill Book Company Inc., 1951), p 288.

[2] David C. Craighead, *Country Lawyer: The Life and Times of James F. Howell*, (Oklahoma City: Oklahoma Heritage Association, 2007), p. 114.

[3] Wayne Atcheson, *Impact for Christ: How FCA Has Influenced the Sports World*, (Grand Island, Nebraska: Cross Training Publishing, 1994), pp. 154-155.

[4] Tony Ladd and James A. Mathisen, *Muscular Christianity: Evangelical Protestants and the Development of American Sports,* (Grand Rapids, Michigan: Baker Books, 1999), p 96. Ladd and Mathisen detail the connection that American and British evangelicals developed with sports during the second half of the 19th century through such movements as the Young Men's Christian Association. They note that this connection was largely severed during the first half of the 20th century as sports became more professionalized and secular and evangelicals grew alienated from popular culture. Don McClanen was in the forefront of re-engaging sport and religion in the second half of the 20th century. His particular innovation was to create a fellowship in which athletes not only evangelized the outside culture but also supported each other in their faith.

[5] Peter King, *Sports Illustrated Greatest Quarterbacks,* (New York: Time Inc. Home Entertainment, 1999), pp. 16-21.

[6] *Impact for Christ*, p. 159.

[7] Ibid., pp. 158-159.

[8] Carl Erskine, *Tales from the Dodger Dugout*, (Champaign, Illinois: Sports Publishing Inc., 2001), pp. 153-154.

[9] These other Christian athletes included the Rev. Glenn Olds, chaplain at Cornell University and a former boxer; Kyle Rote, a running back who had followed Doak Walker to All-American honors at Southern Methodist University and who was now playing for the New York Giants; Bob Fenimore, a two-time football All-American in the 1940s at Oklahoma A & M; and the Rev. Charles Dowell, an All-Conference cen-

ter on the 1950 University of Oklahoma football team.

10 *Impact for Christ*, pp. 164-165.

11 Ibid., p. 164.

12 Ibid., p. 169.

13 Ibid., p. 169.

14 Ibid., pp. 170-171.

15 Ibid., p. 171.

16 Ibid., pp. 171-172.

17 Ibid., pp. 172-173.

18 Ibid., p. 175. Also interview with the Rev. Bob Geller.

19 *Time*, Oct. 7, 1957. Also Sam Mallison, *The Great Wildcatter: The Story of Mike Benedum*, (Charleston, West Virginia: Education Foundation of West Virginia, Inc., 1953).

20 Interview with Paul Benedum Jr.

21 Joseph Dunn, *Sharing the Victory: The Twenty-Five Years of the Fellowship of Christian Athletes*, (New York: Quick Fox, 1980), p. 25. Also *Impact for Christ*, p. 174.

22 Interview with Rose McKee, secretary and director of administration for the Claude Worthington Benedum Foundation.

Chapter Three

1 *Sharing the Victory*, p. 12.

2 "Hero Worship Harnessed," *Sports Illustrated*, Feb. 6, 1956.

3 Ibid.

4 "Religion on the Ball," Empire Magazine, *The Denver Post*, Spring 1956, pp. 12-13.

5 Ibid.

6 *Sharing the Victory*, p. 40.

7 *Impact for Christ*, p. 180.

8 Ibid., pp. 181-182. Also *Sharing the Victory*, p. 46.

9 Transcript of speech provided by Don McClanen.

10 At Branch Rickey's urging, Jackie Robinson followed this counsel and withstood with dignity and self-control a storm of abuse his rookie year, thereby blazing the trail for full racial integration of professional baseball teams. Robinson and Rickey were partners in one of the greatest civil-rights advances of the 20th century. The desegregation of major-league

baseball, after all, was a precursor to President Harry S. Truman's desegregation of the U.S. armed forces in 1948 and the U.S. Supreme Court's ruling in 1954 outlawing racial segregation in schools.

11 *Impact for Christ*, pp. 183-184.

12 *Sharing the Victory*, p. 36.

13 Ibid., p. 26.

14 *Impact for Christ*, p. 190.

15 Ibid., pp. 194-195.

16 "Muscular Christianity," *The Philadelphia Inquirer Magazine*, April 7, 1957, p. 15.

17 Most of the account of Judy's death is from a Gloria McClanen interview with Andrea Wells Miller.

18 *Impact for Christ*, pp. 210-213.

19 Bill Bradley, "...I've Made My Choice," pamphlet reprinted by the Fellowship of Christian Athletes from *The Christian Athlete*.

Chapter Four

1 Landrum Bolling, "D. Elton Trueblood," *Earlhamite*, winter 1995, as quoted on www.waynet.org, October 15, 2007.

2 Elton Trueblood, *While It Is Day: An Autobiography*, (New York: Harper & Row, Publishers, 1974,) pp. 104-124.

3 Catherine Marshall, "What I Learned at Gordon Cosby's Church," *Readers Digest*, December 1953.

4 Elizabeth O'Connor, *Call to Commitment*, (New York: Harper & Row, Publishers, 1963), pp. 4-17. Also O'Connor, *Servant Leaders, Servant Structures*, (Washington, D.C.: The Servant Leadership School, 1991), pp. 1-11.

5 Account of Mary Cosby in Ministry of Money newsletter, No. 86, October 1993.

6 *Call to Commitment*, pp. 55-58. Also, recollections written by Carolyn Hubers for the 40th anniversary of Dayspring.

7 Gloria McClanen interview by Andrea Wells Miller.

8 William R. Parker and Elaine St. Johns, *Prayer Can Change Your Life*, (Englewood Cliffs, New Jersey: Prentice-Hall, Inc., 1957).

9 Don McClanen interview with Andrea Wells Miller.

10 Thomas Keating, *Intimacy With God* (New York: Crossroad Publishing Company, 1994), p. 55.

[11] Another excellent introduction to this type of prayer is Thomas Keating's *Open Mind, Open Heart.*

Chapter Five

[1] "Sod Is Church's Foundation," *The Washington Post,* December 15, 1966, p. F10.

[2] Ibid.

[3] Charles Morgan interview with Andrea Wells Miller.

[4] Charles Morgan as told to Clif Cartland, "Freedom Is Finding Yourself," pamphlet published by The Washington Lift. Also, Andrea Wells Miller interview with Morgan.

[5] "Freedom Is Finding Yourself" and Miller interview.

[6] "Freedom Is Finding Yourself" and Miller interview.

[7] Neely Tucker, "The Wreckage of a Dream," *The Washington Post,* August 24, 2004, p. B1.

[8] Joshua Olsen, *Better Places, Better Lives: A Biography of James Rouse,* (Washington, D.C.: The Urban Land Institute, 2003).

[9] Shirley Letts Stryker, Charles E. Mader, Ward Weldon, *Lift Lab Manual: Theory and Exercises for Leaders of Adult Lift Labs as Used In Washington Lift Laboratories and Workshops,* (Chicago: Trinity Center for Developing Ministries).

[10] Walden Howard, "The Washington Lift," *Faith at Work,* June 1972, pp. 6-8.

[11] "News from the Washington Lift, Inc." (newsletter), July 10, 1972.

[12] As quoted in Ministry of Money newsletter No. 49, August 1987, p. 4.

[13] N. Gordon Cosby with Kayla McClurg, "Radical Newness: The Essence of Being Church," pamphlet of the Church of the Saviour.

Chapter Six

[1] O'Connor, *Journey Inward, Journey Outward,* (New York: Harper & Row, Publishers, 1968), pp. 55-56.

[2] Jan Linn, *Rocking the Church Membership Boat: Counting Members or Having Members Who Count,* (St. Louis: Chalice Press, 2001).

[3] http://www.trinitywallstreet.org, December 26, 2007.

[4] Donald Georgen, "Current Trends: The New Ecumenism," *Spirituality Today,* Winter 1982, Vol. 34, No. 4, pp. 350-361, as seen at http://www.spiritualitytoday.org/spir2day/823446goergen.html on

December 29, 2007. Also, a biographical sketch of Dr. Charles Habib Malik on the United Nations Web site (http://www.un.org/ga/president/bios/bio13.shtml) on December 31, 2007.

5 "The Barna Update," a report from The Barna Group, April 25, 2005, as seen at http://www.barna.org/FlexPage.aspx?Page=BarnaUpdate&Barna UpdateID=187 on January 1, 2008.

6 Other members of the initial steering committee were the Rev. Allen Hollis, a United Church of Christ pastor who had written a book entitled *The Bible and Money*; Allen Green, former executive director of the Irwin Sweeney Miller Foundation in Columbus, Indiana; the Rev. Christopher Raible, a Unitarian minister from Worcester, Massachusetts; and Fred Taylor, a Church of the Saviour member who directed the church's ministry to homeless children in Washington.

7 O'Connor, *Letters to Scattered Pilgrims*, (San Francisco: Harper & Row, Publishers, 1979), pp. 15-17.

8 O'Connor, *Servant Leaders, Servant Structures*, pp. 20-21.

Chapter Seven

1 Information on the Stewardship Foundation from the Web site http://www.stewardshipfdn.org/_form/Foundation%20History-0306.pdf, February 11, 2008.

2 Menninger Clinic Web site, http://www.menningerclinic.com/about/early-history.htm#KarlMenninger, February 2, 2008.

3 Richard Foster, *Freedom of Simplicity*, (San Francisco: Harper & Row, Publishers, 1981), pp. 24, 49-50.

Chapter Eight

1 The phrase is noted in Henri Nouwen, *Gracias! A Latin American Journal*, (San Francisco: Harper & Row, Publishers, 1983,) p. 188.

2 *Gracias!*, pp. 6, 108-109.

3 Jean Vanier, *Be Not Afraid*, (Toronto: Griffin House, 1975), p. 1. Used with permission.

4 Sandy Huffaker, "The Sketchbook Journal," *Fellowship in Prayer*, Lawrenceville, New Jersey, Vol. 37, No. 1, February 1986, pp. 8, 15-16, 26, 29-30, 33, 39, 58, 62-63, 64.

5 From a Bryan Sirchio interview with Andrea Wells Miller.

6 UNICEF report, "UNICEF Calls for More Action to Halt Preventable

Child Deaths Around the World," from Web site
http://www.results.org/website/navdispatch.asp?id=3221, July 7, 2008.

7 Walter Brueggemann, Sharon Parks and Thomas H. Groome, *To Act Justly, Love Tenderly, Walk Humbly: An Agenda for Ministers*, (Mahwah, New Jersey: Paulist Press, 1986), pp. 5-6.

Chapter Nine

1 *Christianity Today*, April 24, 2000, as seen at
http://www.christianitytoday.com/ct/2000/april24/5.92.html, February 4, 2008.

2 Walter Brueggemann, *The Prophetic Imagination*, 2nd edition, (Minneapolis: Fortress Press, 2001), p. 1.

3 Millard Fuller interview in "Where Your Treasure Is," 22nd segment of a TV series by the Bauman Bible Telecasts, Arlington, Virginia, 1981. Also April 21, 2008 letter from Fuller to Don McClanen.

4 Koinonia Partners Web site,
http://www.koinoniapartners.org/History/brief.html, March 14, 2008.

5 Habitat for Humanity Web site,
http://www.habitat.org/how/factsheet.aspx, April 28, 2008. Also Fuller letter to Don.

6 Sojourners Web site,
http://www.sojo.net/index.cfm?action=about_us.history, April 8, 2008.

7 Ministry of Money newsletter, 71st edition, April 1991, pp. 2-3.

8 Web site of the Henry J. Kaiser Family Foundation,
http://www.kff.org/hivaids/timeline/hivtimeline.cfm, March 21, 2008.

9 The Syriac Orthodox Church is a small branch of Christianity whose members live predominantly in the Middle East and India. The church descends from the 1st century church in Antioch.

10 Web site of Mor Gabriel Monastery,
http://morgabriel.org/history.html, March 23, 2008.

11 Henri J.M. Nouwen, *The Spirituality of Fund-raising*, pamphlet based on a September 1992 talk to the Marguerite Bourgeoys Family Service Foundation, published in 2004 by Upper Room Ministries and the Henri Nouwen Society, pp. 3-4.

12 Minutes of July 15, 1993 meeting taken by Dale Stitt, Ministry of Money staff member.

13 Rose Marie Berger, "A Laboratory of Reconciliation," *Sojourners*, Vol. 28 No. 6, November-December, 1999, p. 28. Berger wrote the story after accompanying Don on a July 1999 pilgrimage to Bosnia.

14 Details also from Carole Christopher, "Bosnia: A Journey by Heart," a Ministry of Money pamphlet that reprinted an article from *The Loom*, a newsletter of the Jubilee Community in Comer, Georgia.

15 Tom Osborne, *On Solid Ground*, (Lincoln, Nebraska: Nebraska Book Publishing Company, 1996), p. 130.

16 *The Joy and Rhythm of Giving*, a Ministry of Money pamphlet.

Chapter Ten

1 Quoted in Ched Myers, *The Biblical Vision of Sabbath Economics*, (Washington, D.C.: Tell the Word, 2001), p. 5.

2 *Newsweek*, February 9, 1998.

3 Ralph J. Doudera, *Wealth Conundrum*, (Atlanta, Georgia: Signature Editions, 2005), pp. 1-6, 27-31.

4 Ibid., p. 51.

5 Richard Parker, "Becoming Evangelists of Justice," *Sojourners*, September-October 1999, p. 37.

6 Jaye School, "The Pilgrim: Don McClanen Offers the Wealthy a Different Kind of Freedom," *Barron's*, September 18, 2000.

7 Wayne Muller, *Sabbath: Finding Rest, Renewal, and Delight in Our Busy Lives*, (New York: Bantam Books, 1999), p. 1-2. Muller says, "In the relentless busyness of modern life, we have lost the rhythm between work and rest. ... In our drive for success we are seduced by the promises of more: more money, more recognition, more satisfaction, more love, more information, more influence, more possessions, more security. Even when our intentions are noble and our efforts sincere–even when we dedicate our lives to the service of others–the corrosive pressure of frantic overactivity can nonetheless cause suffering in ourselves and others. A 'successful' life has become a violent enterprise."

8 Daniel Kadlec, "Quiet Giver: America's Best Philanthropist," *Time*, September 17, 2001.

9 Farmer's story is told by Tracy Kidder in his Pulitzer Prize-winning book *Mountains Beyond Mountains: The Quest of Dr. Paul Farmer, A Man Who Would Cure the World*, (New York: Random House, Inc., 2003).

10 Michael A. Hayes and David Tombs, Editors, *Truth and Memory: The Church and Human Rights in El Salvador and Guatemala* (Leominster, England: Gracewing Publishing, 2001), p. 95.

Chapter Eleven

1 Gerald G. May, M.D., *The Dark Night of the Soul: A Psychiatrist Explores the Connection Between Darkness and Spiritual Growth*, (New York: HarperSanFrancisco, 2004), pp. 4-5, 72-73.